D1497463

14 MINUTES

A Running Legend's Life and Death and Life

ALBERTO SALAZAR

and JOHN BRANT

RODALE.

1460
B7

FROM AS:

To my father

FROM JB:

To the good Samaritan

————

Rodale books may be purchased for business or promotional use or for special sales. For information, please write to: Special Markets Department, Rodale Inc., 733 Third Avenue, New York, NY 10017.

Printed in the United States of America

Rodale Inc. makes every effort to use acid-free ♾, recycled paper ♻.

Interior book design by Christopher Rhoads

Library of Congress Cataloging-in-Publication Data is on file with the publisher.

Salazar, Alberto
    14 minutes : a running legend's life and death and life / Alberto Salazar and John Brant.
       p.   cm.
   ISBN-13: 978–1–60961–314–3 hardcover
   ISBN-13: 978–1–60961–998–5 paperback
   1. Salazar, Alberto 2. Runners (Sports)—United States—Biography. I. Brant, John II. Title. III. Title: Fourteen minutes.
  GV1061.15.S33   2012
  796.42092—dc23
  [B]   2012002366

Distributed to the trade by Macmillan

2 4 6 8 10 9 7 5 3 1 paperback

We inspire and enable people to improve their lives and the world around them.

rodalebooks.com

CONTENTS

PROLOGUE

IT TURNS OUT that the white-tunnel stuff is overrated.

Scientists in the Netherlands recently conducted a study of people who'd been resuscitated from clinical death—meaning that their hearts had stopped beating—and only 18 percent reported any sort of mystical experience during the moments they were deceased. On June 30, 2007, the day when I died, I joined the majority. I wasn't transported through a blazing white tunnel, my soul didn't drift out of my body, and I didn't look down at myself sprawled on the thick grass outside the sports and fitness center on the campus of Nike headquarters near Beaverton, Oregon. My death, in fact, was pretty straightforward.

One moment I was walking along with my runners, talking about where to go for lunch, and the next I was in a hospital room, clutching a chain of rosary beads. Between those two moments I knew only blackness and oblivion. That's sort of surprising, actually. Given my extensive near-death résumé and familiarity with miracles, you'd think I would've landed among the 18 percent of the subjects of the study who, at the moment of their seeming end, knew a sense of serene oneness or witnessed their entire lives flashing in front of them.

Maybe I failed to see the white light because I was dead a whole lot longer than the people in that study. Most of the body's organs can survive the loss of circulating blood for up to 30 minutes, and detached limbs can be successfully reattached for up to 6 hours following the dismembering injury. After more than 5 minutes without a pulse, however, full recovery of the brain becomes extremely unlikely. Three hundred thousand Americans die every year from cardiac events, but strictly speaking, they don't perish from blocked arteries or a stilled heart. After a very few minutes—10 at the most—without a fresh supply of blood, your brain starves of oxygen, and that's what really kills you.

I was clinically dead for 14 minutes.

Fourteen minutes is a long time. Abraham Lincoln delivered the Gettysburg Address in much less than 14 minutes. In my competitive prime, I could easily run 3 miles in 14 minutes. You can watch half of a TV sitcom episode, commercials included, in 14 minutes. None of the doctors who treated me, and none of the experts I've consulted since the day I collapsed, have ever heard of anybody being gone for that long and coming back to full health. By all rights, I should've been DOA at the emergency room of Providence St. Vincent Medical Center. At best (or at worst, depending on your viewpoint), I might have hung on for a few days or weeks in a brain-dead coma until Molly, my wife, made the agonizing decision to unhook me from the respirator. If I were really lucky (or, again, if my family was especially cursed), perhaps I'd have survived as a brain-damaged shell of a human being. But instead, on the day after my clinical death, I was chatting to visitors in my hospital room, and 9 days later, with my body whole and my faculties intact, I was back coaching at the same spot where I'd collapsed.

———

In October 1981, I set a world record (or WR, in runners' parlance) at the New York City Marathon, covering the 26.2-mile distance in 2 hours, 8 minutes, and 13 seconds. That performance sealed my standing as the greatest distance runner of my era. I lived a life of extreme athletic excess, as far gone, in my way, as a drug addict or alcoholic. I was famous—or many would say, notorious—for my obsession to outwork any rival and for my absolute refusal to lose. I would later pay a harrowing, decade-long penance for that excess, but at the time, in the late '70s and early '80s, the height of the first running boom, my obsessiveness put me on top of the world. My photo appeared on the cover of national magazines, I shook hands with President Ronald Reagan at a ceremony at the White House, and Nike named an apparel line after me. Now, 25 years later, here I was racking up a second, albeit unofficial, WR: 14 minutes.

———

We were in a loose, celebratory mood on that summer Saturday morning in 2007 at the Nike campus. My Nike Oregon Project team had just returned from the US national track-and-field championships in Indianapolis, where three of our athletes, Kara Goucher, Adam Goucher (Kara's husband), and Galen Rupp, had all placed in the top three in their respective races and thus earned spots at the world championships in Japan later that summer. In a non-Olympic year, this was the professional distance-running equivalent of making it to the Super Bowl, and we were elated.

It had been 6 years since I started coaching the Nike-sponsored Oregon Project. With the full backing of the company's founder, Phil

Knight, and then-president Tom Clarke, I was on a mission to develop an American-bred champion of one of the world's major marathons. Amazingly, only one male American distance runner had won one of the top-tier races since I won New York in 1982 (in 1983, Greg Meyer won the Boston Marathon), and Phil—along with the entire US sports establishment—was hungry for a homegrown hero to challenge the dominance of the Kenyans and Ethiopians. No one knew better than I did what it took to reach this level, and no one knew better the hazards: the various physical, psychological, and spiritual disasters that a runner potentially encountered as he or she approached the edge separating supremely difficult training from self-immolating excess. My job was to drive a handful of elite young American runners to that edge but keep them from tipping over.

On that morning, it seemed like I had struck the winning balance. We had successfully endured the crucible of the nationals. The pressure was off, and I was giving my runners some semidowntime. Kara and Adam weren't running at all for a few days, and Galen was scheduled for a relatively easy workout consisting of a moderately paced 5-mile run followed by a round of quickness- and strength-training drills that he'd go through with Josh Rohatinsky, a promising young runner from Brigham Young University with whom I'd just started to work. Jared, Josh's younger brother, was in town visiting. Jared, Josh, Galen, and I were walking from the parking lot toward the fitness center.

It was a soft, beautiful summer morning, the kind that only seems to occur in Oregon's Willamette Valley. Warm sunshine was burning off the light morning overcast, and the air was so clear that the world seemed to glisten. Days like this are our payoff for the 8 months of gloom. People complain about the infamous Oregon rain, but in general it doesn't bother me that much. A persistent, mild drizzle seems a small inconvenience compared to the blasting winter winds that I grew up with in Connecticut and Massachusetts.

We were headed for the central green to do the plyometric drills, and we were talking about where to go for lunch. I was 48 years old, on top of my profession, and blessed with a happy, healthy family. I was cutting across the gleaming campus of a mighty multinational corporation whose resources lay at my disposal. Nike had even named one of the office buildings after me; you could see the roof of the Alberto Salazar Building from where we were walking. I was with people I cared about, doing the work that I loved. Everything seemed about perfect, and yet I was moments away from dying.

The perfection of that morning was marred by a barely conscious worry about my health. During the previous week in Indianapolis, I had suffered transient stabs of pain in my back and neck and a general feeling of exhaustion. But I was too busy to worry much about these symptoms. I attributed the pain to sleeping in an awkward position on the long flight from Oregon and the weariness to the accumulated stress of preparing my athletes for this meet. Although I'd retired from competition 13 years earlier, I kept myself in excellent condition. I ran 5 miles a day at 7-minute-a-mile pace, lifted weights, never smoked, drank alcohol moderately, followed a healthy diet, and controlled hereditary high blood pressure and elevated cholesterol with medication. Like most fit people my age, I felt invincible.

Still, when I returned home to Portland after the nationals, I reported the symptoms to my family physician. She gave me a thorough exam and couldn't find anything wrong. She then referred me to a cardiologist, who ordered a treadmill stress test, which I was scheduled to undergo the following week. So, healthwise, I had all my bases covered. According to statistics cited by the American Heart Association, 50 percent of fatal heart attacks in men, and 64 percent in women, occur without warning. I had plenty of warning. I was the last person in the world you'd expect to suffer even the mildest cardiac event. I know that middle-aged people who've had heart attacks are always saying that, but in my case the evidence seemed unassailable: I was Alberto Salazar, among the most famous distance runners America had yet produced. The chances of my suffering a massive heart attack seemed as remote as Bill Gates declaring bankruptcy.

But as we made that short walk, the pain that had started in Indianapolis returned, stronger and more urgent than ever. It felt like a blade turning in the middle of my neck. On the heels of that pain, I felt an overwhelming wave of fatigue; suddenly, I could barely lift my feet. The guys were walking in front of me and didn't notice my distress. Galen was explaining to the brothers that the cafeteria at the Mia Hamm Building was closed on Saturdays, so we'd have to go off campus for lunch.

"I know this terrific deli in Southeast Portland," Galen said. "They pile the turkey 3 inches thick in a sandwich."

The wave of pain subsided a notch, enough for me to gather myself and take a breath. I noticed that on the far end of the field, a summer football camp was taking place. I thought again about all the good things happening in my life. I thought about my daughter, Maria, 16 at the time. She was in Texas that week at an equestrian competition, and Molly was with her. I thought about how proud I was of Galen, who was more like a son to me than an athlete. I had discovered Galen 7 years earlier, when he was playing soccer for a high school in Portland. I had carefully nurtured his enormous talent, keeping him from overreaching, refusing to let him make the same mistakes that I'd committed over and over as a young runner, and now he was on the edge of realizing his gift. Finally— funny how the mind works, even at the most desperate moments—I thought about where we should go for lunch.

"Geraldi's," I said, referring to my favorite deli, which was only a 5-minute drive from campus. "They have the best sandwiches in town."

The pain exploded up from my back, filling everything, too overwhelming for me to hide or deny. "Galen, I'm getting dizzy," I said. "I better take a knee." I sank deliberately to one knee, so that if I fainted—

when I fainted—I wouldn't hurt my head. I was still thinking at that
point, still processing the sensory river. Josh, Jared, and Galen had
turned to me, shocked by my transformation. Galen would later tell
reporters that my face had turned purple.

"I knew Alberto was in trouble," he would say. "It was terrible. It was
like watching your father die."

But despite the searing pain—and despite the fleeting realization
that now I'd never complete my mission, never fully transmit my knowledge, never finish building Galen into a runner in my own image—I felt
perfectly calm. It was all right. Whatever happened would be all right.

If I could just rest a minute, I remember thinking, then the pain
might pass. If it didn't, that was fine, too. I wanted to explain this to
Galen. I wanted to reassure Josh and his brother. I tried to speak, but no
words came. The world went black, and I slowly toppled over, landing
softly on my side, setting in motion a wondrous chain of events. Angels,
almost too many to count, leaped into action, as if they'd been waiting
my whole life for this moment. The clock started ticking. My 14 minutes
had begun.

———

I was saved on that summer day by a humbling, mind-blowing combination of science and grace, and I know I've been spared in order to tell my
story. I'm not writing this book for the money. I have enough money.
And I'm not doing it for the fame or notoriety, because I've had plenty of
those things, too. And I certainly don't need the distraction, because the
Oregon Project is in the midst of preparing for the 2012 Olympics, where
Galen hopes to win a medal in the 10,000 meters. During the last few
years, two more of the world's best distance runners—the US marathoner Dathan Ritzenhein and Mo Farah, a citizen of Great Britain—
have joined our team, and now I'm also tending their Olympic dreams.

The business of training a world-class runner is 24/7 now. The time spent on the road is in many ways the least of it. There are drills for every movement of the body and mind. You study what a runner eats, how many hours she sleeps, and the quality of what she thinks. As an athlete, I thought that training was all consuming, but now, instead of just worrying about myself, I'm worrying about a half-dozen young women and men with their dreams, their fears, and their obsessions. For some reason, God has given me some of the most talented, complicated, and damaged athletes to work with. The ones whose gift often troubles them and who can't seem to stop themselves from running over the edge. They feel driven to accomplish this great thing, and maybe this book can help guide them.

———

I keep thinking about that Dutch study of the near-death experience. Maybe the reason I missed the white tunnel wasn't due to the fact that I was clinically dead for 14 minutes. Maybe I'm more like a city dweller who can't see the stars because their shine gets swallowed by the ambient light of the metropolis. Perhaps I failed to see the divine light because, to varying degrees, I've been living in its glow for my whole life.

PART 1

IT SEEMS FITTING that my earliest childhood memory entails strife, conflict, and intense emotion. It also seems appropriate that the Roman Catholic Church was involved. I was 5 or 6 years old. My family was out in Michigan visiting during a summer vacation. I attended a day camp run by a Catholic order, a sort of Bible day camp. I recall the presence of nuns. Another little boy started teasing me. He hit me with a vine, using it in the manner of a whip. This infuriated me. I fought back with a ferocity far beyond the pain I'd absorbed and beyond the bounds of a little boy trying to defend himself.

I jumped on the kid and started pounding him with my fists. When he escaped my grasp, I chased the terrified boy around some picnic tables. The nuns stopped me, but they couldn't staunch my rage, which kept flooding out of me, a deep volcanic upswelling at the injustice of the boy's attack. I wept and thrashed and couldn't be consoled. Eventually the nuns, who despite their experience had never encountered this sort of emotional intensity from a child, had to call my mother to come get me.

I remember that day: the stinging thrash of the vine; the deep green of the grass and trees; the startled white faces of the sisters under their habits; and my outpouring of rage that, even at that young age, I felt coming through me rather than from me. I sensed that I was a conduit of forces beyond my understanding and perhaps beyond my control.

———

My boyhood passed in a similarly tumultuous key. In our family, as in many Latin families, emotions ran high and often exploded into arguments and yelling. We argued about the same things as other American families—time in the bathroom, use of the car, who would claim the last slice of pizza—but the intensity we brought to these disputes was unlike that of other American families. Years later, when we were courting, I brought Molly to visit my family at my boyhood home in Wayland, Massachusetts. Molly is a smart, kind, sweet, blue-eyed and blonde-haired Oregon girl, and her early family life was as orderly and tranquil as the ones that I jealously watched on '70s TV sitcoms. Now Molly endured her first thunderous Salazar family dinner.

I can't recall what the issue was that evening—whether a movie was worth seeing? who was the better all-around ballplayer, George Brett or Mike Schmidt?—but, as was our habit, my brothers and father and I soon escalated the dispute to seemingly life-and-death stakes. We went for each other's throat, shouting arguments that to Molly's ears seemed beyond forgetting or forgiving. But the next moment, it was all gone. It was, "Pass the salt, please." Molly couldn't believe it. She thought the Salazars came from another planet.

———

And we did come from another planet. We came from Cuba. We came from the actual island nation itself, but also from a separate Cuba, a sort of virtual state, the one fashioned by the Cuban exile community in the United States. And my family occupied still another realm of Cuba: the one created by my father, José Salazar.

My father was the primary spokesman for the Cuban exile community in New England. Anything involved with Cuba, my dad was the man you saw talking about it. Politicians consulted with my father. He led public demonstrations. You drove past busy intersections and there would be my father, holding up a sign, shouting into a reporter's microphone, the veins sticking out on his neck. He appeared on televised panel discussions with Senator Edward Kennedy, his political nemesis, whose brother John F. Kennedy had—in my father's opinion—bungled the Bay of Pigs invasion, in which my father had participated (although on a personal level, the two men respected, and even liked, one another; years later, after I won the 1982 Boston Marathon, Senator Kennedy sent my father a personal note of congratulation).

There were constant meetings at our house, often running late into the night. Angry men shouted in Spanish. My brother José and I could hear them up in our bedroom after the lights were out. José, who is 2 years older than me, didn't seem as bothered by the turmoil as I was. He was wired like my father; absolutely sure of himself. José fell asleep easier than I did. Long after he was breathing rhythmically, I'd hear the voices swelling and receding, the deep impassioned vow that these men lived by: *El ano proximo en La Habana!* Next year in Havana.

One night I wandered downstairs, semisleepwalking. Strange men filled our dining room. The air was blue with cigarette and cigar smoke. More than 40 years later, I clearly remember seeing a man stalk out of the house and come back in carrying a machine gun.

———

I didn't realize at the time, of course—in fact, I wouldn't put it together until I was well into my own adulthood—that a sense of deep, visceral betrayal lay at the heart of this intrigue and of my father's rage. I'm not talking about the pallid kind of political betrayal common here in the United States; the disappointment you feel when the candidate you ardently supported gets into office and turns out to be just another cynical, deal-making politician. I'm talking about the head-butting fury of a deceived lover. I'm talking about the soul sickness that comes from your dearest friend violating your deepest trust.

For my father, Fidel Castro wasn't just a picture in the newspaper or a fatigues-clad, cigar-chomping figure strutting on the TV news. My father had been a friend and comrade of Castro's. My father's father had given Castro work when he was a struggling young attorney in the Cuban provinces. Castro and my father shared a dream of justice, along with nights under fire. For hours one harrowing afternoon, they'd breathed the same stale air in a cramped office, waiting to hear soldiers' footsteps coming for them.

And for my father, Che Guevara wasn't just an image silk-screened on a college kid's T-shirt. My father had watched enemies die by Che's hand and had battled enemies himself under Che's orders. Later, my father worked under Che's direction in the revolutionary government. My father gave himself body and soul to the original, democratic vision of the Castro-led revolution, pledging a loyalty that doesn't seem in tune with our times, that is hard for an American living under comfortable, secure circumstances to comprehend.

———

Maybe you remember the scene from the movie *The Godfather: Part II*: Havana in the 1950s, a city under thrall to the American mobster Meyer Lansky; a playground for wealthy Americans sporting in casinos and brothels. The American mafia, along with US sugar, fruit, and mining interests, enriched to obscene levels the US-backed Cuban president Fulgencio Batista and his cronies, while leaving the rest of the nation destitute. Vibrant music, beautiful women, strong rum, a glowing Havana moon: It all sounds romantic, but for the vast majority of Cubans, the scene represented misery and humiliation.

My father was the scion of a family with a long and accomplished history straddling both Cuba and the United States, a line of engineers, teachers, entrepreneurs, soldiers, and priests. The family home in Havana was of sufficient grandeur that, after the revolution, the Soviet government employed it as part of their embassy complex. My father could have been one of the fortunate ones, exploiting his education and family connections to claim a prime feeding spot at the Batista trough. But instead, he chose the harder and more virtuous path. Along with a growing number of patriotic, idealistic young people, my father followed the opposition movement led by a young law student named Fidel Castro.

In 1950, the University of Havana formed the heart of the movement. Castro, who would graduate that year from the university's law school, was active in student politics, and my father headed the engineering students' league. The revolution wouldn't reach its climax for another 9 years, but already the government was wary of Castro. One day, agents came to campus to detain him. My father got wind of the development and sheltered Castro in his small office in the student union building. My father locked the door, and he and Castro moved the desk against it to block passage. Down at the building entrance, in remarkable demonstration of Cuban loyalty, a security guard bravely rebuffed the government agents.

"I don't care about Castro," the guard said. "But José Salazar is president of the Engineering Students' Department, and I cannot let you pass."

A few years later, when the rebel forces had become more of a threat, the agents probably would have forced their way into the building, but now they backed off. A stalemate ensued. Fidel Castro and my father waited out the afternoon in the small office. I heard the story so often as a kid that I didn't register its full significance and drama: my father, sitting cheek by jowl with a man who'd become one of the pivotal figures of the 20th century. The office would have been hot and stifling, its air increasingly rank with sweat and anxiety. The two young men might have talked about all sorts of things during the 10 hours they spent together. Finally night fell, and Castro slipped out of the office and escaped into the darkness.

Later, my father's pride regarding this episode would grow tinged by guilt and regret, but it never completely vanished. My father had behaved impeccably that day, upholding his personal code of honor: loyalty to a friend, service to an ideal, and grace under pressure. Where there was a choice, he always chose the hard path. José Salazar had touched history, and he—and his family—would never be the same.

———

Through the rest of the 1950s, as Castro hooked up with Che Guevara in Mexico and clandestinely returned to Cuba, taking to the Sierra Maestra and building a rebel army of disenfranchised campesinos, my father followed the rebels' progress and did everything he could to support it. At this juncture, Castro wasn't aligned with the Communists, and he had not yet identified himself as a Marxist. He was simply a patriot leading a homegrown movement for justice. It was justice, and not a political creed, that attracted my father and like-minded young Cubans. Castro promised to deliver the nation from foreign and criminal bondage. That was the sum of my father's political ideology.

When the Fidelistas fought their way out of the mountains and were bearing down on Havana, my father joined their ranks, engaging in firefights and other forms of combat. So did thousands of other young professional-class Cubans: teachers and students, businessmen and lawyers, engineers and physicians. It was not an easy decision. Although they were upholding the highest national values, they were also turning against their own vested interests. They sacrificed their wealth, comfort, and, in many cases, their lives.

My father told me stories about the war. Once he was with Che Guevara when Che left a group of wounded enemies to die in the broiling sun without water. A comrade suggested that shooting the prisoners would be merciful. Che shook his head. "These *gusanos* (worms) have nothing to give the revolution but their blood." And then, my father said, Guevara ordered his troops to slit the prisoners' throats.

During the campaign, my father would officiate in battlefield trials of suspected war criminals. One such prisoner was a former aide to Batista, a man responsible for the deaths of many innocent people. The evidence was unequivocal. My father, acting as a first lieutenant military prosecutor, helped secure the conviction of the man and two of his comrades. Although the man's guilt was beyond question, his subsequent execution disturbed my father for years afterward. Finally, just a few years ago, he told the entire story to a priest from the village where the condemned man lived. The priest confirmed that the man had been guilty of the war crimes. That finally put my father's mind to rest.

But at the time, in the 1950s, such incidents were swept up in the tide of war. When the professionals of my father's class fell in with Castro, they helped transform the heroic cadres of campesinos in the Sierra Maestra into a legitimate military and political force, an urbanized, organized movement. On January 8, 1959, the rebels rolled triumphantly down the streets of Havana. Batista departed Cuba in disgrace, along with the mobsters, pimps, and bagmen. Cuba's honor was restored—or so it seemed for a brief, shining moment. I was an 18-month-old child at the time, too young to recall the events, but perhaps the din and clamor of the revolution worked their way into my dreams.

The rebels were now in power. A skilled structural engineer, a man of formidable energy and organizational abilities, my father quickly rose to the new government's top tier of management. He pledged himself to enact the ideals that Castro had championed. Besides being patriotic, my father was driven by a sort of chivalrous impulse, the hunger to subsume himself both to a noble cause and to a leader he trusted and admired. I understand this impulse well. Many years later, I would pledge loyalty to a leader whose vision and talents were, in their way, as far reaching as

Castro's: Phil Knight, the genius behind Nike, a company that has achieved its own sort of global revolution.

My father helped design 49 projects for the revolutionary government, including national parks, public beaches, and hotels. He worked with energy and conviction, living out his belief that now, free of foreign control, all Cuban citizens could achieve dignity and prosperity. Increasingly, however, the new government's leaders, especially Fidel and Che, did not always work in that same disinterested, democratic spirit. Instead, with dismaying speed, they were evolving into doctrinaire Marxists largely controlled by the Soviet Union.

I'm not trying to make a political point here. I know that many say that Castro only turned to the Soviet camp because of the hostility of the US government. And many people contend that despite its failures and excesses, the socialist revolution has been of great overall benefit to the Cuban people. But my father saw events firsthand and reached a different conclusion. His disillusionment culminated about 8 months into his employment with the government, when he drew up plans for a project especially dear to him: a church building that would serve the residents of a small town in the countryside.

Normally, my father's superiors were enthusiastic about his work and approved his plans without comment. But not this time. The plans for the church came back across my father's desk, rejected, with a terse note of explanation from Che Guevara himself: "There is no room for God in the revolution." My father appealed to Fidel Castro himself, who upheld Che's decision, confirming the edict that religion had no role in the new national order.

At a stroke, my father saw the revolution and its leaders in a new light. For my father, and for millions of his countrymen, the Catholic Church was inseparable from the nation of Cuba. If Castro and Guevara were using foreign doctrine as a pretext for restricting or limiting the practice of worship, how were they any less threatening to the nation than Batista or Meyer Lansky? And if the new government was already abridging freedom of religion, which of the basic human rights would it trample next? My father's deepest allegiance was to God, not the revolution. In fact, it was tough to tell where my father's passion for Cuba ended and his love for the Catholic Church began.

———

The Roman Catholic Church had served as the focal point and cohesive force in our family for centuries. It was a faith intertwined with drama, conflict, death, and national identity. Just as the personal loyalty my father evidenced might seem strange and exotic to the average American, so would my father's faith.

His father, my grandfather, was raised in an orphanage by a nun and later attended Manhattan College and College of the Holy Cross in the United States, both Catholic institutions. On my father's side, each of the 11 generations preceding me have distinguished themselves through acts of faith. These acts have tended to be dramatic rather than contemplative, bound up with death, honor, and blood loyalty and, often, with violence.

John Garesché (the Garesché branch of our family, a line distinguished both in Cuba and the United States) was an expert on ordinance and munitions who was born in Cuba in 1836 and came to the States as a young man. By 1858, when he was 22, he was working at a gunpowder company in Virginia. In September of that year, his employer ordered a series of tests at the armory that Garesché knew would be dangerous, perhaps fatally so. He strongly recommended that the tests be canceled, but the employer held firm, and the trials were scheduled for the morning of September 13.

The night before the test, Garesché sat up praying and meditating about his predicament. He could simply not show for work the next morning, but that would be an act of inexcusable disobedience to the man to whom he'd pledged his loyalty, as well as an act of cowardice jeopardizing his underlings, who would be left to carry out the dangerous tests in his absence. Garesché decided to follow his orders, but on the heels of that decision he had an intimation that was as clear as his call to duty: He knew he was going to die the next morning.

John Garesché spent that night in prayer and reflection, alternately studying his missal and a religious text treating the subject of the fate of the soul after sudden death. The next morning, the young man went to his fate, which played out in exactly the manner that his experience as an engineer, and his faith as a devout Catholic, had predicted: There was a terrific explosion, and Garesché died.

———

I heard John's story and the story of Julius Garesché, John's cousin, my great-great-great-uncle, as a boy. I didn't have much use for Julius's story, like other tales my father told, and it never quite registered. But then, years later, as I was browsing in a bookstore, looking through an old volume on the Civil War, I came upon the story and photograph of my legendary forbear.

According to my father, Julius was the first Catholic to attend the US Military Academy at West Point. His grandparents had nearly been killed in Santo Domingo, Cuba, during a slave uprising. Given that history, the boy might have grown embittered and developed racist attitudes, but instead, Julius went in the opposite direction, living a life of service. At West Point, and later as junior officer serving in the US Army, he was known for his diligence, modesty, and piety. While stationed in Washington, DC, he helped found the city's chapter of the Society of St. Vincent de Paul, which continues to serve the indigent to the present day.

At the outbreak of the Civil War, his brother Frederick, a Catholic priest, had prophesied that Julius was going to die in battle within 18 months, during his first engagement with the enemy. Julius was assigned an administrative post, but despite his brother's warning, he chafed to serve on the front lines. He petitioned his superiors for reassignment, and his request was eventually granted. He drew a posting as a Chief of Staff to General William Rosecrans, who commanded the Union forces at the Battle of Murfreesboro in Tennessee in December 1862. On December 31, the Confederate forces launched a full-scale attack. Julius rode into battle beside the general, mounted on a black horse, with a West Point class ring on his finger, a copy of the Imitation of Christ missal in his kit bag, and his brother's dreadful prophecy hanging over him.

A Captain Bickham, who was in the field that day, picks up the narrative: "In the midst of the horrid carnival they were galloping through a tumult of iron missiles. An unexploded shell whipped close by his leader and the head of Garesché vanished with it. Sickening gouts of his brains were scattered upon his comrades, who turned in horror from the ghastly spectacle."

The black horse that Garesché was riding galloped 20 more paces before the headless body finally toppled onto the ground by the railroad. More than 27,000 soldiers, North and South, fell during the battle, making Murfreesboro one of the bloodiest engagements, percentagewise, of the entire Civil War. That night a friend of Garesché's, a West Point classmate, went looking for the body—the spectacular death had been noted even on that horribly violent day—and discovered it with the froth of blood in place of the head. The officer removed the class ring from the corpse's finger and the missal from the kit bag. That day, the legend of Julius Garesché was born.

It is said that if you go quietly into the old battlefield by the railroad at dawn, or in the twilight of evening, you might see an apparition of the headless horseman. I don't discount the possibility; I have a good deal of experience with apparitions. But to this point, I have not visited Murfreesboro. For me, Julius Garesché is more than a curiosity, the prey of tourists—he is part of me. The ideals he lived by—faith, honor, justice, courage, service, sacrifice—I also try to emulate. And these were the qualities that, 50 years ago, Fidel Castro and Che Guevara impugned when they told my father that the church he'd designed could not be built; that there was no room for God in the Cuban revolution.

———

The spirit of the Gareschés lived on in my father. Such was the passionate, deeply ingrained faith that he inherited. Besides the color and drama, he was also drawn to the fundamentals of Catholicism: attending Mass regularly, confessing sins to a priest, observing the sacraments, and praying through the intercession of the Virgin Mary, who in our version of the faith occupies a crucial position in relation to Christ.

My father could not betray this faith, so he made the great turn. In essence, he made the same call that John Garesché had made the night before his death in 1858. But while Garesché followed his conscience by honoring the obligation to his employer, my father turned on his boss in order to honor a far greater contract. In October 1960, my father wrote an open leter to Castro denouncing him for persecuting the Roman Catholic Church and betraying the revolution. Castro sent agents to detain my father, but he escaped just before their arrival and boarded a flight to Miami. A few months later, my mother followed with her four small children.

———

Shortly after our arrival, I came down with a serious case of scarlet fever. For a week or two, I was quite ill, so much so that my life was briefly threatened and, after the crisis passed, my mother worried for my long-term health.

Perhaps her worries were justified. Consider that summer day in 2007, when I collapsed on the Nike lawn. For more than 24 hours after I entered the hospital, the medical staff refrained from calling what happened to me a heart attack. Instead, they called it a "cardiac event," which some people regarded as a euphemism or perhaps even a cover-up. But, in fact, my doctors were only being honest. It wasn't clear what caused my heart to fail; according to my cardiologist, Dr. Todd Caulfield, it still isn't clear today, more than 4 years later.

Most likely my heart spasmed due to coronary artery disease—one main cardiac artery was more than 70 percent blocked—but it also might have been caused by a significant mass of scar tissue that Dr. Caulfield discovered in my left ventricle. This scarring could have precipitated the arrhythmia that led to the ventricular fibrillation that temporarily killed me. And this scar tissue, in turn, might have formed during a number of traumatic events over the course of my life: the searing marathons and other races or, perhaps, the early-childhood bout of scarlet fever, which I incurred during my first days in America.

———

The other thing that happened shortly after our arrival was the infamous Bay of Pigs invasion, the failed CIA-organized attack to overthrow the Castro regime, one of the defining events of the Cold War. My family is among the 1.8 million Cuban-Americans nationwide, making us the nation's third-largest Hispanic group, behind Mexicans and Puerto Ricans. As a group, we are the most educated and affluent Hispanic immigrant bloc, and, due to our history, we have our own way of viewing American politics and culture. My parents, my siblings, and myself, moreover, are among the 270,000 Cubans who arrived in the United States in the 5 years immediately following the revolution and Cuban Missile Crisis.

This first wave contained a large number of professionals and upper-class exiles who had lost their wealth under Castro and who'd fled the island largely out of self-interest. There were also many like my father, disillusioned idealists who'd voluntarily sacrificed their affluence and standing in the name of Castro's initially democratic revolution. Both groups seethed with resentment at their betrayal. They were angry, many were battle hardened, and they possessed resources. When a Cuban expatriate recruiter offered my father the opportunity to avenge that betrayal—and to liberate his homeland from the rule of a man who, by the day, appeared more dangerous than the deposed dictator—he jumped at it. For 6 months during the winter of 1960–61, my father trained for the invasion in the Florida Everglades.

I have a photo of him from that time. He's standing with a group of eight comrades, wearing military fatigues, squinting in the tropical sunshine, looking strong and confident, exulting in his conviction that the US government understood the menace lurking just 100 miles off the shore of Miami. "Next Year in Havana," a return to and restoration of the homeland, now seemed more than a rallying cry. Grinning into the camera, my father saw himself back in his Havana home. He could taste it, smell it, almost touch it. But, of course, that day never came.

Because he was formerly a close ally of Fidel and Che, the CIA regarded my father both as a potential risk—what if he remained secretly loyal to the revolution and acted as a double agent?—and as a potential asset, with his extensive knowledge of the nation's infrastructure. He was thus relegated to the second wave of the attack on the island, which was expected to take fewer casualties. On April 17, 1961, the disastrous affair unfolded. In part due to the Kennedy administration's refusal to commit air and naval support, the 1,400-man invasion turned into a debacle; a total of 114 invading Cuban exiles were killed. Castro's forces repulsed the initial attack, and the long, cold war of attrition, isolation, and embargo—a war that continues to this day—began. My father never left his staging area in Nicaragua. He and his comrades had been humiliated.

According to a story in *Life* magazine: "Havana gleefully noted the wealth of the captured invaders: 100 plantation owners, 67 landlords of apartment houses, 35 factory owners, 112 businessmen, 179 who lived off unearned income, and 194 ex-soldiers of Batista."

———

Twice betrayed, and doubly embittered, my father evolved from a full-time counterrevolutionary into an avocational one. He turned his attention to earning a living for his family in America. When I was 4, he took a job with a large construction company in Manchester, Connecticut, and we left Florida. My father might now have been a part-time activist, but his pride, faith, patriotism, obsession, sense of honor, and destiny had only intensified.

Growing up in New England, trying to make it as a student and athlete and regular American kid, I attempted to tune out the stories, the myths, but they worked deeply into my consciousness. The central narratives: my father saving Castro's life; the trial of the enemy soldier and his subsequent execution; Che's savagery; my father wanting to build a chapel but being denied by Che himself; my father's outrage at repeated betrayals; his guilt regarding his own complicity in bringing Castro to power. Again, I am not trying to make a political point. I'm trying to explain the source of the rage that I grew up with, that frequently stifled me as a boy, and that later fueled my extraordinary competitive fire as a runner.

"Go, Alberto, go!" I can still hear my father, screaming on the side of the high school cross-country course or in the car behind me as I struggled through a 15-mile training run on a blazing summer afternoon. "Go, Alberto! You can't quit! A Salazar never quits!" A snarling bass roar, not to be denied. A voice booming out heavily accented American English, whose roots ran straight back to Havana.

Looking back, I see that I rejected the particulars of my father's agenda, most prominently his obsession with Cuba, but inherited his passion, which blasted straight into me like a bolt of electricity, intensified rather than dissipated by the passage of years and its journey down through the generations.

———

Salters Pond—it was really more of a lake—lay about 200 yards from our house in Manchester, Connecticut, a town east of Hartford. A long, sloping expanse of grass carried down from our back door along two hills to the water's edge. Salters Pond and the adjacent patch of woods formed the kingdom of the Salazar children, Ricardo, José, Alberto, and Maria (Fernando, my youngest sibling, was still an infant at this time). This was the first place I really knew—it was our playground, our battleground, our Neverland. Recalling those early years in Manchester, I'm surprised that I didn't turn out to be a fishing guide or a game warden rather than a marathoner.

At Salters Pond, we shot at squirrels with BB guns, played with bows and arrows, and made believe we were pirates and soldiers. My brothers and I would set traps and check them for muskrats before we left for school in the morning. If we caught one, Ricardo or José would skin it and sell the pelt for a few bucks. We joined the Boy Scouts and were thrilled to go on camping trips. We turned our BB guns on chipmunks, and if we were lucky enough to kill one, we'd eviscerate the animal and stretch its skin, using a technique we learned from reading *Field & Stream* magazine. I'd pretend to be happy about it, but felt secretly guilty about killing little forest creatures. I also felt bad about killing birds, but death was part of the outdoor life that I loved.

Our range of experience around Salters Pond was quite extensive. For instance, we got into shooting at fish with bows and arrows. Bowfishing? I'm not sure what the name is for it, but it turns out there's a real art to killing fish in that manner. You have to use a broadhead arrow that causes massive internal damage. If you actually hit a fish with an arrow, you want to make sure to kill it. And once the arrow got stuck in the fish, it was a messy, slimy ordeal to get it out. The whole business was pretty barbarous. I have a photograph of José and me playing with a bow loaded with a broadhead arrow. In that picture, the arrow is pointed straight at me.

———

José and I were only 2 years apart in age. Like a lot of brothers, we fought like cats and dogs when we were kids, but today he and I are good friends. He works as a supervisor for the Department of Homeland Security, and we see each other often at Mass on Sunday and go out to eat afterward. But it wasn't like that when we were kids. He and I were always battling.

José had the mentality of a football player, and I had the mentality of a runner. José was strong and self-confident and liked to run into and over things. He loved the locker-room camaraderie and give-and-take of team sports; in a word, José had a personality very similar to my dad's. By contrast, I was shy, less sure of myself, and preferred outrunning my opponents to outhitting them. I liked being part of a team and had plenty of friends, but I also liked being by myself, and I tended to draw strength from inward rather than outward sources.

Ricardo, who was 4 years older than me, had a nature more like mine than José's or my father's. Ricardo and I instinctively responded the same way to people and situations. Years later, for instance, after Ricardo and I had started our respective running careers and José was playing football for Wayland High School, José was in the living room, watching a football game on TV. I joined him. Then Ricardo came in. He saw us watching the football game and shook his head. "Why are you watching those guys play?" he said. "They're only doing it for the money. You might as well watch a bunch of plumbers work."

On the day the photo was taken, I was probably 7 or 8 and José would have been 9 or 10. Ricardo must not have been around that day, because he never would have let us attempt such a stupid and dangerous stunt. It must have been winter, or maybe late fall or early spring, because I wore a parka. We were fooling around with our bows, playing like we were cowboys and Indians, having a wonderful time, two little boys without a care in the world—not a whole lot different than how I felt on that summer day more than 40 years later, when I was walking across the Nike campus with Galen and the Rohatinsky brothers.

Somehow we had got hold of a camera. Maybe one of us had saved up and sent away for it, responding to an ad in the back of *Boys' Life* magazine. I pointed the camera at José, and thinking that it would make a cool picture—maybe it was even my idea—José drew his bow, pointing the arrow straight at me. It was the same kind of broadhead arrow that ripped such awful holes in the fish of Salters Pond.

José did not intend to shoot the arrow, of course. But that's what happened. Entirely by accident, he let go the string, and the arrow with the hideously lethal point whizzed by inches from my neck, nicking my nylon parka. I can still hear the clicking noise. A fraction of an inch the other way—the slightest alteration in God's plan—and I would have died that day.

If you're an American kid of comfortable circumstances, you naturally assume that you're immune to death. It certainly doesn't enter into your daily thinking. But the Salazars came from another planet. Compared with average American kids, we were on intimate terms with mortality.

Late one night in 1965—I would've been 6 years old—the phone rang in our house. My father answered, and a moment later, I heard him wailing "Oh no!" in his booming voice (ever since, when I hear a phone ring late at night, I feel an icy dread). His mother, my grandmother, had died in a plane crash. She'd been on a flight to Venezuela. The plane had crashed during the landing approach at the Caracas airport. My father would have to fly to Venezuela to recover the body and make arrangements for burial.

Traveling to South America meant flying close to Cuba. My father feared that the plane would be hijacked, or that Castro's agents would be sent to assassinate him: Given his background and activities, and the perilous state of Cold War politics at the time, he wasn't being completely paranoid. That trip, however, would prove life threatening in a way that none of us foresaw. To protect himself during his journey, my father bought a handgun, a Saturday night special, that he kept in a cupboard above the refrigerator in the kitchen.

———

Of course, my brothers and I found it. My mother, Marta, must have been busy somewhere else in the house. Besides our large immediate family, we frequently hosted Cuban relatives for lengthy periods. My late mother (she died in 2005, at age 76, of pancreatic cancer) was always working around the house. She'd been a lady of substance in sunny Havana, overseeing a staff of domestic workers who cared for the spacious family home, and now here in cold New England she had to scrub, cook, and sew for us. She never complained and was always a loving, kind presence in my life—the calm mother in equipoise to my thunderous father. Although I grew up to resemble my father in so many ways, as a kid I felt closer in temperament to my mother.

She was away from the kitchen when Ricardo, José, and I discovered the gun in the cupboard. The sleek black weapon seemed to vibrate with a power of its own as we passed it around. When it came to me, I automatically, reflexively, gazed down its barrel. Also reflexively, I placed my thumb on the trigger. I was just a 6-year-old boy, my head full of TV images. Ricardo pulled the gun away from me.

"You never do that," he said. "What if that thing is loaded?"

A little while later, my father came home from work. He went to the cupboard and took down the handgun that my brothers and I had just replaced. "Come on, boys, let me show you something," my father said.

We followed him down to the basement, where my father had jury-rigged a mattress into a firing range. "Now I will practice," he told us. Without releasing a safety lock, loading a bullet in the chamber, or making any other adjustment, my father raised the pistol toward the mattress. He squeezed the trigger. The gun's crack was deafening. The stench of cordite filled the basement. Ricardo, José, and I looked at one another, too terrified to speak. My father smiled, thinking that his prowess with his handgun had impressed his sons. We never told him the real reason for our silence.

———

There were other things my father didn't know. He didn't know much about American sports, for instance, but that didn't stop him from playing an active role in my running career—often, too active a role. *"Go, Alberto go!"* my father would scream, often slipping from English back into Spanish.

I remember an indoor track meet during my junior year of high school against one of our main rivals, Lincoln Sudbury Regional High School. The meet was at Wayland High School, where the track measured 10 laps to a mile. Racing there sometimes resembled a roller derby—you had to be willing to take and throw elbows. We were running the mile and one of their top guys, a kid named Bill Gale, accidentally tripped me from behind.

As we were driving home from the meet, my father asked me what happened. I said that some people were claiming that the tripping was no accident, that Lincoln's coach had ordered Gale to interfere with me. My dad slammed on the brakes, maneuvered a screeching U-turn, and roared back to the school. The coaches were still there, my coach, Don Benedetti, and Pat McMahon, the Lincoln coach who'd purportedly ordered the tripping. My father got in McMahon's face and started yelling and screaming, displaying the reflexive fury at injustice instilled by his experience in Cuba. Coach Benedetti had to hold back my father. I can smile at the scene now, and even admire my father for sticking up for me (I take a similarly protective attitude toward my runners today, minus the melodrama), but at the time it was intensely embarrassing.

People were enchanted by my dad. He was handsome, charming, and charismatic. My friends would tell me that I had such a cool old man. But they didn't have to live with him every day. For me, it was often a miserable existence. I couldn't wait to get out of the house. I felt suffocated. I loved my father and desperately wanted to please him, to follow his example and be a man of honor and courage, and yet he was often impossible to live with.

All I wanted to do was blend in with the other children. I didn't want to stick out as the Cuban kid. At home, we spoke mostly Spanish, but at school and out on the playground, the Salazar children only spoke English. Kids have a cruel and unerring sense for finding each others' sore spots. Back in the 1960s, there were frequent TV commercials for a sofa bed called the Castro Convertible. The kids at school used to call me Castro Convertible because I was Cuban, and because my father was constantly ranting about Fidel Castro. Even before I understood what the kids were talking about, I hated being called that name. I hated it.

———

Fernando, the baby of our family, was the only one of us born in the United States. For his fourth birthday, my parents threw a party for him, and my mother put me in charge of organizing the games. The party was held in our basement. I can't recall what game the kids were playing, but one of them accidentally smashed a light. My dad freaked out, got mad at me, and for some reason decided that he had to fix the light right away. He took off for the hardware store to get what he needed for the repair. When he was gone, suddenly, we saw police cars screaming by, their lights flashing, heading for Salters Pond.

I ran down to the pond to see what was happening. I climbed up on a tree branch, one we'd use as a sort of diving board, to get a better look. From listening to bystanders and the authorities, I was able to piece together what had happened. Some boys had lashed together a few logs and pieces of driftwood into a makeshift raft and taken it out on the pond (it could've been my brothers and me, I remember thinking; that's the kind of stuff we were always doing). One of the boys—I didn't know him—had jumped off the raft, hit his head, gone under water, and hadn't come up. Now the police and ambulances had arrived, with divers, to try to find him.

I was up on the tree branch, only 15 feet away, when the divers pulled the boy up. He was dead. He was white and dripping. They tried to resuscitate him in the manner that, 40 years later, on the Nike campus, bystanders and paramedics would revive me, but this was different. The boy had been under too long, sucking in water, and he was gone, as dead as one of the fish we speared by broadhead arrow. The men on the ambulance vainly worked over him. His skin was a terrible blue-white color. I sat motionless on the tree limb, fascinated, terrified. Finally, my fear overcame my fascination and I ran, screaming, to my mother.

"Am I going to die?" I demanded of her, sobbing.

Meanwhile, my father had come home from the hardware store. My dad told me that the boy's death was my fault, because I had allowed the children at the party to break the lamp. If he had been here at the house, my father said, then he could have saved the boy. Looking back, I can see that this twisted logic was a product of my father's shock at the terrible accident, combined with his embarrassment at overreacting to the busted lamp and guilt about leaving the house. But as a 9-year-old child, of course, I didn't understand any of that. I took my father's charge to heart, and it affected me profoundly.

That night in bed, I prayed as if my own soul were at stake. I didn't pray to be spared from death, which I suppose is what most children would've requested under the circumstances. I did not pray to avoid the inevitable or for magic. Instead, I prayed to the Holy Mother for intercession (in the Catholic Church, you are taught to pray both to Mary, the intermediary, as well as to her son directly; you appeal to the soft, forgiving feminine as well as the stern, judging male). The words of my prayer came to me by their own accord. I didn't formulate or plan them.

Please, Mother, when I die, don't let me be afraid. Bring me straight to heaven to your son Jesus.

———

This episode at Salters Pond taught me that death was real; the intensity I felt when I prayed afterward convinced me that the Holy Mother was real. As real as that poor boy being pulled to the pond's surface, as white and lifeless as a fish skewered by a broadhead arrow.

When I die, don't let me be afraid. Bring me straight to heaven to your son Jesus. I would say that prayer constantly, every night through my boyhood, long after the shock of that day wore off. Those words became the thing I uttered before sleeping, and they refrained all day on the edge of my consciousness, grooving into my brain like a chant or mantra. The prayer protected me and comforted me. It has been my companion all of my life.

Fast forward to the Falmouth Road Race of 1978. I was 20 years old at the Falmouth race, during which I suffered a near-fatal case of heat-stroke and was rushed to the medical tent. I was submerged in a tub of ice water, but my temperature wasn't coming down. *"106 . . . 107 . . ."* I heard the docs reading off the dreadful numbers on the thermometer. *"I think we might be losing him."*

Through the fog of my fever, through the shock of the ice, I could hear the voices clearly. *Okay*, I thought, *I'm gonna die now.* Suddenly I went from feeling panicky to getting really calm. I said my special prayer. *Please, Mother, when I die, don't let me be afraid. Bring me straight to heaven to your son Jesus.* The prayer made me feel calm and accepting. *Here I come, Lord*, I thought. I was ready. My prayers had been answered. My moment of death had come and I wasn't afraid.

———

Jump to June 30, 2007, the day of my cardiac arrest and my clinical death. I lie in the hospital room after being resuscitated. My sons Tony and Alex are in the room with me (Molly and Maria are on their way back from the equestrian competition in Texas). I don't recall this exchange; my sons told me about it later. I had been asleep, in a type of drug-induced coma. Suddenly I awoke and calmly looked at my boys.

"Guys, I need to go away now," they reported me saying.

Tony and Alex grew frightened. They thought for sure I was dying. "Where do you have to go, Dad?" Tony, my elder son, asked.

"I don't know," I said. "But there's a woman calling me, and I need to follow her."

———

I am a man of science and technology. As a coach, I am famous—many would say notorious—for seeking a scientific basis for all training and competitive issues. Running a marathon is in many ways an imponderable enterprise. No matter how thoroughly you prepare, there is always an element of discovery and surprise, sometimes gratifying; more often, unfortunately, otherwise. But I think—I know—that the percentage of distance running that remains a mystery is far less than we imagine.

At the same time, we are just scratching the surface of empirically training the human body. That's why I have introduced technology such as the altitude chamber and the antigravity treadmill; why we're drawing the blood of our runners to measure every possible training variable; why I've hired a sports science expert to join the Oregon Project coaching staff; why I've developed stride mechanics into a separate discipline; and why my ambition, more than producing a new American marathon champion, is to establish a database of empirical training knowledge that athletes and coaches can employ far into the future. Moreover, on a personal level, I have extensive experience with doctors and medical science due to my many injuries and illnesses, physical and emotional.

So I know all the physiological and psychological explanations for the peace that descended on me at Falmouth and for the woman's spectral appearance following my virtual death in 2007. I know that my visions can be explained away as blips in my brain chemistry, as a result of a sudden drop in my blood-oxygen levels or a spike of my hormone levels, or as a product of presuggestion, wish fulfillment, or pure moonbeam fantasy. And yet I also know that the woman I saw after my virtual death was the Holy Mother. *It's not your time*, she told me. *You're coming back.*

By the same token, I know that Mary heard my prayer and saved my life at Falmouth. The conflict between science and religion never bothered me that much. Maybe that's because my encounters with death removed belief from the equation. The spirit is a fact; a discipline. God's hand is behind every movement of your life, but you have to look hard and long for it and accept that most of the time the touch will remain ineffable. The harder you work to see it, often, the more it fades from view, a paradox that the greatest minds through the ages have explored. I am simply a distance-running coach who acquired death as a teacher. Maybe death is like any other human skill or endeavor. If we practice death, we get better at it. If we are familiar with death, we fear it less.

———

A generation ago, almost nobody who suffered cardiac arrest outside of a hospital survived. Today, the survival rate stands at around 8 percent. That translates into thousands of people each year being pulled back from death. The quantum-leap gains in technology and medicine— everything from cell phones to defibrillators to new surgical techniques, all the scientific advances that came together to save my life—increasingly deliver us to face-to-face encounters with the spirit. People walk back from death and report profound insights and visions. Responsible scientists are starting to investigate a phenomenon for which there doesn't seem to be an explanation.

During clinical death, our brains cease electrical activity; they stop processing sensory data and generating thoughts. And yet, with increasing frequency, individuals report lucid and verifiable thoughts and impressions during a time when, according to science, their brains aren't capable of producing them.

Even my cardiologist, Dr. Todd Caulfield, Harvard educated and a scientist to his fingertips, increasingly observes the near-death experience in his patients. "These individuals don't report a feeling of bliss as much as one of serenity," Dr. Caulfield says. "They come back convinced that death is okay, and by extension they know that life is okay, too."

I didn't see the white light when I died, but somehow my belief was strengthened. It requires faith to see God's hand. I don't regard faith as a passive virtue but as a praxis, a habit of the heart and mind, which we build through effort and over time. I think that in order to see the light, you most often have to spend a long time stumbling around in the dark. There is nothing cheap or easy about it. In my experience, miracles grow out of faith, and not the other way around.

————

From my background—the Cuban heritage, the relationship with Castro and the great currents of history, the implicit sense of drama around our family and my precocious encounters with death—you might think that a portentous air surrounded our household, that we wandered around the rooms with sacred music playing. But, of course, that wasn't the case. When there wasn't a recently arrived Cuban exile staying with us or my father wasn't hosting some kind of political meeting, we kids busied ourselves with school and sports. My father worked long hours at various construction projects; my mother ran the house. My sister and brothers and I hung out with friends and explored the woods around Salters Pond, fooling around with muskrat traps and fishing poles.

My father always stressed that there was a divine plan for everybody in the family, that the Salazars were subject to a momentous destiny, but I never felt that way. I don't feel that way now. If I can use my fame as a runner or standing as a coach to positively influence the people around me, great. If my influence radiates farther than that, better still. But as a little boy, I never had the idea that I'd be supergreat at anything. I harbored no delusions of grandeur. I was a good student and okay athlete. I had my brothers and my sister and my friends. And then running came along.

My first experience with the sport was when my brother Ricardo started running cross-country at East Catholic High School in Connecticut. At that time, I was a fifth grader at St. Bartholomew's Elementary School. My brother talked about how great running was. He got a stopwatch and started timing the kids around the neighborhood in 50-yard dashes up and down the sidewalk, or he would clock us running around the house, with a big oak tree in our front yard serving as both starting and finish line. I was a fast runner, but not the fastest, especially not in the sprints and shorter races.

In PE class, the teacher had us run all kinds of races in a parking lot and field beside the school. At recess, we played games like Red Rover. We dodged and sprinted and changed directions quickly to avoid getting caught. I was no better than okay at that game. We also played an extended form of tag in which everybody eventually became "it" and went after the last kid who remained at large. This game could range over the entire field, and I was always the last one caught because I figured out that I could run forever. I found the seams and followed paths to the open ground. The other kids grew weary of chasing me and eventually gave up. That brought me great satisfaction. I suggested to my classmates that they form a system of relay teams to come after me. I suppose that's when I showed my first inclination to coach. I just had this idea that I was a distance runner.

When I completed fifth grade, St. Bart's closed due to lack of funds and I transferred to Bowers Elementary School in Manchester. At the end of the year, the school held a field day with a 600-yard run; the PE teacher had measured out a three-lap course around the baseball backstop along the edge of the fields. I wasn't the fastest in the sprints, but I had hopes for the longer distance. My chief rival was a boy named John Lacy, the big hero of the school and the sweetheart of all the girls. It was John Lacy this, John Lacy that; he was good at football and all the other sports. The girls in my class jeered at my ambitions to win the 600-yard run. "You can't beat John Lacy," they told me. "No one can beat John Lacy."

The day of the big race came. I started fast and led at the end of the first lap. But then disaster struck: My shoelace came untied. As I bent down to tie it, all the other kids flew past me. I stood up and ran as hard as I could. By the end of the second lap, I caught up with the leaders, including the great John Lacy. During the third lap, I pulled away and won by a 50-yard margin. After the race, the PE teacher came up to me. "Alberto," she said, "I think you might have a future as a distance runner."

I walked on air the rest of the day. After school, I rode the bus home. We lived at 54 Tracy Drive in Manchester. The bus dropped us off at the foot of the drive, and we had to trudge up the long hill to the house. José and I always complained about that climb. But that afternoon, I flew up the hill, elated, clutching my blue ribbon. "I beat John Lacy!" I shouted. "I beat John Lacy!"

I was a runner.

———

Ricardo's stopwatch served as both tool and toy, and he was an exemplary first teacher. He stressed the significance of the personal record, or PR. Winning and losing were important, of course, but because other runners were involved, victory was to a certain degree out of your control. But a PR—bettering your previous best effort at a given distance—was entirely a matter of individual resolve. Even when Ricardo wasn't around, I would take his stopwatch and go out alone to time myself running around the house or on the various routes around our neighborhood. I would run around the house and try to touch the oak tree in less than 26 seconds.

I loved these private time trials. And I loved racing the half-mile loop around my house against the other kids from the neighborhood. Running wasn't easy in the beginning (maybe running is never easy). The first time Ricardo showed me the route, I couldn't make it around the block. For a 10-year-old boy, a half-mile might as well have been a marathon. The first time I tried it, I had to stop halfway and sit down on the curb to rest. Ricardo wondered what was taking me so long and cut across the block to find me.

He ordered me to stand up and get moving. I would try again and fail again. Ricardo didn't allow me any slack. He jeered that I'd never become a distance runner because I wasn't tough enough; I had no tolerance for pain. I'd stand up and keep working at it. I wasn't going to let my older brother down or let him think that I wasn't tough. And eventually, I learned to love rather than dread that half-mile loop.

———

I played other sports, but I was middling. I was never good enough in baseball to make Little League, so I played PONY league instead. Ironically, I played catcher, the position on the diamond where the biggest, slowest kid is usually placed. We moved to Wayland, Massachusetts, a suburb of Boston, when I was in seventh grade. I got cut from the basketball team at Wayland Middle School. In the spring, however, when we finally got outside after the long winter, track and field came up on the PE curriculum, and with it the 600-yard run. That was my chance to shine. The bigger, stronger boys, the ones who starred on the Little League baseball team and made the cut in basketball, gasped and struggled to keep up with me. Near the end of the school year, we had a field day, and I won the 600-yard run outright, beating all the seventh graders.

That fall, Ricardo came home from a high school cross-country meet—he was one of the top runners both in the school and league—talking about Richard Smith, a good runner at a rival high school. Ricardo told me that Richard Smith's younger brother, an eighth grader like me, had competed in a high school JV race, in which he'd placed third. "You better watch out," Ricardo told me. "Richard Smith's brother is getting the jump on you. . . . You better start training." Don Benedetti, the Wayland coach, agreed to let me do the same as this other boy—run a JV race for the high school team. (Today they would never let a kid do that. There would probably be lawsuits if you tried such a thing.) I ran with the high school kids and did even better than Richard Smith's little brother: I won the JV race. Meanwhile, Ricardo won the varsity race. The achievement earned us a photo in the sports page of the local paper. Our father just about popped with pride at the success of the Salazar brothers.

I was starting to show up on people's radar screens. When the league championship meet came around, I was permitted to compete. My dad picked me up at school that afternoon and drove me to the meet. We were running late, and I was just about the final athlete to arrive. All the kids massed at the starting line in their uniforms, warming up. Suddenly, I froze. I could not stand the thought of going out there and having all those other guys staring at me.

"Come on, Alberto, get out there," my father said. "They're all waiting for you." But I couldn't move. I was so shy and embarrassed. My father cajoled and threatened me, but I refused to get out of the car. The idea of being the center of attention petrified me. I stayed inside the car, and they ran the race without me. My dad was furious.

But I quickly bounced back. That winter, I won a few indoor races against high school competition, and that spring, I broke the Wayland Middle School record for the 600-yard run.

Meanwhile, Ricardo had developed into one of the top 10 prep runners in the state of Massachusetts. He was also an excellent student; my father wouldn't countenance anything short of superior grades from his children. Ricardo considered going to Massachusetts Institute of Technology in nearby Cambridge but instead accepted an appointment to the US Naval Academy (echoes of our illustrious forbear, the headless horseman Julius Garesché, one of the first Cuban graduates of West Point). Ricardo progressed into a 4:07 miler at Annapolis and as a senior was elected captain of the Navy cross-country team. Ricardo was my hero. He had introduced me to the sport and shown me the magic of the PR. He would also soon introduce me to the legendary distance-running program at the University of Oregon. He would describe the mythic exploits of Steve Prefontaine and his coach, the godlike Bill Bowerman. Had it not been for Ricardo, my life would have unfolded in an entirely different direction.

Of course, growing up near Boston, the first capital of American distance running, helped. Long before the running boom of the 1970s, a man named Fred Brown, president of the North Medford Track Club, instituted a summer series of road races, 5-mile or 10-mile races through the back lanes of the colonial stone-fence suburbs, winding along routes that Paul Revere once rode and where King Philip's War raged during the 1600s. We lived in a ranch house built in the 1950s, on a quiet street called Snake Brook Road. While the backyard of our house in Manchester sloped down to Salters Pond, our backyard in Wayland slanted up toward a broad outcropping of New England granite. In the years ahead, I would run the local roads in all lights and weathers, but those early summer road races molded me.

At least once a week—10 or 15 times over the course of a summer—I would hitch a ride to the race's start from a neighbor. As a 15-year-old kid competing against grown men, there was no way I could challenge the leaders. I ran in the middle of the small fields of serious athletes; no one showed up at a road race just to finish in those days. I simply focused on notching a PR, on beating my previous best time. We'd pound through Natick and Medford, Wellesley and Wayland, and afterward tuck into hot dogs, corn, watermelon, and cookies. My stomach was always sensitive after these races—I always ran them hard—but I couldn't resist the spreads of summer food. I remember some epic stomachaches.

I had great fun at these road races. I was piling up the reps. By the time he's 14 years old, a boy from Kenya's Rift Valley or the sheepherding uplands of Ethiopia will have already run and walked thousands of miles, encoding running deep into his brain and muscle memory. Add that natural training to genetic predisposition and living at altitude, and you have an incalculable training advantage that even the most brilliantly talented American kid can never match and has to compensate for by other means. I'm not saying I ran nearly as much as an African kid, but there was an element of that spirit in my early immersion in the sport. Combined with the fire that I'd inherited from my father, I was branded for distinction as a runner. But that's jumping ahead of the story.

———

Besides Ricardo, my earliest running heroes were Dave Bedford, the British runner known for his extreme workouts and toughness, and Steve Prefontaine. This was during the early and mid-1970s, and the cult of Pre was growing nationwide. But I had a personal connection.

My brother's coach at Navy was a man named Al Cantello, the former
world record holder in the javelin. Cantello and Bill Dellinger, who had
recently succeeded Bowerman as head coach at Oregon, had been teammates on the 1964 Olympic team. They stayed friends and would trade
workouts for their respective teams. Cantello would send Dellinger
workouts for throwing events, and Dellinger would send running workouts to Cantello. My brother would say how great the University of Oregon distance program was. "If you're serious about the sport," he told me,
"Eugene's the only place to go."

My brother spoke in reverential terms about Prefontaine, the fiery,
charismatic Oregon middle-distance star who'd finished fourth in the
5000 at the '72 Munich Olympics, and who would die in a car crash in
May 1975, with tragic echoes of James Dean's death. In both substance
and style, Prefontaine was the standard against which all American runners were judged. Along with sending workout plans for distance runners, Dellinger would sometimes ship boxes of lightly worn Nike
prototype training and racing shoes to Annapolis. The Navy runners
were thrilled; perhaps the great Prefontaine himself had worn a pair. It
was almost as if they were the relics of a saint.

From Dellinger and the U of O, via Ricardo, I learned about
peaches and toast. Legend had it that that was the special meal Dellinger always fed his runners before a competition. The story turned
out to be true. A few years later, when I was running for Oregon, Dellinger insisted on peaches and toast for our prerace meal. The team
would gather at the dining hall or a restaurant, where plates of the stuff
would be waiting for us. Apparently, when Dellinger was a high school
runner in Springfield, Oregon, he'd been visiting his grandparents
before a big meet. He looked in the pantry for something to eat, and all
he could find were a can of peaches and a loaf of bread. So he dined on
peaches and toast, then went out and ran a record time at the track
meet. Ever since, both for himself and his athletes, Dellinger stuck

with peaches and toast. It was mostly for good luck, but the idea was also nutritionally sound. Peaches and toast actually make a pretty good combination of tasty, easily digestible carbs.

Here I am, a freshman in high school, just a kid, and all of this stuff is funneling through me. Peaches and toast. Summer road races against grown men. Dellinger's workouts. Prefontaine's used racing flats. And it began to have an effect. In the fall of that year, I finished 19th in the state cross-country championships.

Meanwhile, the running boom was building across America. At the 1972 Olympics in Munich, Frank Shorter had won a gold medal in the marathon. The United States was going through a crisis of confidence due to the Vietnam War and other social upheavals, and Shorter had proved that an American could prevail in a race of supreme difficulty, against the best that the rest of the world—including the steroid-laced Eastern bloc nations and the altitude-advantaged Africans—had to offer. Americans also learned about distance running from the philosophical essays of Dr. George Sheehan, from the practical advice offered by Jim Fixx in the bestselling *The Complete Book of Running*, and from the health-based arguments offered by Dr. Kenneth Cooper in his popular book *Aerobics*.

For the first time in history, Americans in mass numbers were voluntarily moving, and moving fast. These newly hatched citizen-runners weren't simply content to practice the same sport as Shorter, in the manner that high-handicap duffers played the same sport as Jack Nicklaus; they aimed to become Frank Shorter, or at least to train nearly as hard as he did, and to a great extent they succeeded. You were either on the bus or off the bus in those electric days, and America turned out sub-2:30 marathoners by the barrelful.

———

But I proceeded independent of the boom. I didn't subscribe to *Runner's World* (well, maybe I did in the beginning, but if so I skipped the meta-physical Sheehan column and went straight to the meat-and-potato training material). Health was never my motivation for running. I never worried about losing weight, and I certainly wasn't into the sport's psy-chological benefits. I wanted to run fast. I wanted to better my PR. I wanted to make my father proud, and I wanted to escape the atmosphere of rage around my house that my father had engendered. It looked like I had a future. I finished second in the state as a sophomore in the 2-mile on the track. Then in the fall of my junior year, after a summer of honing my speed on the local road-race circuit, I blew through an unbeaten cross-country season that culminated with my finishing second at the state championship meet.

My success continued during the first part of the winter indoor sea-son. One day after a meet, a man named Kirk Pfrangle came up to me. Kirk was a friendly guy in his mid-twenties, and I could tell from his build and demeanor that he was a runner. He said that he was a member of something called the Greater Boston Track Club, and he invited me to participate one of the club workouts. I said sure. I was vaguely aware of the GBTC, but I didn't know a lot about it. I didn't realize that Kirk's invitation was the equivalent of a high school shortstop being invited to play with the Boston Red Sox, or of a garage-band drummer being invited to sit in with the Rolling Stones.

———

January 1975. My first magical transformative year had begun. I started tagging along with Kirk Pfrangle to GBTC workouts. In the space of a car ride from Wayland to the field house at Tufts University in Medford, where the club held its winter workouts, I went from being a good high school runner to training with the best distance runners in the world. The group included the man who was going to win the Boston Marathon in a few months and soon thereafter become a household name across America: Bill Rodgers. Like many of the other guys in the club, Bill was sort of an oddball hippie outcast, a long-haired conscientious objector to the military draft. Before he turned to running, he was a somewhat marginal character who smoked cigarettes, rode a motorcycle, and earned his living as an orderly at a hospital morgue. Guys like Bobby Hodge, Dick Mahoney, and Randy Thomas were equally obsessed runners who lived and breathed the sport 24 hours a day. (Kirk, gainfully employed as a middle school teacher, was somewhat of an exception.)

These starving-artist-style outcasts had been redeemed in 1972 when Shorter won the Olympic marathon; suddenly, what they did mattered. And their coach, the best marathon coach in the world, was a one-of-a-kind man named Bill Squires. He was tall, around 50, with a classic Beantown accent pitched to be heard in the most clamorous Irish barroom. Squires came from the Casey Stengel school of management and elocution. He wouldn't use one word if 10 would do, and there was no such thing as a straight line or a simple answer. But Squires was whip smart, a Notre Dame grad, and you underestimated him at your peril. No coach understood the marathon in general, and the Boston Marathon in particular, better than Coach Squires. Years later, Rodgers would joke to a reporter that he started to worry about his mental health when he began to understand what Squires was talking about.

The first GBTC workout I attended was at the Tufts indoor track. Rodgers was there and Bobby Hodge and various other top performers from the Boston running scene, but also a few serious but less-talented citizen-athletes. Squires called this latter group the Guppies, and Rodgers and the other guys the Sharks. The coach looked at me—a pale, painfully skinny and shy kid, maybe 110 pounds, who looked more like an altar boy than an athlete—and pointed to the Guppie group. "Go over there with them, kid," he said.

But Pfrangle pulled the coach aside. Kirk remains a close friend of mine. I'll sometimes host him at big races like the New York City Marathon or the Olympic trials so he can see the Oregon Project athletes. Kirk has been following Galen Rupp's career since Galen was a soccer player at Central Catholic. Just as I recognized something special in Galen, Kirk recognized something in me; something I didn't even know about myself—at least not yet.

"The kid doesn't belong with the Guppies, coach," Kirk told Squires. "He's a runner. He belongs with my group." Squires looked skeptical, but he agreed to let me run with the Sharks. That evening, we hammered repeat 400-meters at a hard pace. Had I known more about who I was running with, I might not have hung in so doggedly. The first several repeats were no problem, but as we worked into the middle of the session, I started to labor. Kirk told me I should back off. Coach Squires came up to me. "Nice work, kid. Now ease up a little bit so you don't pop a valve, for chrissakes."

But there was no way I was going to back off, no way I wasn't going to prove that I belonged with the Sharks. By the end of the workout, I was sore and white and gasping, but I'd kept up. From that day forward Coach Squires knew where I belonged. I would never be mistaken for a Guppy again.

———

Once Squires saw my toughness and level of commitment (qualities that I equate with "talent" in distance running), he accepted me as an equal to his other runners. Squires was the mad scientist, speaking a language that was hard to understand on one level but made perfect sense on another. A former All-American miler at Notre Dame, Squires became a teacher and coach in his native Boston area and continued to compete on the club level. He ran the 1961 Boston Marathon, logging a very creditable 2:47. He was the kind of coach—the kind of adult—who seemed common at the time but is so rare today: a man molding young people through the full-hearted but ethical pursuit of a sport, with no ulterior motives or hidden agenda.

Squires didn't make much money from his coaching; he earned his living as a professor at Boston State College. Running was his passion, but he went about it in a madcap way, holding court in various taverns and coffee shops, writing down workouts on paper napkins. He blended the two irreducible components of training—speed and distance—into inspired combinations.

––––––

Distance-running training is really very simple: A program consists of running fast and running long. You run short distances to increase your speed, and run long distances to build endurance. But you can mix these two ingredients in endless variations. You can run short-short for intense speed, for instance, or medium-short to blend speed with a tinge of endurance. By the same token, you can run long and deliberately for pure endurance, or run long at a little faster pace to add a touch of speed. Squires's system was based on running fast, semilong intervals; that is, running fast for as long as possible.

He believed that speed came first, and the high-mileage endurance training could come later. It was necessary to amass a base of high mileage if you were going to succeed at the marathon, but high mileage could also be a source of misery, frequently yielding injury and burnout. Moreover, the window for running first-rate marathons was very small. The distance tore you up so much that you might be able to run just a few at your peak (athletes like Rodgers and the late Grete Waitz, who won nine editions of the New York City Marathon, were exceptions proving the rule). So Squires preached

patience. Extreme patience. He recognized that I possessed the basic ingre-
dient of a good marathoner: the willingness and capacity to suffer.

————

My nickname was "the Rookie." I would work out 2 evenings a week with
the GBTC and go to races with the group on weekends. The other guys
in the club were at least 5 years older than me. We'd go to eat at a coffee
shop and one of the guys would start telling a raunchy joke, and as he got
to the punch line, another guy would say, "Wait, hold on, we got the
Rookie with us." Squires would tell stories that could go on for an hour.

Almost from that first workout, the coach saw that my future lay in
the longer distances—that my gift was endurance—which meant that
eventually I would turn to the marathon. Squires calibrated all my
training toward the long term. He said that I shouldn't even think
about the marathon until I was out of college. Until then, I would focus
on quality rather than quantity in training. Then after college, in my
twenties, when my body had strengthened and matured, I could add
heavy volume to the base of speed and finally fulfill my destiny in the
marathon.

This sounded good to me on an intellectual level, but I didn't fully
understand the fate that Squires had prophesized for me. I didn't really
understand the marathon until Bill Rodgers showed me.

————

Rodgers: a sweet, friendly, ragamuffin guy; a hippie with a dirty-blond
ponytail. When he wasn't running, Bill seemed like the gentlest—and
spaciest—guy in the world, but once he laced up the training flats, the
starling turned into a swooping bird of prey. Bill just soared on a breath-

taking, light-footed stride. Still, I didn't realize how good he was until, just a few weeks after I started working out with the GBTC, he traveled to the world cross-country championships in Morocco and finished third. This long-haired dude that I hammered intervals with 2 nights a week at the Tufts track was one of the top distance runners in the world. Then about a month later, on Patriots' Day in April, the 1975 Boston Marathon came around.

I'd been aware of the race before then, of course—my family lived less than 2 miles from the midpoint of the course—but I'd never gone to watch it. This year, I went out with my father and Ricardo to take a look. We drove to three or four spots along the course between the village of Hopkinton and downtown Boston. We made a point of stopping at Wellesley College, around the midway mark. This is one of the most celebrated places on the course, where the Wellesley girls all come out to scream at the top of their lungs as the marathoners pass, forming this deafening, thrilling chute of noise that blasts the runners along.

My father, Ricardo, and I stood on the edge of the road waiting for the lead pack to arrive. Pretty soon we heard the doo-wop warning blast of the motorcycle-cop sirens. Then we saw the orbiting misery lights, and the Wellesley girls started to jump up and down, shrieking out such pent-up energy that I got goose bumps. And here comes the leader, and it's Bill Rodgers. Skinny, spacey Bill, with his long hair flowing in back of him, the guy I'd eaten BLTs with at Friendly's ice-cream restaurants. He's wearing white tube socks that stretch up to midcalf and a pair of shoes sent out from Blue Ribbon Sports in Oregon, the forerunner of Nike. He's wearing a ratty T-shirt on which he's crayoned the letters GBTC. Despite this motley getup, Bill is wailing. He's opened a 400-yard lead in the most prestigious marathon on earth, and I can see very clearly that nobody's going to catch him.

"I know that guy!" I shouted to my dad and brother. "I run with that guy!" But mostly I'm shouting this amazing fact to myself, and at that moment, like a bolt, it comes to me: This is the marathon; this is what Coach Squires promises is waiting for me. At that moment, I resolved— at that moment, I *knew*—that I was going to grab that destiny with both hands. I knew with every fiber of my being that I was going to become the greatest marathon runner in the world.

———

Witnessing Bill Rodgers at the Boston Marathon, catching that bolt, broke a dam inside of me, and after that day my running progressed with lightning speed. Once I established my marathon goal, everything fell in place around it. For a few months, Squires had been telling me that my talent lay in the distances, that I possessed the physical and psychological characteristics that would take me to the top ranks as a marathoner, but I didn't pay full attention; not until Patriots' Day 1975. Then I understood that my destiny lay in distance; the longer the better. That I had happened to fall in with Squires and the GBTC was an incredible stroke of good fortune, almost like Elvis Presley stumbling into the Sun Records studio in Memphis and going to work with Sam Phillips.

Rather than high volume, Squires based his system on long intervals; that is, running long but not prohibitively long distances at the maximum speed possible. My weekly mileage topped out at around 70, but a high percentage of those miles were logged in the long intervals, run in the company of older, more experienced, and more accomplished athletes. This mode of training is far different from the "long slow distance" philosophy then in vogue among citizen-athletes. The concept of "junk miles" (that is, dawdling workouts that look impressive in a training log but do nothing to increase your speed) was anathema to me. I devoted each moment of my running—each moment of my life—to getting faster.

In late April, just a few weeks after the Boston Marathon, I finished second in the high school 2-mile at the Penn Relays in Philadelphia, one of the most prestigious track meets in the country. Later that spring, I won the distance in the Massachusetts state championship meet. I was rapidly evolving into a very good high school athlete, but I'd still done nothing to differentiate me from many other good prep runners around the nation. That was about to change.

In late June, Coach Squires entered me in the USA junior outdoor track-and-field championships, for athletes 19 and under, held in Knoxville, Tennessee. I did not win the 5000-meter race—I again finished second—but I competed against athletes significantly older than me, including guys who'd just finished their freshman year in college. Moreover, my 14:14.6 time tied the US runner Craig Virgin's mark as the fastest ever by a 16-year-old. Virgin and I were the fastest 16-year-olds in the world at that distance. That performance—my first WR—took me to another level. People regarded me differently. More important, my expectations for myself changed.

———

Something else happened that spring: At the end of May, in Eugene, Oregon, Steve Prefontaine died in a car crash at the tragically young age of 24. On the evening after a track meet at Hayward Field, Prefontaine had dropped off Frank Shorter at the house where Frank was staying, then had blasted back toward a postrace party. Pre never made it; he crashed into a rock outcropping and died under his overturned MGB sports car. The legendary Pre, my hero and role model, who brought passion and meaning to running, a style that would later infuse and inspire Nike and guide so much of my life—was gone.

I remember where I was when I learned the bad news. For me it was like knowing where you were when you heard about JFK's assassination.

In school, before seventh period, this kid named Ralph came up to me and asked if I'd heard about Pre.

"Heard what?" I said.

"He's dead," Ralph said. But Ralph was a big joker, a bullshitter, and I didn't believe him. This couldn't be true. The previous day, Pre had won a big 5000-meter race against Frank Shorter. I went home that evening, turned on the TV news, and discovered that this time Ralph had been straight. Pre was dead. The news hit me in the gut. But I was 16 years old and, despite my nightly prayer to not be afraid at the hour of my own death, I was sure that I would live forever.

————

My performance at the national junior meet earned me a spot in the junior US–USSR track meet held later that summer in Nebraska. In those late Cold War years, the meet against the Russians was a big deal. Maybe not as big a deal as it had been during the 1960s, when, for the senior elite meet, 50,000 fans filled the Los Angeles Coliseum and a national TV audience watched avidly, but it still drew major attention. My father regarded it as the most important sporting event in the world. Due to Russia's support of Castro's Cuba, he despised the Soviet Union with a special vitriol.

It was 110 degrees on the track that day in Lincoln, at the University of Nebraska. The 5000-meter race would be my first in extreme heat. I came through. I won the race, defeating both the Russians and a highly touted American runner named Ralph King. My dad thrilled at the photo of me in the newspaper.

After the race, I ended up in the medical tent, hooked up to an IV as I was treated for dehydration. That scene would be repeated several times over the course of my career. My success that day under difficult, high-pressure conditions fed my building notion that I was a tougher runner than any of my peers.

My father interpreted the victory as an expression of fate, of the special Salazar destiny. I accepted it as my due for hard training with the likes of Bill Rodgers and focused on my next workout. I had aced my first international test, but already I'd determined that I wasn't going to stop to smell any roses. I did not intend to be that kind of athlete. If I started congratulating myself now, I might lose my edge. This win in Nebraska formed only one early step in a march that, according to Coach Squires, would take years to culminate.

That meet was special for another reason; there I met Rudy Chapa, who would become my lifelong best friend. A Mexican-American kid from Hammond, Indiana, Rudy was the same age as me, a rising high school senior, and he was as promising in the 1500 as I was in the longer distances. Rudy's father's had come to the United States through the bracero guest-worker program and settled in Gary to labor at a steel mill. Rudy and I connected right away, in part due to our common Hispanic heritage, but mostly because we instantly recognized that we shared a hunger for running—a physical, mental, and emotional committment. I thought Rudy was a far more talented athlete than me; in fact, I was a little in awe of him. We got to be friends and stayed in touch after leaving Nebraska. Over time, we decided that we'd go to the same college, which turned out to be the University of Oregon.

So the spring and summer of 1975, when I was 16, turned out to be a momentous and productive period for me. Now I recognize this as a pattern: high-cycle spates of time in which my purpose in life burns clear, when God's hand, normally hidden, becomes manifest. Within a 5-month period, I had watched my training partner Bill Rodgers win the Boston Marathon; logged a world record; defeated the Russians in my first international track meet; and met my lifelong best friend. People in the sport had started to notice me. I was no longer an anonymous Cuban-American kid from a small town in Massachusetts.

But the inner change was the most important. I was quickly building an unshakable conviction that no opponent would push harder than me. Maybe, like Rudy, a runner would be more talented, but he wouldn't be tougher.

In 1975, about the same time that I watched Bill Rodgers win the first of his four Boston Marathon titles, Dr. Thomas J. Bassler, a pathologist in California, cockily put forth the hypothesis that training for and completing a marathon guaranteed that an individual would not suffer a heart attack. Unsupported by research, Bassler's claim was immediately challenged by his colleagues. But the media took it and, well, ran with it. The hypothesis seemed to ring true, and countless newly hatched adult runners fervently wanted it to be true. So mainstream Americans largely lived and ran under that false assumption, which wasn't unequivocally disproved for another 9 years, when Jim Fixx, author of the bestseller *The Complete Book of Running*, died of a heart attack while running at age 52.

In 1975, however, the age of cardiovascular innocence—the magical thinking that a healthy lifestyle could permanently trump genes and other factors—was blossoming. As a teenager, of course, I was oblivious to all this. I felt invincible. Nothing could ever touch me—certainly not heart disease. However, according to Dr. Caulfield, my cardiologist, heart disease often starts as early as one's teenage years. Autopsies conducted on young American soldiers who'd died in combat in Vietnam show streaks of plaque already clinging to the nascent lesions in the corpse's arteries.

It is therefore reasonable to hypothesize that during those golden few months in 1975, when my life flowed in its first full tide, when I saw my future in glorious, diamond-hard clarity, I was already in the process of dying. I was already moving toward my 14 minutes.

One night in Nebraska, Rudy Chapa and I were talking—talking in that first thrilling rush of discovery you get with a new and close friend—and I told him my secret, my resolution: I was going to bag the WR in the marathon one day. Rudy didn't laugh. He believed me. But it wouldn't have made any difference if he hadn't, if he thought I was a blowhard and fool. What was important was that I believed my own dream. I wasn't just some kid on a pathetic, delusional fantasy trip. I had evidence. I had watched Bill Rodgers up close every day for months. I had goofed and traveled and eaten with him, busted through the same killer 6 x 1 mile interval workouts with him. I knew how hard he trained, the way he approached a race, the texture of his mental toughness—and from all this I knew that, some day, I was capable of matching what he'd achieved.

Moreover, Bill Squires had laid out a concrete, detailed, long-range plan for me to meet this goal. Belief itself is hardly enough for you to embody a dream, but if you don't state your goal, there's no chance at all that you'll meet it. Once I declared my intention to Rudy—once I believed it myself—I had no choice but to do everything within my power to achieve my very specific desire. Mastering the marathon became the supreme goal of my life.

During the fall of my senior year, I won the individual state cross-country championship and finished third in the junior national cross-country championships; the following winter, I dominated on the high school indoor circuit, all the while continuing to train with Squires and GBTC. Don Benedetti, my coach at Wayland High School, allowed me to log hard workouts with the club and rejoin my high school

teammates for the easy days of their training schedule, with the stip-
ulation that I'd never miss a high school race or competition. This
arrangement allowed me to continue to develop on a world-class level
in the company of Rodgers, et al., while at the same time keeping me
humble.

Indeed, despite my grand ambition, my opinion of myself was any-
thing but grand. In my mind's eye, I was still just skinny Alberto Salazar,
the Castro Convertible kid ridiculed by his classmates and cut from the
Little League baseball team. I was still the boy who prayed to the Holy
Mother every night that, at the hour of his death, he wouldn't be afraid.
In April of my senior year, the Penn Relays came around again in
Philadelphia. This year, 1976, I won the 2-mile race in 8:53. But the
very next day, at Coach Benedetti's insistence, I returned to Wayland to
compete in a big relay meet for my high school.

It wasn't hard for me to stay humble, at least privately, but it proved
difficult for me not to grow impatient and overreach. I came back from
the Penn Relays with the idea that I had to run more miles, like most of
the nation's other top schoolboy runners, even though I'd just prevailed
over them. So I bumped up my miles dramatically over the next week and
as a result came down with a sore leg and dragged through my GBTC
workouts.

"Lemme see your training log, Rookie," Squires said.

I showed him the log, he looked at all those miles, and went ballistic.
"You damn fool!" Squires said. "Do you want to ruin yourself?" He
stressed again that I wouldn't get to the marathon until after college, and
that until then I had to be patient, stay focused on the track, and build
my speed. Once that was established, I could think about adding miles. It
was like the voice of God speaking to me. Squires made it very clear that
despite my accomplishments, I was still the Rookie, and he was going to
look after me.

———

I was the Rookie, the phenom with the golden future, but the veterans on the team weren't jealous (elite runners tend to be the least jealous of any professional-level athletes; they know that in an event such as the marathon, the distance, and not their competitors, is their true opponent) and treated me kindly, taking me under their wing. Kirk would pick me up in Wayland and drive me to the workouts. We had good conversations. I regarded him as a mentor. Bill Rodgers was also like a big brother to me. In fact, Bill saved my life once.

I was out on a long run with the GBTC, about 18 or 20 miles around the town of Natick. We ran by this big mansion set far back from the road, and suddenly a huge Great Dane, a dog from hell, comes tearing out at us. We're running in a pack, and this Great Dane, this monster, instinctively homes in on the weakest and most vulnerable member—which, of course, is yours truly, the 110-pound Rookie. Snarling, snapping, slobbering, the beast closes in on me. I'm terrified. I'm frozen. I can't move. But just as the dog is about to spring—it's just like the movies—he yelps in pain and slinks away. I look over, and there's Bill. Among his eccentricities was the fact that he always ran carrying this heavy key ring—I never realized why until that moment (although, being Bill, he might not have realized why he carried it either). He had chucked the key ring at the dog and scared him away. We continued our run. Bill Rodgers had saved my life.

Meanwhile, my life at home, while in some ways loving and affectionate, continued to be contentious, tumultuous, and combative. It seemed like my father was always snarling at me like that Great Dane, except at home there was no Bill Rodgers or key ring. I couldn't wait to get out of there and escape to college. I knew that my father supported me and loved me and was raising me in the way that he thought best. There were no shades of gray in my father's worldview. Things were either black or white, good or evil, and at every moment, a man had to choose between the two. I admired my father's moral rectitude, but living with him was exhausting, suffocating. I couldn't get any room. All I wanted was to get away, and running gave me the opportunity, literally and figuratively.

How did all this happen? What accounts for my sudden unlikely leap from good high school athlete to a world-record-setting distance runner? It certainly wasn't due to physical talent. In fact, I was notorious for my awkward stride. Squires likened my crabbed stride to that of a little old man's, and later, at the University of Oregon, my coach Bill Dellinger would note that I failed to kick my feet back on the follow-through; I looked like I was sitting down and running at the same time. Dellinger often half-joked that he worried that I would fall over in midstride.

So the advance wasn't due to pure physical ability, and with the exception of my brothers Ricardo and José, there was no history of athletic excellence in our family. However, as I've pointed out, I did inherit the family traits of obsessiveness, pride, and toughness. Although I rejected my father's notion of a singular and heroic Salazar family destiny, I privately felt chosen to attain my lofty ambition. I had inherited by father's religious faith, and with it his willingness to sacrifice.

But I paid a price for my obsession. Running was all I had; or, more accurately, all that I thought I had. I defined myself by the sport. At school, I wasn't in the hip crowd; I was a classic nerd. At least that's how I regarded myself. My friends were other runners and the smart bookish kids who got good grades. I did not hang with the football players or other cool guys. I might have beaten John Lacy in the 600-yard run, but John Lacy (or his surrogate) was still the dreamboat whom all the girls loved. Outside of running, I was an awkward kid, excruciatingly shy. To say the least, I did not date.

I had a crush on a girl named Pam Murch. Pam was on the school swim team. I would go and watch her at swim practice; I lurked outside the fence beside the pool and waited for her to get out of the water. But I could never summon the courage to say anything to Pam, and she never knew of my devotion to her. I had a total of one date in high school. I pretended not to be interested in dating or girls, but inside I was a cauldron of intense adolescent emotion, juiced by my passionate Cuban genes.

I remember junior year going to a '50s-theme dance dressed as a greaser. I went wild on the dance floor, jumping around, trying to impress this girl named Aileen Flynn, whom my brother José also had his eye on (the archetypal high school girl who got away; almost as powerful a psychic force as my father). After the dance, I hated myself for being such a dork. Maybe I was a dork, but I was also a runner. I could run the 5000 meters as fast—or faster—than any 16-year-old boy in the world. Even as I hung around the pool suffering over Pam, or made a fool of myself on the dance floor in front of Aileen, I carried that bright coin in my pocket, that shining, saving knowledge that I was good at something, damn good, and I was going to get even better. I was going to be the greatest marathoner in the world.

That knowledge formed my lifeline. It also gave me an excuse for not having the nerve to simply walk up to Pam or Aileen and ask for a date. Instead of being too shy to go out with girls, I told myself I was too busy and disciplined to go out with them. I didn't have time, I rationalized. I didn't have time to go to my senior prom because I had the regional track meet the next day. I didn't even have time to go to my high school graduation ceremony, because I was away at the national junior track championships. This identity—this growing sense of myself—made me stronger. At least, it made me stronger as a runner.

———

I was really good at something. The numbers didn't lie. But I wasn't any good with girls. I'd had one date, kissed one girl, all the way through high school, but that didn't matter because now I was among the best teenage runners in the world. Why was I so good? I wanted it more. That's the only way I can explain it. It wasn't because I had a longer or more elastic stride, or because my blood was less acidic and I could recover from a hard effort faster. And I'd known since I was a fifth grader and getting beat in games of Red Rover that I wasn't special as a sprinter.

I was a special distance runner because I wanted it more. I sacrificed more. I did not go out with Aileen Flynn. I didn't go to my high school graduation. And if I didn't win—if I didn't perform in a race the way I felt capable—I was miserable. Actually, "miserable" isn't strong enough a word. After a bad race, I questioned who I was. I didn't want to see anybody. I didn't want to eat, and I couldn't sleep. I would go into black funks that could last for days. All I could think about, when I wasn't hating myself, was getting back on the track so I could redeem myself—shed this awful weight that defeat had placed on my shoulders.

This might sound extreme, perhaps even a little deranged, but I don't think you can make it to the very top rank in any sport if you don't have a similar aversion to losing—a visceral, physical loathing. I look for this trait in an athlete, although the hatred of losing has to be balanced by a certain degree of realism, an ability to step back just enough so that you can process your disappointing performance and learn from it. That's where a coach can help. A coach can provide that perspective, but he or she can't manufacture that black hatred and self-disgust that comes with losing. And a coach can't provide that willingness—that hunger—to sacrifice.

I don't mean sacrificing once or twice a week at a race, or even sacrificing every day during the season. I mean sacrificing all the time; rejecting everything that comes between you and your goal of becoming the best runner in the world. You never shirk a task that will make you stronger. But at the same time, you can't let your hunger cloud your judgment.

There's a fine line between hating losing for its own sake and hating defeat in order to motivate you to an ultimate victory.

The great runner continually interrogates himself. How badly do I want it? How much of my soul am I going to put into this? How lost am I willing to feel? To what degree will I fight against the natural defense mechanism that protects me against losing and pain? How bitterly will I reject failure?

———

I don't want to misrepresent the nature of high-level distance running. Along with pain and effort, the sacrifice, and the sense of self-loathing that arrives when you fail to perform to your own expectations, the sport is also a tremendous amount of fun. Actually, "fun" is way too pallid a word. The sense of exhilaration you feel when you're riding your pain, when after long and exacting work you've become pain's master rather than its servant, is almost indescribable.

Often these peak moments arrive during training rather than in competition. Maybe you're running a series of 10 x 800-meter repeats in which each rep is run faster than the previous one. At the end of the sixth rep, you know you're maxed out, that you can't possibly run the next two laps around the track any faster or harder. But after your minute's rest, you throw yourself into the next rep and something happens by the backstretch of the first lap, some instinctive switch gets flipped. You reach the edge that you intellectually know you can't go past, but instead of easing back from the edge, you find yourself taking one small step over it. That step is terrifying at first; any rational person would move away from the edge.

But a runner born, like the Kenyan and Ethiopian athletes, or a runner made, the kind that I was, learns to move toward it. Over time, you even learn to welcome it and then eventually crave it. What you assumed to be your ceiling actually forms your floor. You look in the mirror and feel better about the person you see. All you can think about is running back to the edge, and moving one more step beyond it. You are moving on pure will. The journey to the edge becomes intoxicating; dangerously so.

———

By the time I was a junior in high school, I was climbing that seemingly endless ascending ladder. In fact, I'd already climbed into a cloud. If I'd taken a moment to glance down, I might have noticed that I could no longer see the ground. But I never stopped to look down. I only looked up, my eyes fixed on the next rung.

During my teenage years, I often came down with painful strep throat infections, a condition, of course, exacerbated by continuous hard training and its attendant strains on the immune system. On one bitter winter day—the kind of permeating, bone-chilling cold that seems peculiar to New England—I was laid low by strep and stayed home from school. I lay in bed all morning but eventually, even through my pain and exhaustion, I felt the itch to run. Or more accurately, I felt the command to run. There was no choice involved. I absolutely had to log my daily quota of miles. But getting my fix wouldn't be easy. My bedroom was on the second floor of the house, and my mother would be guarding the door downstairs.

I very quietly rose from bed and slipped into a sweat suit, watch cap, and running shoes. I moved to the window and raised it just enough to slip my skinny butt through it and onto the sloping snow-covered roof overhanging the front porch of our low-slung ranch-style house. I inched down the roof to its edge and softly leaped to the snow-covered lawn. So far so good; I hadn't twisted an ankle, and my mother hadn't noticed my escape.

I turned and started running down the snowy streets, into the bitter wind, ignoring my pain and fever and weakness, stuffing them down into the hole in my psyche where I deposited all negative thoughts—along with all negative facts—detracting from my running. During my work-out, it started to snow, and when I arrived back home an hour later, my cap and sweat suit were caked. Icicles hung from my nose, and I shivered uncontrollably. Any further subterfuge was inconceivable; in my condition, there was no way I could climb back on the roof.

So I rang the doorbell. I'll never forget the look on my mother's face when she opened the door and realized that this shivering snow-covered wraith was her son. My mother screamed and pulled me inside. She hugged me close and wept.

All through high school, the strep throat never quite went away. It might recede for weeks or even months, but it would always bloom again. I remember that after one race my throat felt like it was on fire. I couldn't swallow. My glands were swollen as big as chestnuts. I went into the locker room where no one could see me. Now it was my turn to weep.

———

Today, 40 years later, my mother is gone and my father lives in Florida. For the past few months, we've been at war over the upcoming wedding of one of my nephews. The bride and groom are planning a non-Catholic ceremony, which infuriates my father. He says he's going to boycott the wedding and threatens to shun any of his children who decide to attend. We discuss the issue—we go to war over the issue—every time we talk on the phone. I make all the logical arguments. I explain how times have changed, and that a non-Catholic ritual does not constitute a sacrilege, or even a breach of faith. But my father, thus far, remains unmoved. He dis-plays the same stubbornness, the same iron-clad conviction that every-thing in life is either right or wrong, that drove me crazy when I was a kid.

Now it's getting worse, but now I'm able to view his behavior in a more charitable light. Now, in fact, I recognize that same quality in myself. When I was in college and high school and starting to excel in the sport, my father declared it was because of the "Salazar blood." It made me want to crawl and hide with embarrassment, but now I know there's some truth to my father's assertion. My drive had to come from somewhere. By the same token, I have come to respect (although I know I'll never match) my father's ferocious adherence to principle and his unfailing readiness to stand up for what he believes. It might be a product of tunnel vision and bull-headedness, but it also reflects a certain virtue.

———

Now my attention started to turn to college; or, more accurately, to college running. I already had announced my number-one choice: the University of Oregon, where, along with my new best friend Rudy Chapa, I could run in the footsteps of Prefontaine. But now there were other contenders.

My father got to be friends with the track coach at Harvard University, and for a time my dad entertained every American parent's dream—that his son would go to the nation's premier institution of higher learning. The dream was all the more potent for my father, an immigrant who came to this country with nothing and in less than 20 years had achieved a remarkable success. More specifically, he envisioned me as a Harvard-trained physician. Alongside his more reasonable daydreams, my father conjured nightmares in which the Soviet Union "took over" America. No matter what the political and economic system, went his thinking, people always needed doctors.

I was a good student and took academics seriously, but my main goal was running, one area in which Oregon clearly trumped Harvard or any other of the Ivy League colleges. Also, going to Harvard would mean staying home in the Boston area, and I desperately wanted to escape. I received offers or letters of interest from every top college running program in the nation, but I eventually narrowed my choices to two universities on the West Coast: Oregon and Stanford.

Such was the fame and reputation of Oregon's program that its coach, Bill Dellinger, who'd recently succeeded Bill Bowerman, almost never made recruiting visits. It was the obligation of the fortunate recruit to make the pilgrimage to Eugene, where tradition-soaked Hayward Field and the general ambience of Track Town USA were usually enough to sell the kid. But in my case, and also that of Rudy Chapa, Dellinger made an exception.

During the winter of my senior year, the coach traveled to Massachusetts to recruit me in person. He came out to a GBTC workout at the indoor track at Tufts. I badly wanted to impress Dellinger, and probably because I was pressing, I tripped during a repeat and went sprawling. But I jumped up with a vengeance and resumed running, which, Dellinger told me later, impressed him even more than if I hadn't fallen at all. After the workout, Dellinger came to the house in Wayland, where my father insisted on showing him some home movies. "Don't worry," my father told the coach. "I'll only show this one reel—it's all of Alberto running." But, of course, my dad couldn't locate the reel, and Dellinger ended up watching hours of family vacations and Thanksgiving dinners. When he finally left our house, the poor man was cross-eyed. He probably never made a recruiting visit again.

It turned out that Dellinger's trip, while flattering, was unnecessary. Once I saw the Oregon campus, I was hooked. At the time of my visit, I was still undecided between Stanford and Oregon. In fact, both schools pooled resources to sponsor my recruiting trip out to the West Coast. I visited Stanford University first, and I was impressed by the sprawling, magnificent campus at the base of the coastal foothills, with its eucalyptus-lined walks and mission-style architecture. Payton Jordan, the distinguished coach who'd led several US Olympic track and field teams, showed me the trails through the foothills on the edge of campus where I would train and the famous 85,500-seat Stanford Stadium where I would compete. With California stars glittering in my eyes, I flew north to visit the University of Oregon in Eugene.

There couldn't have been a greater contrast between the two schools. Where Stanford was private, Oregon was public. Where Stanford was sunny, Oregon was gray. Where the Stanford Stadium was a vast bowl, big enough to host a Super Bowl (which in fact it did, in 1985), Hayward Field was an unprepossessing, almost homely green-painted structure that could hold only about 10,000 spectators. But what the U of O lacked in grandeur, it more than made up for in tradition and soul. For a runner or track fan, Hayward represents what Fenway Park or Wrigley Field means to a baseball player or fan.

Fenway or Wrigley can't compare in amenities to modern high-tech stadiums, but as soon as you step inside one of the vintage parks, you feel like you're entering the true realm of baseball. That's what Hayward represented to me—this was the house that Bowerman and Prefontaine built. This was the mythical place I'd been hearing about since I was a little kid, when Ricardo first started telling me stories about the U of O. But Hayward was clearly much more than a museum.

You could feel right away that Eugene served as the beating heart of distance running in America. Dellinger had carried on the U of O tradition. In the entire 20th century, the school had had only three permanent head coaches, and all were named Bill: Hayward, Bowerman, and now Dellinger. The Ducks had won a string of recent NCAA track and cross-country championships, and Hayward Field was scheduled to host the '76 US Olympic track-and-field trials. The school was recruiting a prospective freshman class featuring some of the nation's top prep runners, including Rudy and me. Unlike Stanford, Oregon couldn't offer spectacular trails through the coastal foothills, but it did have Pre's Trail snaking along the Willamette River and the Amazon Trail cutting through the south end of town. These trails bulged with runners day and night.

Most telling, Hayward Field lay at the actual—and symbolic—heart of the U of O campus. At Stanford, running was just one of the riches that the university and region had to offer. At Oregon, and in Eugene, by contrast, running lay at the center of everything. I knew where I wanted to go to college—where I was destined to go—and Rudy decided to join me. It was a fateful choice. From that day forward, my life became inextricably bound up with the University of Oregon, both its reality and its legend. The mystique would continue to radiate from the campus, crossing over to affect the Nike ethos and culture, which was just beginning to build. And through the agency of Nike, of course, the spirit of Oregon distance running—the idea that a passion for sports in general, and running in particular, were available to anybody—would eventually spread around the world.

———

In the fall of 1976, I enrolled as a freshman at Oregon. It was an auspicious time in the sport of running. A few weeks earlier, at the Summer Olympic Games in Montreal, Frank Shorter, the defending Olympic champion, finished second in the marathon behind the East German Waldemar Cierpinski, who was later documented to be part of that nation's notorious doping program. From that point on, doping would play a major role in the sport, and from that point forward, American distance runners would no longer dominate international competition. We would have to share the prizes with the drug cheats and, more significantly, with the gifted African distance runners who had just started to make their presence known and who would arrive en masse once the sport turned professional shortly thereafter.

Apart from running, the counterculture was then in full bloom, and Eugene served as one of the main stops on the hippie highway. On campus, the ethos of running coexisted with the one of sex, drugs, and rock and roll. Pretty strong stuff for a conservative, straitlaced Catholic kid from Massachusetts. I might have found it overwhelming, but I had a built-in community of runners to tap into and keep me grounded. I was also lucky to have Rudy Chapa as my roommate and best friend.

Rudy would later tell me that three things made him curious about me when we met at the junior US–USSR track meet in Nebraska in 1975: my Hispanic surname, the fact that I was toothpick-skinny (I weighed only 120 pounds at the time), and my terrible running form. Rudy was amazed that despite these latter two deficits, I could run so fast. By contrast, Rudy had a beautiful stride and was a fine all-around athlete. I still think he's one of the most talented American runners ever. More important, he was a good kid—smart, funny, charismatic, and kind. I felt like I was none of those things. Maybe we got along so well because we were so different. We got assigned to the same room in the University Inn, the athletes' dorm on campus. That first night, we got into an epic but friendly argument.

We turned out the lights and were lying in bed and somehow started debating the question of who was the world's greatest athlete. I said it was Bruce Jenner, the American who had just won the decathlon at the Montreal Olympics. Rudy said no, the best athlete in the world was Julius Erving, Dr. J, the superstar NBA basketball player. We really got into it. I listed my reasons, Rudy ran down his. The argument grew pretty heated; we also got very specific. I was premed at the time, and Rudy was prelaw (he would later become an attorney), so we both put great stock in objective evidence and in our own abilities to marshal it. We had a blast, and the hours flew by. We argued until 3 o'clock in the morning, fighting it out to a draw. We hadn't settled anything, but I think we both drifted off to sleep that night knowing that we'd made a friend for life.

————

Often a freshman is initially disappointed in his college, but I wasn't let down at all by the U of O. In fact, it exceeded my expectations. It was good academically and a perfect place to run, and that's what I was there for. In the fall of '76, the Ducks were putting together another NCAA championship-caliber cross-country squad led by Terry Williams, Dave Taylor, and Don Clary. As a freshman, I was only a spear-carrier on the team, but it was still a great experience, and I was learning every minute. In most ways, Bill Dellinger's training philosophy jibed with what I'd been getting from Bill Squires back at the Greater Boston Track Club; a stress on quality rather than quantity, and a lot of long, fast intervals. The personalities of the two men, however, differed.

Squires would discuss anything with you, but once you understood what he wanted, and you'd agreed to it, he would jump on your case if you didn't follow through. Dellinger, as Rudy would say, sometimes gave you enough rope to hang yourself. Not because he didn't care, but because he believed in treating us like adults. The bronze medalist in the 5000 meters at the '64 Olympics, Dellinger was an old-school, tough-as-nails military veteran from small-town Oregon who'd put himself through school working in lumber mills. He told us what he wanted and left the rest up to us. He never yelled or screamed. During a race, Dellinger often sat up in the stands and watched; Bill believed that by the time the meet came around, the coaching was essentially over.

That approach suited me perfectly. I was obsessed by running and was always looking for ways—some of them off the wall—to improve. A more controlling coach—Bowerman, for instance—wouldn't have tolerated a freshman's schemes for a moment, but with Dellinger I had room to experiment. Rudy was also mad about running, but even he was amazed by the stuff that I came up with. For instance, I would pry the soles off my training shoes and then put them back together, using Shoe Goo, in a mad-scientist attempt to balance both shoes to the exact millimeter. When a fad arose around something called "static stretching," in which you hold a muscle-twanging position for up to a full minute, I hopped on the bandwagon. At a time when very few distance runners bothered with any strength or core training, I would pump out hundreds of pushups and situps every day. I went so far as to make my own yogurt according to a recipe I'd read about in some magazine. When I injured my ankle and had to cross-train in the pool, I swam so obsessively that I developed tendinitis in my shoulders. Rudy, who was a witness to all this, would just smile and shake his head. He was dead serious about the sport, too, but kept it in better perspective. Rudy understood that running had given him the shot at a college education, and he wasn't going to blow the opportunity. He was equally committed to books and sports. At night, he wanted to sit up studying, and I wanted to get my sleep for the next day's training. Finally, he rigged up a lamp in our closet, so we both got what we needed. Not that I was an academic slacker—during my freshman year as a pre-med major, I took bone-crusher classes like organic chemistry—but I had a good memory and had learned to be an efficient student. I discovered that if I listened very closely in class and took careful notes, I could do well in tests—and running could comfortably remain my priority.

Despite our shared Hispanic heritage, Rudy and I came from widely divergent backgrounds. Rudy's father had come up from Mexico to labor in the steel mills of Hammond, Indiana. Rudy was the first kid in the family to go to college, and he took the long view: Elite-level running would only last 4 or 5 years; it was what came afterward that was really important. Your family and your professional career would define you as a person. By contrast, I came from a long line of accomplished, well-educated professionals. Ricardo was a graduate of the US Naval Academy, one of the most prestigious universities in the world. Merely graduating from college and pursuing a successful professional career wasn't going to distinguish me in the eyes of my father—or at least so I thought. I burned to stand out in a different way, and running was it. I couldn't imagine a life beyond the sport.

From a competitive standpoint, my freshman year proved a mixed bag. That fall at the NCAA cross-country championship, I made a dumb rookie mistake. The night before the meet, which was held in Denton, Texas, I went out for dinner and ate a huge steak. The lump of animal flesh was still sitting in my gut when the race started the next morning, and after a fast opening, I began to cramp up. I tried to fight them off, but the cramps got worse, and I was forced to drop out after 3 miles, contributing no points for the team. I felt miserable. I fell into one of my black funks; I felt the kind of shame that can only be alleviated by a redeeming race. During track season the following spring, however, I suffered a series of nagging injuries that lingered for nearly 3 months. But I recovered in time to finish third in the 5000 at the Pac-10 championships and ninth at the same distance at the NCAA championships. Those late-season successes confirmed that I was on the right track. The future looked bright, and my destiny remained clear.

That summer, I returned home to Wayland and went back to training and hanging out with Bill Squires and the guys from the Greater Boston Track Club. I was still the Rookie, guys like Kirk Pfrangle and Bill Rodgers and Randy Thomas still would playfully bust my chops, but now I'd been away, gotten some seasoning, and further proved my mettle. We would go out to eat after a workout, and from time to time they would sneak me into bars—I was still under the legal drinking age. At home, things were a little less tense. I had my driver's license now, I had my own life going and didn't feel trapped in my father's shadow.

Our relationship improved. In fact, I had a job that summer working for my father's construction company. I'd get up at 5:00 a.m., go for a run, and then we'd drive together to the job site. We were working in Nashua, New Hampshire, putting up the new headquarters for the Digital Equipment Corporation. I worked as a helper on a surveying crew. The guys would always rag me because I fell asleep so easily. I could sleep anywhere. When we drove 5 minutes across the construction site in the pickup truck, I would conk out for a 5-minute nap.

It wasn't the work that was wearing me out or having to get up so early. Every afternoon, on the drive home, my dad would let me out of the car 7 miles from home, and I would run the rest of the way. By the time I rounded the corner onto Snake Brook Road, showered, and ate dinner, it was 7 o'clock. I'd be in bed by 10. It was a good, tough summer that culminated in August with my second-place performance at the 7.1-mile Falmouth Road Race on Cape Cod. A few weeks later, when I went back to the U of O preseason training camp at Odell Lake in the Oregon Cascades, I was a much stronger runner.

———

By the end of my sophomore cross-country season, I was one of the top runners on the team, and the Ducks were in contention for another NCAA championship. Two of our biggest rivals were Washington State University, which was led by Henry Rono, the peerless Kenyan runner who would eventually hold world records in distances ranging from 3000 to 10,000 meters (all of them set within a single 3-month period), and the University of Texas at El Paso, whose team also was built around athletes imported from Kenya and other African nations.

Today, because of the relatively abundant opportunities to win prize money in road races around the world, the most talented young African distance runners—and every year the flood of them increases—forego educations to make as much money as they can as fast as they can on the pro circuit. But in the 1970s, distance running was still a primarily amateur sport, and Kenyans such as Rono jumped at the chance to come to the United States and compete on the collegiate level.

Many Americans took exception to this practice, accusing the universities of essentially hiring ringers to deliver them championships, construing the foreign athletes as some kind of carpetbaggers. But at Oregon, we felt differently. At least Rudy and I did. We stayed up late one night talking about it, but unlike our freshman-year argument about the world's greatest athlete, this time we agreed. We both welcomed Rono; we would have welcomed competition from Mars, if that planet produced runners with sub-29-minute 10-K speed. "How could you call yourself the best," we asked one another confidently, "if you didn't test yourself against the best?"

———

The 1977 NCAA championship cross-country meet was held in Spokane, Washington, on a late-autumn day when the temperature was around 8 degrees. I had never been colder in my life, even on that day back in Wayland as a teenager, when I ran through the snow with a strep throat. This was in the days before university athletic departments signed deals with shoe companies to provide all their gear. For that meet, we wore uniforms designed by the mother of Bill McChesney, one of the guys on our team. The shorts were made out of thin, filmy material, with especially flimsy liners; we felt like we were literally freezing our balls off. And, of course, I had virtually zero body fat to provide insulation.

I tried to zone out the weather and focus on the race. I had finished second to Rono in both the Pac-10 championships and NCAA western regional meet; and now, at the national meet, I thought I was in shape to break the top five. The gun cracked and I started strongly, jumping into the lead pack of about five runners. We had proceeded a good distance into the 10-K course, at least 600 meters, when the gun sounded again, a signal for us to stop running. Something had gone wrong at the start, somebody must have jumped, and now we had to start over. During the wait for that second gun, I couldn't stop shivering. I felt cold and tight and miserable. The gun sounded a third time. Now the race was finally on, but I couldn't hit my rhythm, my chance was gone.

I languished in around 30th place for most of the race but rallied over the last half-mile to finish ninth and score some significant points for the Ducks. It didn't appear to be enough; UTEP finished just a point or two ahead of us, and we flew back home feeling empty and frustrated. When we stepped off the plane at the Eugene airport, however, we found out that the officials had made a mistake. When they retabulated the results, they discovered that Oregon had actually won the meet. We went wild celebrating what was my first NCAA championship.

———

By sophomore year, I was also settling into college life. I switched my major from biology/premed to marketing and finance, mostly on the advice of Terry Williams, who'd been cocaptain of the cross-country team during my freshman year. Terry was also a premed major, and he told me it was hard enough balancing Division 1 distance running and premed academic pressure as an undergraduate; it would be virtually impossible to continue to run seriously while going to medical school. That's all I needed to hear. I didn't care if my father was convinced that in some fantasy USA overrun by the Soviets, medicine would offer a secure livelihood. I had already established my postgraduation career plan. Anything that might possibly interfere with running, I didn't even want to consider.

There was one exception to my rule, of course: girls. Or, I should say, women. In another 2 or 3 years, a writer from a national publication would portray me as veritable babe magnet, "with the looks of a young parish priest that made all the housewives flutter." Was he writing about the same guy? Remember, my high school babe-magnet totals amounted to one date and one girl kissed. My freshman year at the U of O didn't dramatically add to that tally. Not that I was a prude or a complete loser in the romance department, but let's just say that I was not exactly part of the wild vanguard of the sexual revolution. In part this was due to my Catholic upbringing, but mostly my shyness had to do with a lack of self-confidence. I still saw myself as that geeky high school kid hanging around outside the swim practice, waiting for Pam Murch to climb out of the pool. I wasn't a big confident football player like John Lacy, or even like my brother José. I was just skinny Alberto, the Rookie, a kid who became a runner because he wasn't big enough, fast enough, coordinated enough to make it in another sport. I had driven myself to excel as a runner to compensate for a deep insecurity.

I wished that I were a solid, squared-away guy operating on a balanced, healthy combination of measured self-confidence and realistic self-doubt, like my best friend, Rudy Chapa. But instead, I was this weird, haunted, obsessive *Cubano* nut. And then I met Molly, and it was love at first sight.

———

Molly Morton was a talented freshman on the cross-country team. She was blonde with blue eyes and a fresh, friendly, easy manner. If I was all dark, East Coast ethnic, tortured weird, Molly, a native of Portland, Oregon, was all open, sane, WASP, Western normal. Molly was a knockout, and I thought about her all the time. She was a happy, well-balanced sorority girl, a good student, and a good athlete. Although a fine runner—she once held the U of O women's school records in the

3000, 5000, and 10,000—Molly didn't approach the sport with a fraction of the obsession that I showed. Rather than being turned off by that, I found it attractive. I felt instinctively drawn to her balanced, healthy approach. We started dating, but I came on way too strong at first and scared her away. We broke up at the end of sophomore year. But she remained always on my mind. (The next year, when I went out with another girl, I committed the cardinal sin and called her Molly by mistake.)

Meanwhile, Molly was testing the water with other guys. She went out with a pole vaulter on our team named Tom Hintnaus. Tom was a good guy and good athlete. He was also extremely handsome; so good looking that he worked as one of the first models in those famous ads for Calvin Klein underwear. If you visited Times Square in Manhattan in the 1970s, you might have seen Tom's seminaked body sprawled across a huge billboard. So my claim to fame is that (eventually) I beat out the guy who was the model for Calvin Klein underwear. Although at the time, it seemed that I'd blown it with Molly, driven her away with my intensity. I was heartbroken, and for consolation I turned to my unfailing source of comfort and identity. I reached for that bright coin shining in the bottom of my pocket, the certainty that I was going to become the greatest marathoner in the world.

———

That spring, Henry Rono was on his record-breaking binge, setting world-best marks in distances ranging from 3000 to 10,000 meters—all of this while still competing for Washington State University, one of the Ducks' big rivals. The previous winter, I'd briefly butted heads with Dellinger—he picked a few other guys over me to run the 2-mile in a big indoor meet and I'd been livid—but now I was over that. Washington State came into Hayward for a big dual meet. Everybody on our team hated Washington State. I was entered in the 5000 meters, running against Rono. Before the race, he and his teammates were trash-talking, playing mind games. Then the race started, and the jostling and maneuvering continued. Rono was working with his teammate Joshua Kimeto, another Kenyan athlete, and Rudy and I were working together for Oregon. At the finish, I threw down a strong kick (by that time Rono had dropped out of the race) and won in 13:26. That was my big race of the spring. It was a great moment, although that season ended in disappointment.

At the Pac-10 championships, Rono got his revenge. I finished second to him in the 10,000. At the NCAA Championships, Rudy won the 5,000 meters while I finished a distant sixth. I was happy for Rudy but disgusted with my own mediocre performance. I felt puzzled and frustrated. I was doing everything Dellinger asked of me, yet I seemed stuck on a plateau. All during my serious running career, starting with Squires and the GBTC in high school, my coaches had been telling me to hold back, pace myself, not risk burning myself out, keep my eyes on the distant prize, think about the future, etc. Well, I was tired of waiting for the future. I had seen the future, and it was Henry Rono coming to America from Kenya with his blazing natural talent and setting four world records. It was my best friend, Rudy Chapa, fulfilling the promise he'd shown when we were running together at that US–USSR junior track meet in Nebraska. When was I going to make good on my promise? I was tired of waiting. The future was *now*.

———

I made a mental adjustment and decided that I could push harder. Part of my obsession with running had been to meticulously follow the instructions of my coaches. They had told me to proceed deliberately. When I encountered injury or undue pain, they counseled me do the common-sensical thing and back off. But now I wondered what would happen if I responded to pain by moving into it rather than easing away; what if I regarded pain as a signal that I was doing something right, and that I should pile on more of what was causing it rather than cut back? As hard as I'd trained, as much as I had suffered, as successfully as I had raced, I still harbored deep doubts about my toughness. Maybe I wasn't as tough as I thought—or as I hoped. When I got home to Wayland that summer after my sophomore year, I took a big piece of poster paper and a felt-tipped marker. "You will never be broken again," I wrote, in stark bold lettering, and I nailed that vow on my bedroom wall.

That summer, I got a job as a "product tester" for a running shoe company. The money was good and the duties light. So I didn't have to go back to working for my father's construction company. No more 5:00 a.m. wake-ups, holding up surveyor's rods, catnaps in the truck, or 7-mile runs home in the sweltering afternoons. Now I was free to train all day, and now I didn't have a Squires, Dellinger, or anybody else warning me that I might be overdoing it. I greedily seized the opportunity. I ran all the time, training twice a day around my house, and also at a running camp put on by Squires. Soon my weekly training mileage had rocketed up to 120, when my previous high had rarely exceeded 90. Predictably enough, I soon paid the price for my excess, developing a stress fracture in my foot. I went to the doctor, who said that the fracture had affected a bone in my foot that was essentially non–weight bearing, and that I could train through the injury. I thought this was the best news in the world; in the long run, it was the worst thing I could have heard. For years afterward, I had the idea stuck in my mind that I could cheat pain and find a way to train through an injury. It was the same kind of magical thinking that allowed people to believe that if they ran marathons they would never have a heart attack. You latch on to whatever piece of good news fits your purposes—whether it's from Dr. Thomas J. Bassler or from my doc in Wayland—and disregard the mountain of evidence telling you unequivocally that there is no magic.

My competitive goal that summer was the Falmouth Road Race on Cape Cod in August. The previous year, I'd finished second to Bill Rodgers there; this year, I aimed to win. The Falmouth race was important for all sorts of reasons. It formed the summer bookend for the New England running calendar. The Boston Marathon was the traditional serious event, run in the spring but more associated with winter because you had to train for it then, and Falmouth was almost shorthand for summer. The race seemed to represent all that was best about the time and the place. Although sadly, at the age of 19, I was too wrapped up in my own agenda to really enjoy it.

The Falmouth Road Race was the creation of Tommy Leonard, the classic friendly ribald Boston barkeep. But Tommy was also a very serious citizen-runner, equally dedicated to his miles and his beer, a uniquely Boston-area combination. Tommy spent summers on Cape Cod, and the distance from the Captain Kidd Bar in Woods Hole, where he hung out, to the Brothers Four in Falmouth Heights, where he stood behind the stick, measured 7.1 miles. Tommy conceived a road race between the two bars, and the first edition, in 1973, drew a field of 92, mostly fellow bartenders and buddies of Tommy's, along with early adaptors to the nascent running boom; only a year had passed since Frank Shorter's gold medal marathon at the Munich Olympics, and the wave was just beginning to build. That early Falmouth was a fun, funky blend of a smackdown for bragging rights among the small, close-knit Boston running community and an excuse for a blowout summer party—as if Tommy and his pals really needed an excuse. The buzz around Falmouth built, especially among the guys that I knew at the Greater Boston Track Club, and the race soon became a can't-miss event.

Indeed, by August 1978, 5 years after the maiden race, the first wave of the running boom was cresting, and it seemed like the entire world wanted to come to Tommy Leonard's excellent beach party (in fact, people were heartbroken when their applications for entry were denied; they would show up at Tommy's bar and tell him sob stories, trying to gain special entry). The field had swelled to 4,000, prompting Kenny Moore to write in a feature story about the race in *Sports Illustrated* that "the sport is rapidly outgrowing its Thoreauvian roots." Falmouth '78 represented a sort of coming-out party for distance running in America. It wasn't the climax of the boom—that wouldn't come for another few years with my marathons in New York City and Boston. Falmouth marked more of an arrival.

For my part, I was interested in neither the beer blast nor the "Thoreauvian" aspects; I wanted to win. I wanted to prove my toughness, both to myself and to my old GBTC friends who still thought of me as the Rookie. That summer, I was still thinking about Molly—about how I'd scared her away with my intensity, and how she'd ditched me for the pole vaulter—but I was dating a girl named Nancy Robinson. Nancy's father was a doctor, and the family owned a house on the Cape, which is where I stayed that weekend. Between the crush of runners there for the race, and the normal horde of August tourists, the Cape was overrun. My father and Ricardo had driven out from Wayland to watch the big race.

The morning didn't seem overbearingly hot—the temperature hung around 75 degrees—but the humidity felt off the charts. It was the kind of muggy East Coast humidity that made summers tougher on me than the most bitter winter—the type of humidity that people hope to escape by coming to the Cape in August. Besides Rodgers and me, the field included Rudy, along with the standout American runner Craig Virgin, the reigning national champion in the 10,000 meters.

The gun sounded, and we went out fast, the elite pack bolting ahead of the 4,000 runners behind us. Rodgers, Virgin, and I ran in front. Bill was then at the height of his fame. Besides his streak of Boston Marathon wins that had earned him the moniker Boston Billy, he was also on a roll at the

New York City Marathon, riding a streak of four consecutive victories. Bill's spaced-out, easygoing demeanor belied a competitive drive every bit as fierce as mine. Bill wanted to put me in my place, to prove that he was still the master and I was the Rookie. He led the pace from the first mile of the hilly course, going out at 4:25, hitting the second mile in 8:55 and the third in 13:43. I locked in on his shoulder, a half step behind.

I felt strong, both from the months of extra training mileage and from my daily study of the vow on my bedroom wall: "I will never be broken again." I also drew confidence from my closing speed—I knew that Rodgers, who ran exclusively on the roads, couldn't match the speed that I'd honed on the Hayward Field track. And finally, as I'd soon dramatically learn, I was fortified by the prayer I'd been repeating each night since I was 7 years old, since that terrible afternoon when I saw the body of the boy being pulled from the waters of Salters Pond: *Mother, when I die, don't let me be afraid. Let me go straight to your son Jesus.*

A prayer I had voiced so often that I'd long since stopped focusing on the words. Yet a peculiar power of prayer, I have learned, comes in its cumulative effect. Even a prayer offered by rote, with minimal concentration, works its way into your mind and spirit. By the same token, as I blasted along through the race's middle miles, I repeated another phrase whose words were about to take on a chillingly literal meaning: "Nobody pulls away from me," I told myself. "I'll die before letting anybody beat me." Even Bill Rodgers.

————

At the 4-mile mark, we were still wailing. Rodgers rocked steady, a half step ahead of me. "Bill, you've been doing all the work," I said to him—meaning that he'd been setting the pace and breaking the force of the breeze blowing off of the Atlantic and into our faces. "Why don't I take over for a while?"

That's the last thing I remember about that race, the last image that would seem real for a long time. All I can do now is piece together an account of what followed from media accounts, spectators, medical personnel, family members, and my fellow athletes.

Bill Rodgers glanced over his shoulder to accept my offer, but I was no longer close to him. I had suddenly fallen 10 yards behind, and I lost more ground with each step.

I was drifting, confused. The world looked strange. It was fuzzy and had dim patches. But I kept going. I kept running, even though it seemed that other runners were inexplicably passing me—runners who weren't nearly as fast as me, who had no business blowing by me. Then I did something very strange, although I have no recollection of it.

Randy Thomas, my teammate from the GBTC, later said that I came to a dead stop, turned slowly around in a circle, and then resumed running. Randy must have been completely creeped out. The little kids watching from the sidewalk must have been frightened. Somehow, I kept running. More competitors passed me, which normally would have driven me into a rage, but now it didn't bother me a bit. I would later learn that I finished 10th in the race, but it might have been 510th, for all that I knew or cared at that moment.

The next thing I remember is hearing a voice calling out numbers: "104 . . . 106 . . . 107 . . . it's not going down! I think we're going to lose him!" I realized that I was no longer running. For some reason, I was lying down in the medical tent. The objects in my field of vision remained fuzzy. What appeared to be doctors and nurses moved around above me. I could tell that they were very worried. "One-oh-eight," one of them said in a hushed voice. It occurred to me that the voice was talking about my temperature. One hundred eight degrees? Was that possible? Shouldn't that hurt? How could I be so hot if I wasn't feeling anything?

I was lying completely submerged in a tub of ice water. I drifted out of consciousness again and came back. And then, like an ice-pick stab in my throat, I realized that I was going to die. I panicked. I tried to push out of the tub of water, but I could not move. I started to scream and yell. I felt a hand on my shoulder. "You're in the medical tent," a voice said. "You're going to be okay."

But I knew that wasn't true. "I want my father!" I yelled. "I want to see my father!"

There was some scrambling, some hushed conferencing, and then they were calling my father's name over the public-address system. My fear ratcheted into terror. The doctors had stopped calling out my temperature readings. I heard scraps of conversations: "brain damage . . ." "he may die. . . . " My panic intensified.

And then my father was there. My father stood above me. He had found two wooden sticks, tongue depressors, I suppose. He crossed the sticks over me in the shape of a crucifix. "Concentrate on this, Alberto," my father said. "Just focus on this, and you'll be okay."

He spoke in a calm voice. I wondered where that calm and strength came from. In earlier crises—the boy drowning at Salters Pond, the middle-of-the-night phone call in which he'd learned that his father had died in a plane crash—he had been anything but calm, but now my father seemed strong and sure of himself, and I felt protected. In that instant, my panic subsided. I remained certain that I was about to die, but I was no longer frightened. I suddenly felt as calm as my father's voice.

This is it, I'm dying now. I'm coming to you, Mother. I was half-talking to myself, half-praying. *I'm coming now. Please forgive me for my sins.*

A profound feeling of peace came over me. My boyhood prayer had been answered. The time of my death had come and I wasn't afraid. The action in the room, formerly so frantic, now seemed to slow. I looked up at the jury-rigged crucifix, and above that at the face of my father, and beyond that at the shapes of doctors and nurses moving around the medical tent. I saw all that, or sensed it all, and I waited . . . I waited . . . and then, as suddenly as the fear of death had drained out of me, I felt wildly, excruciatingly cold.

Everything started moving very fast. I was lifted out of the tent and into an ambulance. My father and Ricardo were in the ambulance with me. I remember IV bottles swinging and a general atmosphere of chaos that included a series of smashing noises; Ricardo would later tell me that in his haste to get to the hospital, and amid the throngs of people around the finish area, the ambulance driver clipped off several side mirrors of parked vehicles.

I shivered uncontrollably. I finally understood what had happened. I had suffered heatstroke out on the course. The ambulance delivered me to the hospital—more rushing around, more chaos. And then a priest appeared. Perhaps this was a vision related to my feeling of serenity, the assurance from the Holy Mother that I needn't be afraid. I blinked, but the priest was still there. He was no figment of my fever, but a real priest, and he was giving me the Last Rites of the church. I found this puzzling. Didn't the father know that I wasn't going to die?

Over the next hour, as I continued to be fed fluids intravenously and bathed in ice water, my temperature plummeted below normal, and I had to be swaddled in blankets to bring the reading back up to 98.6. Once I was rehydrated and my vital signs stabilized, I was released from the hospital. Astonishingly, except for some bruises around my arms and elbows, where the medics had jammed in needles, I was none the worse for wear. And yet, on the inside, I was a different person that afternoon than I'd been in the morning.

I felt exhilarated, and not merely by the fact that I'd narrowly escaped a brush with death. My thrill ran deeper; I had learned something from death. I had learned, through the agency of my lifelong prayer, that I wasn't afraid of death. I realized that this made me different from the people walking by me in the street. More important—at least to me in the midst of my obsession—it made me different from other runners. I no longer doubted my toughness, not after running myself into the ground, not after running myself to the point of death. Why would I have to fear anything again? I was not content to accept my survival as a gift from God; I interpreted it instead as divine affirmation of my toughness.

———

In many ways, the events at Falmouth that day conform to the classic near-death experience. According to my cardiologist, Dr. Todd Caulfield, people undergoing a near-death experience often witness a powerful, warm light. An air of comprehensive acceptance distinguishes the NDE, accompanied by an overwhelming sense of well-being. I experienced all of these things during that August morning on Cape Cod. I saw the light, I knew that the Holy Mother was waiting for me, and that everything was going to be okay.

Preliminary scientific studies show that compared to the general population, people who have been through an NDE are less afraid of death and have a stronger belief in life after death. They exhibit a greater interest in spirituality and willingness to explore the deeper meaning of existence and feel a heightened awareness and intuition regarding the needs and emotions of others. In my post-Falmouth period, I think I showed most of those traits. In one crucial way, however, I differed from the typical near-death-experience veteran. According to the 2010 book *Consciousness Beyond Life: The Science of the Near-Death Experience*, by Pin Van Lommel, MD, the Dutch cardiologist who published the 2001 study of the subject, people who have been through the near-death experience "attach less importance to status, money and material possessions, and distance themselves from the competitive elements in contemporary society."

Status, money, and material possessions were never my prime motivators. Competition, however, was a different story. Instead of dampening my competitive drive, I'm sorry to report, my first NDE sent it off the charts.

Perhaps it was due to the arrogance of youth, or maybe it was due to the emotional fallout from the near-death experience, coupled with the intense emotional energy I had invested in running that summer; or maybe it was simply divine plan, a responsibility that God apportioned me as companion to the privilege of sparing my life and the key to unlocking my greater destiny. Whatever the causes, instead of being humbled by my NDE, I felt infused with power and pride.

I was so obsessed with running—so intently focused on my goal, my calling, of becoming the greatest marathoner in the world—that instead of regarding my spared life as a gift, I saw it as God telling me that I was special and strong. "Man, am I tough," I thought. "Man, am I cool. Now I'm going to be the most unbelievable runner in history! I don't have to be afraid of anything or anybody!"

I felt grateful to God not for sparing my life but for sending this apparently clear, unequivocal sign. I went to a party that night, and my friends touched the bruises on my arms—the marks left by the IV needles—as if they were the wounds of a saint. I felt like I was walking on air. Now I knew, beyond the shadow of a doubt, that I'd been correct in pursuing my destiny. I had been chosen.

———

What an idiot, you might think; what an egotistical ass. Perhaps. But greater forces seemed to be at work. Except for the occasion after the junior meet in Nebraska in which the temperature soared above 100 degrees and I required rehydration in the medical tent after the 5000, I hadn't experienced particular difficulties running in the heat; certainly nothing approaching my life-threatening experience at Falmouth. Looking back now, I realize that in the excitement of coming to Cape Cod and seeing a bunch of old friends, I failed to drink adequate fluids the day before the race and grew dehydrated.

Still, the severity of my collapse seems out of proportion to that lapse.

I think that God's hand was visible in my fall. Had I not suffered that breakdown in Falmouth, I might have enjoyed a longer career, but I probably wouldn't have reached the heights I attained. That egotistical yet sacrificial sense of being chosen for a great destiny, and of viewing every experience through the prism of my sport, goaded me to several years of transcendent performance—and also led to my early exit.

Had I interpreted my near-death experience in a rational way, thanking God for sparing my life and choosing to train and race more prudently in the future, I certainly wouldn't have achieved my marathon dream so quickly. Moreover, as Dr. Caulfield hypothesizes, the trauma of Falmouth '78 may have created the scar tissue that, nearly 30 years later, precipitated my 14 minutes: the apparent catastrophe that now seems a blessing in disguise.

———

That August on Cape Cod, however, with the running boom coming of age and my coming of age as a man and competitor—the message seemed crystal clear: I was on my way. I was a changed runner and a changed person. A few weeks after Falmouth, I went back to Oregon brimming with confidence for the start of cross-country season. I didn't believe I was a better runner than anybody else, just tougher. I stormed through the cross-country season: the dual meets, the invitationals, the NCAA regionals. Henry Rono and I stalked each other like two fighters who knew our title bout approached.

The showdown came at the NCAA championship meet in Madison, Wisconsin. It was another freezing early-winter day, much like the one in Spokane the previous year, except now we ran in a swirling snowstorm. And much like the '77 championship meet, this one featured a fiasco at the start. Henry and I went out hard at the starting gun, spurting far ahead of the rest of the field, but somehow, maybe because of the snow or some miscalculation of the officials, we took a brief wrong turn—we went off course for 50 yards, which in a race of that caliber amounted to a huge deficit. By the time Henry and I got back on course, the field had mostly passed us.

This was the kind of setback that a year earlier would have finished me. I would have lost my temper, internally cursed the officials, thrown a fit, wasted my energy—and given myself license to let up and give up; to embrace an excuse for losing. Now, however, after going through the crucible of Falmouth, I accepted the wrong turn as a challenge rather than a disaster. I settled back to my pace, drawing on the physical and mental strength I'd accrued during the summer. One by one, I picked off the runners in front of me until I'd regained the lead. Meanwhile, Henry Rono hadn't responded as well. Henry was every bit as tough as me, but he was also notoriously moody and temperamental. On this day, the early misfortune did him in. He languished far back in the pack, while I went on to win my first individual NCAA championship.

Rudy Chapa noticed that I was a changed runner post-Falmouth. He also recognized that I behaved differently around people. I was more direct and less afraid to say what I thought. Together with the attention I was getting for being a national champion, this led some people to think that I was growing arrogant and bigheaded. But the people closest to me—my fellow runners—knew this wasn't true. I was more confident as an athlete but not as a person. I was still searching. Except when I was around my teammates, I felt like the shy introvert; my newfound brusqueness was in part a defense moat to keep people away. I went out with a few girls, but no sparks flew. I still carried a torch for Molly. During the spring of 1979, I finished third in the 10,000 at the NCAA outdoor track-and-field championships. And then, for the first time, I entered the gravitational pull of the Olympics.

For a national-class runner, the Olympics are the only real game in town. The Games are how you establish your reputation, and if you're a professional, that's how you make your real money. Prior to my breakthrough in Falmouth, I was just a good Division 1 college athlete. But after Falmouth and that NCAA cross-country championship, I became a favorite to make the US team for the '80 Games in Moscow. That meant for the next 2 years, insofar as my commitment to Oregon allowed, I would arrange all my training and competition around the Olympic schedule.

The US system for determining its Olympic team is notoriously egalitarian, making no exception for reputation or past performances. The top three finishers in the various events at the Olympic trials qualify for the team, and everybody else has to wait another 4 years until their chance comes around again. The US Olympic track-and-field trials are held in June or July, about 4 or 5 weeks before the Games, and the marathon trials are held in January or February so the three qualifiers have time to recover and train for the Olympic event. For the 1980 Games, which were to be held in Moscow, I wasn't quite ready for the marathon—as Squires said, the marathon required patience—so I set my sights on the 10,000 meters.

I redshirted the 1980 track season (most college teams accommodate the training of their Olympic hopefuls, realizing that producing Olympians is a prime way to build the reputation of the program). In January, to escape the Oregon winter, I went to Kenya to train full time for a month. My time there was quite instructive. I was less impressed by the physical training—in quantity and quality, the Kenyan runners weren't doing much different than their American counterparts—as their mental approach. The Kenyan runner projects an aura of almost preternatural calm, both while running and at rest. They don't beat themselves by succumbing to stress and anxiety. Because they regard running as a business proposition, they view the sport more objectively. They don't let their egos affect their judgment. Instead of hating themselves after a bad race—the source of my competitive fire—Kenyan runners merely shrug. There's always another race, and another paycheck. And as soon as they've won enough prize money to buy a farm or build an apartment house in Kenya, they simply walk away from the sport.

Meanwhile, the movement built for a US boycott of the Games. At least it built in the White House, where President Carter sought a way to protest the Soviet invasion of Afghanistan. We hoped that he wouldn't use us athletes as a bargaining chip, but all we could do was focus on our training and hope for the best.

Returning from a month in Africa, I trained through the spring in Eugene. As the prospects for a boycott grew, my hopes for making the team sank—I developed a painful and stubborn case of tendinitis in my knee that virtually kept me from running at all. The combination of the injury and the political games put me in a foul mood. I knew intellectually that the world didn't revolve around me, and that on a larger scale running around a track amounted to very little. But I felt that I'd been chosen for a special destiny, and I had little patience for the obstacles standing in my way.

Looking back now, I can clearly see a pattern. I would undergo a period of intense confusion and self-doubt, and after long effort and prayer, I would experience an epiphany in which God's plan for me finally seemed clear. It had happened the day Kirk Pfrangle brought me to my first GBTC workout, the day I watched Bill Rodgers win the '75 Boston Marathon, and the day I barely averted death at the '78 Falmouth. After each of those experiences, I felt ready to jump out of my skin: *Get out of my way, Lord, and let me take over; I see the road ahead now, and I'm ready to drive.* But no sooner had I charged off down this clear new path than I'd slam up against another roadblock, retesting my faith and reminding me that I wasn't privileged with a direct line to the spirit.

At Falmouth, I believed, God had settled my doubts about my toughness and shown me that I could suffer more, endure more, than any other distance runner. The success I'd had since then provided further validation. The '80 Olympic Games were clearly supposed to be the next rung of my ever-ascending ladder, but instead political gamesmanship threatened to cast me back to the bottom. What was the matter with these fools? Why were they standing in my way? If a reporter asked my opinion about the boycott, or about my chances for making the team, I told him what I thought: The boycott was misguided, and I was going to make the team. I wasn't bragging. My assertions weren't based on fantasies. I had beaten the likes of Henry Rono. I had seen with my own eyes how Bill Rodgers trained and knew that I trained harder. And yet here I was in the summer of 1980, temporarily unable to run, and with no place to go even if I was healthy. The boycott seemed a lock, and I'd already decided to redshirt the 1980 cross-country season at Oregon. What was the point of risking further injury at the Olympic trials, which were scheduled for Hayward Field a few weeks later?

So, feeling immensely sorry for myself, I loaded up my car outside of my apartment in Eugene and started driving east. My plan, such as it was, was to drive home to Wayland, hang out there for a while, let my injury heal, and then figure out my next move. I left Eugene in the early afternoon and drove over the Cascades to the central Oregon town of Bend. I was off the freeway and traveling on US Highway 97, which carries through the center of town. I stopped at a red light on a steep hill; the sun was setting in a red fiery ball behind me, which seemed to mark both the end of the day and of my Olympic hopes. Then fate nailed me once again.

The pickup truck ahead of me at the light rolled backward—the driver must have misstepped on the clutch pedal—and slammed into my car, smashing the headlights. By the time we got the mess sorted out, all of the auto repair shops were closed for the day. I didn't know anyone in

Bend and, at the very start of my cross-country road trip, didn't want to blow my limited funds on a motel room. I had only traveled a few hours from Eugene, and there were several hours of daylight remaining. I decided to drive back home, sleep in my apartment, get the headlights fixed the next day, and be on my way.

I made it back to Eugene just as my roommates were sitting down to dinner. I told them what had happened, and they didn't seem all that surprised. In fact, they had set out a plate for me at my usual place at the table. "We thought you might be back," my roommate said, in a rather Twilight Zone tone of voice. The next day, while my car was getting fixed, I went out for a run. My knee felt inexplicably better; a lot better. I ran again in the afternoon and felt even less pain in my knee. I forgot about driving east. The plan, clearly, was for me to stay in Eugene and resume training for the trials.

I had about 4 weeks to get ready for the meet, and I committed to a crash course of training (during this time President Carter invoked the boycott; the meet would be run as scheduled, and the top 3 finishers in each event would be recognized as Olympians, but they would not compete in Moscow). I jacked my weekly mileage up to 110, which amounts to more than 15 miles a day. I expected my knee to give out under the strain and my hopes to again fall through, but my knee held up, freeing me to trash the redline. Dellinger gave me most of my workouts, but I'd invariably juice them. Every third day, I'd log an over-the-top speed workout, say 6 x 1 mile at 4:25 per mile. The ceiling for one week's training became the floor for the next week. My work, and my latest dance with fate, again paid off: I finished third in the 10,000. My 28.10.42 performance brought me home almost 25 seconds behind winner Craig Virgin, and more than 7 seconds behind second-place finisher Greg Fredericks. Moreover, an air of anti-climax permeated the entire meet (the great US discuss thrower Al Oreter commented that he knew it wasn't a "real" Olympic trials because he was able to sleep that week).

Nonetheless, at age 21 and still an undergraduate, I had become an Olympian.

The satisfaction I felt at my accomplishment was further undercut by the fact that Rudy Chapa had been injured and failed to make the team. I sent a letter to Rudy saying he deserved the spot more than I did, and that my achievement felt hollow because he wasn't there to share it. Such was the bond of our friendship, and such was the chemistry among the U of O runners. Of all the teams and training groups I have ever been a part of, those were the tightest. Beyond the disappointment of the boycott, moreover, and feeling bad for Rudy, the emptiness I felt at making the Olympic team also reflected the depth of my obsession and my almost total inability to savor my triumphs. All I could focus on—all I could think about—was proving my toughness all over again at the next workout, the next race.

The feeling from Falmouth stayed with me. My sense of toughness had nothing to do with having a high pain threshold. It's not like I possessed a yogilike ability to walk across hot coals, and when I went to the dentist, I accepted all the novocaine they offered. My toughness came from desire. I wanted it more. I needed it more. I needed running because I wasn't good at anything else. I was not a balanced person. Thank God, my own children, Tony, Alex, and Maria, have not inherited this trait. They are well rounded, popular, smart; they have a wide circle of friends. But I wasn't well rounded. All I had—all I wanted—was running. And the farther I traveled with my running, the more I invested in it. When I ran badly, I felt worthless; when I ran well, I was on top of the world. My goal remained to become the greatest marathoner in history, to set a world record at the distance and win an Olympic gold medal.

That dream sounded crazy when I said it to myself watching Rodgers at Boston in '75, and it sounded brazen when I told Rudy about it when I first met him. It still sounds crazy now. Again, simply declaring your goal won't help you attain your dream, but unless you declare it—unless you believe in it—you have no chance of attaining it. A sense of destiny might be more curse than blessing. Pursuing your destiny forms life's greatest adventure. But it's also a path that can take you straight over the edge.

The two important people in my life at the time, Molly and Rudy, were also runners—excellent runners—but they possessed balanced, grounded personalities. By this time, I had started to date Molly again. I think it was a combination of my wearing her down, time softening some of my roughest and geekiest edges, and her recognizing that we really were meant to be together. We had a strong natural attraction, and our personalities complemented each other. I wasn't a detail person (except when it came to running) and lacked a firm handle on the practical aspects of life, while those things came naturally to Molly. We forged a tacit understanding that she would support my running career. For Molly, running was a sport to enjoy; for me, it was a reason to live. Similarly, as the Olympic year of '80 passed and Rudy remained dogged by injuries, he started planning to go to law school. He wasn't ready to give up on serious running, but at the same time he could envision a life beyond it. That seemed amazing. I envied Rudy for adopting an attitude that seemed totally alien to me.

———

I loved to run, pure and simple. When you're hitting it right, to run feels like an effortless float. On the other hand, it's so exhilarating to look back after a race at the point you thought you were finished, dead in the water, and know that you pushed beyond that point. You can live easier with yourself, remembering moments like that. It's not the same as managing a sharp, clearly defined jag of pain. The pain of distance running is more like a comprehensive, bodywide exhaustion. Your will drains out of you; every fiber in your being tells you to stop. Your thoughts go muddy. The world looks foggy. You are just about ready to give up, to stop struggling and sink beneath the water.

And maybe you do give up, for a fraction of a moment, for just long enough to taste the bliss and terror of surrender. But then you take another step. You discover that the point of exhaustion and surrender that you were sure you'd reached in fact lies up the road another mile. You realize it's okay to feel awful; feeling awful becomes your new normal. You can take feeling awful in your hands and shape it to your will. If you're very lucky, during a few golden moments over the course of a career, you can seize control over your suffering to the extent that you're playing with it. This is the most wonderful—and dangerous—feeling in the world.

Years later, when I started coaching, I thought I could impose this type of toughness in my athletes, much in the way that a drill sergeant imposes discipline and toughness into his troops during basic training. But I've since learned that for an athlete, the toughness has to come from within—from some sort of hunger, crisis, or need. You can coach nearly any other quality or skill into a runner, but you can't coach that.

———

In the summer of 1980, after the Olympic trials, which in that unfortunate year formed a bridge to nowhere, I went to compete in Europe, where track and field remains a major spectator sport and the big summer meets fill stadiums. There I logged a 13:23 PR in the 5000 meters and a breakthrough personal best in the 10,000, dipping under 28 minutes for the first time with a 27:49 performance. In the process, however, I strained a hamstring muscle, and when I got back to Eugene at the end of the summer, I was basically in recovery mode. One day, I was going through a light workout at Hayward Field when a short, wiry little guy with a bushy beard and a painter's cap motioned me over to the stands. The man was Fred Lebow, the founder and organizer of the New York City Marathon.

The NYC marathon was then in its 10th year. Unlike the Boston Marathon, which began in 1897 and whose traditions and importance accrued over the decades, the result of contributions from countless groups and individuals, the New York City Marathon was a pure product of the running boom, and its success was largely due to one man: Lebow. Fred had organized the first edition of the race in 1970, laying out a course confined to Central Park, and 127 runners—who the rest of the city regarded as masochistic eccentrics—showed up to run. Each year thereafter the field swelled exponentially. In 1976, Fred and other race organizers moved the course out of Central Park and ran it through all five boroughs. The marathon quickly evolved into an iconic Big Apple event that stitched together the entire city. That same year, Bill Rodgers started his 4-year string of victories. On a national scale, the race had become a major event. And now here was Fred Lebow, personally inviting me to come run it.

Fred, who died of brain cancer in 1994, was a great salesman. And like all great salesmen, he believed in his product—he was passionate about running in general and the marathon in particular—and he had done his homework regarding his customer. In this case, the customer was me. Lebow knew that I had my sights set on the marathon for years; that I was a hot commodity due to my college performances and recent strong races in Europe; and that I wasn't competing for Oregon that fall (I had used up all 4 years of cross-country eligibility, although I still had one season of track eligibility remaining in the spring). I wasn't doing anything else this autumn, so why not run the New York City Marathon at the end of October? Fred finished his pitch, patted my knee, and told me to think it over. He also left a piece of paper on which he'd jotted down the time he'd projected for me: 2:10, which was the marker of a world-class performance.

So suddenly, out of nowhere, my dream moment was in reach. My investment in Oregon running had been total, but at the same time these last 4 years had been prologue for what I believed to be my true calling—the marathon. You'd think that melodramatic organ chords would've been sounding in my brain at that moment, but no music played. In part, this was because I was taken by surprise. The marathon was always something I'd envisioned for the future, certainly postcollege. Was the future of my marathon now? Also, it was tough to get excited because of my lingering hamstring injury—how could it heal in time for me to adequately prepare for the marathon, less than 2 months away? Finally, the organ didn't bellow due to the warrior mentality I'd developed, my absolute, iron focus on the workout or race at hand, and my refusal to get caught up in any glamour or hype involved with the sport—not that there was that much, and even if, as in this case, the hype was justified.

On the flip side, Lebow's offer intrigued me. I had absolute confidence that I was ready to run a first-rate marathon; primed to meet the prediction that Fred had scribbled on the slip of paper. It all depended on my hamstring holding up, and the only way to tell was to probe the pain. After the smashed headlights in Bend had caused me to return to Eugene earlier that summer and run through my knee injury, I felt confident about coping with any injury. The day after receiving Fred's invitation, I gave myself a test, going out for a hard tempo run along the Willamette in Alton Baker Park. My hamstring pain was manageable. After talking it over with Molly and Dellinger, I called Lebow and accepted his invitation. I was going to run my first marathon.

———

But I had only 5 weeks to prepare. As a rule, the minimum buildup for a seasoned distance runner would be 3 months, and many runners spend 6 months or more training for a marathon. You must acclimate your musculoskeletal system to the pounding, your energy-delivery system to the depletion of glycogen stores, and your mind to the overall challenge. Earlier that summer, however, in my buildup for the Olympic trials 10,000, I had already logged the 120-mile training weeks that are the staple of marathon training, and my breakthrough races on the track in Europe proved that I possessed the necessary speed and strength. I would be adjusting my training rather than starting from scratch.

I didn't read any marathon-training manuals. I just talked it over with Dellinger, who, as always, broke the enterprise down to its essence in clear, simple terms: In the marathon, you run the first 20 miles and race the final 6 miles. All my training would be geared to that tactic. I immediately started hitting those 120-mile weeks, with greater emphasis on long, steady-pace runs rather than 6 x 1-mile repeats; I already had the speedwork under my belt. Overall, I think that the highly compressed training cycle worked to my advantage. It didn't give me time to overthink or worry. I only had time to focus on my next race.

I flew to New York on the Thursday before the race, which would take place on Sunday morning. You'd think I would have been petrified. I was a 22-year-old kid coming to the media capital of the world to run my maiden marathon. I arrived with no coach or entourage; Dellinger was busy back in Eugene with the Ducks cross-country team. And yet I wasn't afraid. I was familiar with New York City. I had visited and raced there numerous times when I was living in Massachusetts, and just the previous February, I'd run the indoor 5000 at the Millrose Games in Manhattan.

Also, the media spotlight didn't bother me too much. I had long inured myself to tune out the hype accompanying any big race. I knew what I was capable of on the strength of my recent races and workouts. Although my specific marathon training had been brief, I'd in fact been preparing for the distance for 5 years, ever since the day I'd watched

Rodgers win Boston. Indeed, Rodgers's coach had been my coach; *I knew how Bill trained, and I knew that I trained harder.* Finally, I wasn't afraid because I knew I was the toughest runner in the race. I didn't care what nation they came from or how fast they'd run in the past: Nobody wanted it more than I did. I had run myself into the ground at Falmouth, I had run to the point of death, and I hadn't been afraid. What did I have to fear now?

Beyond the forces at work in my own career, I arrived in New York at an auspicious time for the sport. Running had grown to the point where it had become part of the mainstream culture, and yet it was still new enough to seem fascinating. The American running community already boasted Shorter and Rodgers, along with Prefontaine, its tragic, James Dean–like figure. But there was room for a new talent, a young distance runner who would build on the accomplishments of those older men, set world records and win Olympic gold medals, and seal American dominance in this new sport—this new phenomenon—that was sweeping much of the world. My personal destiny to become the world's greatest marathoner, in other words, was merging with a current of collective destiny. Fred Lebow recognized this. He saw my marketing potential. In my mind's eye, I was still a shy, insecure Cuban-American kid desperate to win his father's approval, who'd kissed one girl in high school and had hung around outside the swimming pool hoping to get a look at Pam Murch.

But what Lebow and the world saw, apparently, was a talented young athlete, confident to the point of cocky, possessed of dark, exotic good looks, ready to take the world by storm. At the prerace press conference, when reporters asked me what time they thought I was going to run, I didn't dissemble with self-deprecating platitudes about "respecting the distance," or "taking the race a mile at a time." I responded honestly. "Barring the unforeseen," I told the reporters, "I should run under 2:10."

Moreover, I delivered this highly quotable line while wearing a black leather jacket that I'd bought the week before in Eugene. The reporters loved it. The skinny kid from Oregon had morphed into a swaggering upstart in a black leather jacket, guaranteeing a big day, like a distance-running version of Joe Namath or Muhammad Ali.

———

This media juggernaut might have flattened me if I'd paid any attention to it, but I was in a zone, oblivious, thinking only about the job at hand. My parents and Fernando, my youngest brother, 14 years old at the time, drove down from Massachusetts to watch the race. In an indication of how relatively small-time running was at that point, even in New York, my parents stayed in another hotel in Manhattan, but Fernando bunked with me in the hotel at race headquarters.

On the night before the race, I wasn't exactly anxious, but I was too keyed up to sleep. Typical for a teenager, Fernando was hungry. At 1:00 a.m., we got dressed and went out to the street and I bought him a slice of pizza. A few hours later, at a predawn breakfast, I met Amby Burfoot, the champion of the 1968 Boston Marathon who was writing for *Runner's World*. It was a cold morning, and I asked Amby if I should wear a long-sleeve jersey under my singlet. He told me to put on a T-shirt over my singlet, and then as the day warmed up, I could peel it off. Now all that was left to do was start running.

———

It felt so easy. After all the years of anticipation, all the hype, all the dream-ing, the marathon felt ridiculously, almost laughably easy. In the lead pack at a 4:52 pace, I felt like I was jogging. I followed Dellinger's simple plan: Run the first 20 miles, race the final 6; husband my energy for the final sector of the race, where I'd rely on my track-honed closer's speed to deliver victory. Simple in theory, often so difficult in practice. Your mind can play so many tricks over the course of 26.2 miles. There are so many points where you can fall prey to either your panic or your exultation.

Patience isn't always rewarded—it's possible to start too conservatively, lose contact with the lead, dig yourself too big a hole to climb out of—but 9 times out of 10, you have more time than you think. At the 10-mile mark, I pulled up to Rodgers, the great maestro of the distance, the friend who'd saved my skinny butt back home in Boston on the day he fired his key ring at the dog from hell.

"Billy, this feels so easy," I said to him. "When does it start to get tough?"

"Don't worry, Rookie," Bill replied. "Your time will come."

Rodolfo Gómez, the great 29-year-old Mexican runner who'd finished sixth in the marathon at the Moscow Olympics, took the lead at the 18-mile mark. At about the same time, I developed a painful side stitch, not enough to slow me down, but enough for me to be aware of it. If the stitch were still there when crunch time came over the last few miles, I might not be able hit full throttle. I parked myself 20 meters behind Gómez and hung on, waiting for the stitch to work itself out.

You try different breathing techniques. You try relaxing your diaphragm, fully exhaling each breath, and relaxing the rest of your mind and body. I employed all these fixes but my side remained on fire. Nineteen miles, no change; 20 miles—the supposed notorious "wall" when your glycogen stores play out and you bonk—the stitch was still there. But I stayed 20 meters on Gómez's stern, ready to pounce when the pain left me. Finally, at mile 21, as quickly and mysteriously as it had appeared, the stitch vanished. I stuck with my game plan, however, hanging 20 meters back, gathering myself for the decisive move. After another half-mile with no pain, I was ready. After 22 miles, the race had begun. Everything got easy again. I was in control. I felt the way a lion must feel, running down a springbok in the African veldt.

I pulled up on Gómez's shoulder and hung there. I could have blown past him at that point, but I decided to wait. I stayed even with him until the course entered Central Park in Upper Manhattan, letting him think about me; letting him surmise, maybe, that this was all I had, that maybe if he kept grinding, the kid would break. A water station appeared up on the right, the last chance for water before the finish. The crowds were thick and roaring at this point, but I couldn't hear them. All I thought about was Gómez. He broke for the water station. I saw my opening. The day was cool, in the upper 40s; I didn't need water. I waited for Rodolfo to slow ever so slightly to grab a cup of water, and then I made my move. I threw a surge that opened up a 30-second gap between us. Gómez didn't have an answer.

I throttled back down to my 4:52 pace, and rode it on home. I hit the line in 2:09:41, making good on Fred Lebow's bet, making good on what I'd told the sportswriters, making good on what Bill Squires had recognized in me, and making a hefty down payment on the contract I'd made with myself when I was a nameless kid standing among the screeching Wellesley women in April 1975. At age 22, I was the New York City Marathon champion. Moreover, I had recorded the fastest debut marathon ever, and the second-fastest time ever by an American (Rodgers still held the AR, 2:09.27, set at the 1979 Boston Marathon).

I crossed the line thinking, "Yes, I am home! This is what I've been waiting for! The marathon truly is my event!"

Also, I crossed the finish line thinking, mistakenly and to my ultimate sorrow, that the marathon wasn't magical or even all that special. After the race, talking to reporters, I said, "I don't want to add to the myth of the marathon. It's just a distance, not a shrine. I didn't think you had to run it a lot to run it well. But everybody told me you did. 'It's different, Alberto,' they would say. 'Those last miles.' But it wasn't much different from the pain I've known before. I don't think I proved anything to myself, but I imagined I did to a lot of others."

By the same token, as a result of this attitude, which my critics portrayed as arrogant but which I thought was simply matter-of-fact, I was not overly impressed by my accomplishment. I did not pause to savor the distance I had traveled from my boyhood in Wayland or, even further back, from my roots in Havana. I had neither the time nor the interest in congratulating myself for merely racing well in the most recent event on my calendar. In fact, I didn't realize the full import of what I'd done until I arrived back in Eugene.

Bill Dellinger convened a meeting of the track team to discuss plans for the spring season, my final season of eligibility as a Duck. The meeting was held at McArthur Court, the university's basketball arena. I was running late, and by the time I arrived, the rest of the team was sitting in the bleachers, and Bill was standing in front of them. When the guys saw me, they spontaneously rose as one and gave me a standing ovation—Coach Dellinger included. I got goose bumps. Tears came to my eyes. That was the proudest moment of my life up to that point. Recalling it still gives me goose bumps.

But even that moment did not return me all the way to reality. Or more precisely, that moment didn't distract me, in a brief, healthy way, from my obsessive focus. I failed to gain some perspective and wisdom regarding what should come next. My New York City victory proved that I was attuned to the marathon and that my approach to it was correct. The win failed to satisfy me, however, because my two-pronged goal was to set the world record for the distance and win a gold medal in the Olympic marathon. Derek Clayton of Australia set the WR in 1969 at a race in Belgium with a 2:08:33 clocking. I was less than a minute away from that mark, and I knew I could run much faster—the New York effort had been so easy for me. The Fukuoka Marathon—a venerable race, the Japanese equivalent of the Boston Marathon—was scheduled for December, just 6 weeks after New York.

Again, for elite-level distance runners, the minimum recommended interlude between marathons is about 3 months; 6 months to a year is considered optimal. Nonetheless, bursting with youthful hubris, I sat down and wrote a letter to the Fukuoka officials, requesting entry to the race. I excitedly showed the letter to Bill Dellinger, who, of course, was aghast. He told me I was nuts; I needed months to fully recover from New York. In what was turning into a habit, unfortunately, I ignored Bill's advice, ramping up my training when I desperately needed to rest. Luckily, my body rebelled before I could do serious damage. I contracted a raging case of bronchitis that forced me to shut down. Otherwise, I would have plowed straight over the edge, then and there.

———

That 1980 New York City Marathon victory completely altered the course of my career. Before then, I was well-known in the collegiate track community, and somewhat of a celebrity in Eugene, Track Town USA, but now I catapulted into nationwide attention. Again, the timing was fortuitous. The running boom continued to build; Jim Fixx's *The Complete Book of Running* topped the national bestseller lists. The average Joe-six-pack American sports fan was learning about a sport that heretofore seemed masochistic and weird. Perhaps he even bought a pair of running shoes and started pounding the pavement himself.

I was also lucky because the rigid, unwieldy, and often hypocritical amateur system that had presided over American track and road racing was at last beginning to crumble. For the first time, an American distance runner could openly pursue a professional career, with an income derived through a combination of prize winnings, appearance fees, and, most important, sponsorship from a shoe company. The International Olympic Committee also began to reconsider its strict amateurs-only stance. As a result, I could look forward to a professional career—perhaps a lucrative one—in which I could focus entirely on my sport, a luxury that previous great American runners, from the milers Glenn Cunningham and Jim Ryun to the distance runners Frank Shorter and Steve Prefontaine, could never enjoy.

College athletics, however, remained strictly amateur. Because I had one more track season remaining as a Duck, I had run the New York City Marathon as an amateur, wearing a motley uniform consisting of Nike shoes, Adidas socks, and a University of Oregon singlet.

That spring track season of 1981, the spring before I graduated, I was recognized everywhere for my accomplishment. At meets, the announcer introduced me as Alberto Salazar, New York City Marathon champion. I won both the 5000 and 10,000 meters at the Pac-10 championships and hoped to finish my collegiate career with a win in the 10 at the NCAA championships. But the meet was held in Baton Rouge, Louisiana, on a brutally hot and humid day. I died in the heat, seeing double, and finished a disappointing fourth behind three African runners who thrived in the heat. But that proved a minor blip on an otherwise triumphant 4 years at the U of O.

I had arrived in Eugene as a shy, insecure kid from the East trying to escape my father's shadow, and during my time here I had grown into a man. I was coming out of school with a bachelor's degree in marketing and a future bride; Molly and I planned to marry that December. I had found a home that I loved in Eugene, made lifelong friends, won individual and team NCAA championships, become an Olympian, set an American record, and won the New York City Marathon. I had also come close to dying and recalibrated my position with the spirit.

I should have been proud and grateful for all that had happened over the past 4 years, and on an intellectual level I did feel that way. On a deeper emotional level, however, I remained hungry and unsatisfied. All of my success, I felt, wasn't true success. I still hadn't unequivocally proven that I was a man of honor like my father. I had only begun to redeem the blessing I'd been vouchsafed as a boy on the banks of Salters

Pond and that I had sealed by my near-death experience at Falmouth. During my time in college, I hadn't lost or seriously questioned my Catholic faith, but in the absence of my father and his goading, I had definitely let it slide.

I still went to Mass and periodically to confession. I still said my nightly prayer to the Holy Mother, asking to be spared from fear at the hour of death, but I participated in these sacraments, and voiced these prayers, by rote rather than with feeling. By the measure of the average American college kid in those postcountercultural times, I was as straight and devout as could be, but not by the standards ingrained in me by my father and by generations of forbears stretching deep into my family's Cuban past. I unconsciously realized that I was putting off my appointment with my faith.

At the same time, my success as an athlete had only left me burning for more. Finally, in the chambers of my heart muscle, the linings of my arteries, and the synapses of my nervous system, the seeds of disease that would manifest decades later, during my 14 minutes, were silently taking root. Equally silently—and equally surely—so were the seeds of the miracles that would save me.

PART 2

IN THE SUMMER of 1981, I began the campaign to defend my crown—and improve my time—at the New York City Marathon in October. Unlike the previous year's buildup to New York, I had no significant injury issues and had ample time—12 full weeks—to prepare. Again I stuck to a simple, basic training plan, consisting of 120-mile weeks, most of the mileage coming on the trails and forest roads around Eugene, and two or three hard speed workouts, either along the woodchip Pre's Trail in Alton Baker Park along the Willamette River or on the track at Hayward Field. The most significant difference between marathon and 10,000-meter training is the extralong weekend run.

Today, a good chunk of marathon training consists of finding the optimal methods for ingesting fluids and calories, but 30 years ago, we didn't think that was so important. By the same token, we didn't worry much about strength or flexibility training, spend much time on the chiropractor's table, or consult sports psychologists. Mostly we just ran, hard and long. I was living in an apartment near the Amazon Trail in south Eugene. Most of the top American distance runners were also based in Eugene, or spending a lot of time there, including the middle-distance great Mary Decker and the perennial US steeplechase champion Henry Marsh. Athletics West, the Nike-sponsored elite running team, was also based in Eugene. Other than wearing the red and white AW singlet, getting an occasional massage, and being tested by the exercise physiologist Jack Daniels, however, I didn't have much to do with the program. I still consulted with Dellinger, who wrote out my basic workout plan, but mostly I coached myself. The joke around Eugene at the time was that I would take whatever workout Dellinger suggested and double it. That was an exaggeration, of course, but like most such distortions, it contained an element of truth.

That September, I traveled overseas to the World Cup track meet in Rome, where I ran 27:41 for the 10,000, which was both a PR and the second-fastest time ever recorded by an American. The performance was significant in and of itself, but it also registered as a giant confidence booster for the marathon. At the time, as a rule of thumb, a male marathoner had to be able to break 28 minutes for a 10,000-meter race on the track in order to be considered world class; without sub-28 minute track speed, you lacked the horsepower to surge and kick in the marathon with sufficient force to put you in contention for victory. I had just blasted the 28-minute barrier to smithereens. With the exception of Rob de Castella from Australia, no other marathoner in the world could match my 10-K speed. (Kenyan runners such as Henry Rono were not yet running the marathon in significant numbers because, in that era, marathons didn't offer rich enough paydays; training for, racing, and recovering from a marathon meant missing the chance to earn money at races of shorter distances.)

In short, I was primed to break Derek Clayton's very approachable record of 2:08:33. My assault on the world-best mark would come on the world's biggest and brightest stage: New York City.

———

Meanwhile, I hired an agent, Drew Mearns, from the International Management Group, to help me negotiate a shoe-company sponsorship contract. My choice was basically between the two industry leaders, Adidas and Nike. At that time, Nike had not yet developed into the giant that it is today—a state of mind as much as it is a shoe and apparel manufacturer. Because the company had been founded at the University of Oregon by Bill Bowerman and Phil Knight, there was a tight connection between the university and its athletes, but it wasn't ironclad or automatic. In fact, a Nike-related rift had developed between Bowerman, the renowned retired U of O coach, and Dellinger, his successor and former athlete.

Dellinger had designed a weblike sole for a training shoe that he tried to sell to Nike, but the company had already decided to go with its recently developed air-sole technology, which of course soon became a mammoth success. So Dellinger sold his invention to Adidas, Nike's big rival, which angered Bowerman. Both men were careful not to place athletes in any crossfire, but since I was closer to Dellinger than Bowerman, I remained open to Adidas. Both companies made more or less identical offers: a base salary of around $50,000, with ample bonuses for national and world records and for winning performances at high-visibility competitions. Each company pledged that for marketing purposes, my name would be attached to a line of performance running apparel.

The main difference between the two offers was that Geoff Hollister, the Nike executive who was negotiating with Drew, held out the possibility that some day, after I retired from competition, I would be considered for a job with the company. Since my degree was in business and marketing, this idea appealed to me and tipped the balance so that I signed with Nike. That almost casual throw-in of Hollister's would eventually prove fateful. My life would be probably playing out much differently had I signed with Adidas.

————

Once again, I stepped into the lion's den of New York City. But now, in 1981, I couldn't slip in under the radar, a slim, dark-haired, Cubano wearing a black leather jacket. I was the defending champ, a swaggering winner, the kind of guy New York City liked, who said things straight and carried a little bit of a chip on his shoulder. This wasn't who I really was, of course, but the media had painted my portrait, and consciously or otherwise, I played into it.

When the reporters asked, as they'd been prompted to by Lebow, the impresario, if I was going to set a world record, I told them the truth: If the day went as planned, barring the unforeseen, then a world record was likely. I wasn't bragging, and I wasn't making anything up. I was only interpreting what the numbers said, just as I had the year before. Then the gist of the media stories had read, "Salazar Guarantees Sub-2:10." Now it was "Salazar Guarantees World Record."

To my mind, my "guarantee" was merely a statement of common sense: You raced the way that you trained. When I trained properly, I knew that it was very difficult to beat me. In 1980, I'd had 5 weeks of injury-free training before the marathon. Training for the race on a wood-chip trail in Eugene, I had logged a workout consisting of 5 x 1-mile repeats in 4:42 per mile. For the '81 New York, I'd enjoyed 12 weeks of focused, injury-free training, and over the same wood-chip loop I had nailed a 6 x 1-mile workout in 4:30 per mile. Off of my truncated 1980 training, I had run a 2:09:41 marathon. Now, on the strength of significantly enhanced training, wasn't I capable of finishing the marathon in a time 46 seconds faster?

Most athletes refrain from putting themselves on the line before a major competition, because if they don't produce, they look foolish. But I wasn't bragging. I wasn't saying I was the greatest. While capable of breaking the WR in the marathon, I was hardly invincible; I took my lumps in the 5-K and 10-K. Moreover, I had grown up watching Bill Rodgers, I had run beside the guy who'd won Boston four times, and I knew I was better than him. I had a very good idea of what it took to be the best in the marathon.

I realized that the image painted by the media was distorted, but at the same time, I no doubt came across as arrogant. It was the hard-won, honest arrogance of a Michael Jordan or Tiger Woods at the top of their games. I knew I might lose an occasional race, but there was no doubt in my mind that, overall, I was the best.

———

This time, Molly traveled with me to New York (we had set our wedding date for December 21, in Portland). My parents drove down from Massachusetts to watch the race. My father remained unchanged in his intransigence, his imperiousness, and his obsession with Cuba and the Castro regime, which had now been in place for more than 20 years. He continued to live in unwavering faith to the church and his vow of "Next Year in Havana." After what he considered to be the 4 lost years of the Carter administration, my father was upbeat about the nation's new leadership. He had avidly supported the candidacy of the staunchly anticommunist Ronald Reagan, and the presidential inauguration earlier that year had touched off a celebration in Wayland.

Meanwhile, he and my mother were bursting with pride at the success of their American children. Ricardo had graduated from the Naval Academy and was now flying fighter planes off the aircraft carrier USS *John F. Kennedy*. José had graduated from the University of Massachusetts and my sister Maria Cristina was beginning her career as a professional translator. The previous year, after my NYC win, my photo had appeared on the cover of *Sports Illustrated*, a laurel wreath of victory on my head. Now I'd returned to New York, intent not on merely defending my title in one of the most prestigious foot races in the world but setting a world record in the process.

My father approved of the confident predictions I made to the media, but privately he almost jumped out of his skin with anxiety. Molly was also anxious; she knew that there were so many ways a marathon could go wrong, and that now, if I achieved anything less than a world record, I would be perceived as a failure. Of all the people in my camp on that October weekend, I was by far the calmest. I had faith in my numbers, my workouts, the seasoning resulting from the previous year's race, and in my toughness. I did not fear the marathon, nor did I regard it as a shrine. And finally, unlike my loved ones, I could discharge my stress in the act of running. I slept soundly the night before the race, while Molly told me she stared at the ceiling. I told her not to worry. I knew the race would go the way that I planned.

———

Race morning broke cool and misty, a no-excuse morning, perfect for running, and the atmosphere at the start was electric. Even I was affected by the grandeur of the start of the New York City Marathon.

Runners are transported by bus or ferry to the Staten Island end of the Verrazano-Narrows Bridge, where the atmosphere is like that of a great military encampment. The mighty bridge soars over the water, and you can feel the structure vibrating; I admired its combination of function and beauty—perhaps something of my father's engineer genes juiced my appreciation. That morning, there was another record field on hand. A total of 14,000-plus runners might seem meager today, when numbers three times that run the marathon, but then it seemed like a revelation.

Adding to the buzz, the New York City Marathon would be televised nationally for the first time. ABC-TV trucks idled on the ramp by the toll station. The renowned sportscaster Jim McKay prepared to call the action. Waiting in the elite athlete's area, I could sense the collective air of anticipation—the sense that something great was about to unfold. As I stepped to the starting line, I whispered my prayers and punched the timer on my watch, secure in my faith in God and the numbers.

———

In some races you are intensely aware of the clock, while in others—an Olympic or world championship race, for instance, when victory rather than time is the only objective—you barely give the timer a glance; you concentrate solely on overcoming your opponents. In the case of NYC '81, I was almost totally focused on the clock. The other runners didn't matter that much. I know that sounds cold and haughty, but the attitude reflects a subtly different quality. It's akin to the mentality with which the best pitchers in baseball practice their craft. When they're at the top of their game, when everything is flowing and clicking, they stop seeing the batter. It doesn't matter if the guy at the plate bats righty or lefty, if he's hitting .400 or .200. The pitcher is so locked in that all he can see is the target his catcher sets up with his mitt. The game slows down, turns very clear and simple. The pitcher feels like he's a kid again, playing a game of catch.

That's the way I felt on October 25, 1981. In order to break Clayton's mark of 2:08:33, I had to average 4:54 or better per mile. The danger in that kind of marathon, where the conditions are so favorable and the expectations so high, is going out too fast, burning too much energy, and leaving nothing in the tank for the late stages of the race, when the true competition begins. Our lead pack of eight runners passed the 5-mile point in 24:15, a 4:51 pace, which was just right—a little bit faster than optimal, but not prohibitively so. An Irish runner named Louis Kenny spurted ahead of the lead pack, but we let him go. We knew he couldn't hold that pace.

The crowds on the streets were enormous and deafening. It felt like you were crossing the finish line with every mile. People recognized me and shouted out my name. "You can do it, Alberto!" they hollered, referring to my record attempt. Just ahead of us, the TV truck rolled, its camera trained on us. Every few minutes, a fan would jump off the sidewalk and run beside us for a few yards, hoping for an instant of nationwide exposure. It was a wild, raucous, New York City scene, and I rocked steady in the heart of it, intent on hitting my splits.

I hoped to hit 10 miles in 49 minutes. We nailed it at 49:05; perfect. At the halfway point, 13.1 miles, my WR prospects looked even better:

1:04:10. There were still eight guys in the lead pack at that point. At mile 15, when we reached the Queensboro Bridge going from Queens to Manhattan, the pack had whittled to four: myself; Rodolfo Gómez, who had pushed me in last year's race; a Polish runner named Ryszard Marczak; and José Gómez (no relation to Rodolfo), Mexico's record holder in the 10,000 meters, who was running his first marathon. But unless one of them was prepared to break the WR—and none were—I wasn't going to worry about them.

Besides marking the transition to the final decisive miles of the marathon, the Queensboro Bridge stands out because it's the only quiet place on the course. Spectators aren't allowed on the bridges. A protective carpet covered the bridge's steel grating, muffling our footsteps and slightly slowing us down, as if we were suddenly running on the beach. Coming off the bridge, the lead pack had dwindled to two: José Gómez and me. I respected Gómez's speed but questioned his endurance. I decided to get rid of him, throwing in a long surge, my specialty, a tactic I'd learned from Bill Squires years earlier and had honed to near perfection over the long summer's training in Eugene.

Gómez held on until 86th Street in Manhattan, around mile 18 and then dropped away. At that point, I knew I had the race won. A few minutes later, when I hit the 20-mile mark in 1:37:29, I knew the WR was in the bag.

I was running all alone now: It was just me; the clock with its big, beautiful, digital numbers; the TV truck beaming my image across the nation; and the people of New York City, going wild on the sidewalks. All I had to do was hold my pace. This year there were no side stitches or other specific pain points. The pain was there, of course, but I was riding it; playing with it. I ran 4:55 for mile 22, 5:02 for mile 23, and 5:06 for mile 24. I had slowed down on purpose, holding something back in case some unforeseen pain hit me in the final miles. I left Harlem and entered Central Park. The noise from the crowd was wild, jubilant. Helicopters clattered overhead, horns blared. No reason to hold back now, because nothing could stop me.

I hit mile 25 in 4:52 and mile 26 in 4:58. "He's going to do it!" Jim McKay screamed to the millions watching on TV. "Salazar is going to set the world record!"

In the video clip, you can see Fred Lebow, ever the impresario and showman, sprinting behind me, flailing his arms like a dervish, urging me on. I hit the line in 2:08:13, surpassing the old record with 20 seconds to spare, dead on the numbers, just as I'd predicted, and just as I'd planned.

———

Molly kissed me. My dad fought through two NYPD cops in the finish line area to give me a congratulatory hug. In his story about the race in *Sports Illustrated*, Kenny Moore wrote: "[Salazar] crossed the finish line in Central Park in 2:08:13, ending all speculation in this, his second attempt, as to who is the greatest marathoner who ever lived."

At age 23, just 6 years after the idea first came to me, I had achieved my dream. You'd think I would've been exultant, that that night I would have partied like a rock star in the finest New York City fashion, but I felt strangely subdued. I thought that I would transform into a different person after setting my world record—stronger, wiser, calmer, more mature. But I was the same person as I'd been that morning, with the same insecurities, the same hungers. I called Rudy back in Eugene. He was ecstatic for me, but I told him it didn't mean anything if he wasn't running well, too. I think I was looking for a way to downplay my achievement, to distance myself from it. Owning a world record was a privilege reserved for great champions, men of honor and distinction; I was just skinny Alberto from Wayland, the Castro Convertible kid.

Moreover, my entire MO was based on moving forward, on subsuming everything to attaining this seemingly impossible goal, and now that I'd attained it, what was I supposed to do? Who was I supposed to be? The only solution, the only way to cope, was to not change. Somehow, I had to treat my WR as if it were just another entry in my training log; the old ceiling that would form the new floor for pursuing my next goal. But along with reflecting my emotional insecurity, this attitude had served me well as a competitor. If I had trained for the marathon as if it were something special, paradoxically, then the results might not have been as spectacular. Twenty-six years later, during my 14 minutes, that curious and powerful dynamic would come into play again.

The paramedics had scooped me up in front of the Lance Armstrong Center on the Nike campus and had delivered me to the emergency room at Providence St. Vincent Medical Center. Dr. Todd Caulfield was the cardiologist on ER call that day. He was working in another wing of the hospital when word reached him that an ambulance was on its way, bearing a cardiac patient barely clinging to life, and whose chances for survival appeared slim. Hustling down to the ER, Dr. Caulfield noticed an unusual flurry around my gurney.

As he closed in on the scene, Dr. Caulfield saw that the patient was Alberto Salazar. He wasn't superfamiliar with my career, but he knew about me. Most people in Portland recognized my name. Dr. Caulfield felt a pop of adrenaline—a common reaction, he would tell me later, when your patient is a celebrity. "But then I immediately let that go and focused on my job," Dr. Caulfield would say. "I didn't treat you differently than any other patient. That's how you get the best outcome. When a doc starts trying too hard, or attempting to do things that he wouldn't normally, a case tends not to end as well."

By treating my world-record win as if it were just another long run, I tried to cultivate a similar attitude, although my motivations weren't as disinterested and uncomplicated as Dr. Caulfield's. The truth was that achieving my goal frightened me. How could I identify myself now? Also,

I'd always thought that world records were set by extraordinary athletes who were slightly larger than life. I knew that I was just an ordinary athlete driven by extraordinary hunger. My cocky, black-leather-jacket persona was just a facade. If *I* could set a world record, then how hard could it be? Still another part of me—a small, dispassionate voice—told me that for all that I'd invested in the marathon, it wasn't very important at all. This thing to which I'd dedicated my life did not require great courage. It wasn't like landing a F-14 fighter jet on the pitching deck of an aircraft carrier or battling into Havana beside Fidel Castro. Nor had I achieved something lasting and noble, like teaching a child how to read or setting a broken femur.

As soon as I notched my WR, these unsettling voices rose. The only way I could think to silence them was by moving the goal line back now that I'd crossed it. I decided that I'd try to set two more WRs, in the 5000 and 10,000. Then I wouldn't be merely the greatest marathoner of all time but the greatest distance runner, period.

———

But there was no way I could shut out all the attention that came at me. The first blast was the loudest, and most irresistible: an invitation to the White House to be recognized by President Reagan. The word came the day after the marathon. Today, these White House visits by champion sports teams have evolved into ritualized photo ops, often occurring many months after the Super Bowl or NCAA championship game, whenever the president can fit it into his schedule. Thirty years ago, however, such invitations were rare, granted only to athletes and teams of especially exceptional achievement. The spontaneous nature of the invitation added to its value—the president wanted to see me right away, on the Tuesday after the marathon.

Of course I accepted. Nike helped make arrangements, including FedExing a pair of size 12 running shoes for me to give Mr. Reagan.

When we learned that my family was invited to the ceremony, my father nearly hyperventilated. As I mentioned, President Reagan was a hero to my father, due to his staunch anti-Castro position and unwavering support of a strong military. Ricardo had told my father how, at the end of the Carter administration, he often had to fly fighter-pilot missions without live ammunition. Now that Reagan was in office, Ricardo reported, he went on missions fully armed. I was going to be honored by my brother's commander-in-chief, and my father was thrilled. Since my parents had traveled by car to New York City, we decided—probably, my father decided—that we'd all drive down to DC in his vehicle.

We set out early the next afternoon. As a younger man, my father did everything hard and fast. He talked fast, thought fast, worked fast . . . and drove fast. Sitting in the backseat, I warned him about the state troopers on the New Jersey Turnpike, but of course he waved me off and continued blasting south at about 80 mph. Sure enough, a few minutes later, we saw the light orbiting in the rearview mirror. I anticipated what my father would try to pull next, and I wasn't having any of it.

"Keep me out of this, Dad," I warned him. "Don't use me to try to talk your way out of a ticket."

"Don't worry, Alberto," he said. "I would never embarrass you like that."

We pulled over, and the trooper approached our car. My dad rolled down the window and blurted, "Officer, I'm sorry, I know I was driving a little fast, but I'm very nervous."

"Why are you nervous?" the trooper said.

"Do you know who that is sitting in the backseat? That's my son, Alberto Salazar! Yesterday he set the world record at the New York City Marathon, and now we're driving down to Washington so President Reagan can congratulate him!"

The trooper gave a little smirk, obviously thinking that this guy was feeding him a crock. Then he looked in the backseat and gave a double take—my picture had been all over the TV news and on the front page of the papers. I managed a weak smile, thinking that I'd murder my dad, that this was the most miserable moment of my life.

"That is Alberto Salazar!" the trooper said.

Rather than giving my father an expensive, richly deserved speeding ticket, he asked for my autograph, which I was happy to provide. The trooper warned my dad to slow down, told us congratulations and good luck, and went on his way. I was furious at my father, but at the same time, I couldn't really be angry. I realized how proud he was of me, and this whole episode was so much in character for him that my getting mad would be like getting angry at a robin for pulling up worms.

We maneuvered back onto the turnpike, and within moments my dad was going 80 again. A minute or two later, we passed the trooper who had stopped us. He had just pulled over another motorist. He saw us blasting by but just waved us on.

———

The next day, all of us—my parents, Molly, and I—dressed up and went to the White House. An aide named David Waller met us and outlined the game plan. President Reagan would meet with us briefly in the Oval Office, followed by a short ceremony in the Rose Garden in which I would receive my official congratulations and give the president the pair of Nike shoes. "You get 20 seconds per person in the Oval Office," Waller told us. "Just enough time for a quick handshake."

We went through in a line. My mom and Molly first, then me, and finally my dad. I told you he could talk fast? Well, you should have seen him talking to the President of the United States. In his 20 allotted seconds, my father crammed in the story of Ricardo's blank-ammo missions under President Carter and how much more effectively Ricardo and other pilots functioned under Reagan's command. My father urged the president to hang tough on sanctions against Cuba. My father spoke so quickly and heatedly that spittle flew out of his mouth. I was mortified, and as we left the office and headed for the Rose Garden, I apologized to Waller for my father's behavior. The aide waved it off.

"The president loves hearing that kind of stuff about the fighter pilots," he said.

A few minutes later, however, it was my turn to make a gaffe among the most august company imaginable. Reagan gave a short speech commending me for my victory and world record. He said that I was a fine role model for Americans in general and for first-generation American young people in particular. Then the president paused, and Waller signaled for me to go to the podium and give Mr. Reagan the gift pair of Nike shoes. But it turned out that the president wasn't finished talking.

"Can't you wait a minute?" he hissed sotto voce as I approached. Mortified again, I slunk back to my seat. But a moment later, I gave him the shoes, and the Salazar expedition to the White House concluded on a warm note.

———

I don't think my father's anti-Castro activities played a significant factor in President Reagan's extraordinarily generous acknowledgment of my achievement, but I'm not so naive to think that politics didn't play a part. In 1983, President Reagan delivered a speech in Miami to an audience comprised mostly of Cuban exiles, in recognition of the Cuban Independence Day.

"The list goes on and on," the president said, referring to the contributions of immigrants to the United States. "People from every walk of life, of every race and family background, have made their mark in just about every corner of American society. A few months ago, I was honored to welcome to the White House a famous runner, Alberto Salazar. I didn't know what to say. He gave me a pair of running shoes (laughter from the audience), but I'm not sure what kind of race he wanted me to run in." I thought I had left Cuba far behind, but it was still part of me.

The post-world-record celebration continued when I arrived back in Oregon from the East. Nike held a reception in my honor in Portland, where I met Phil Knight for the first time. My formal relationship with the company was only a few months old, but I'd been using Nike gear through my career at the U of O, where Phil's partnership with Bowerman—the coach inventing the revolutionary shoe technology using his wife's waffle iron, Knight selling shoes out of the trunk of his car—was part of Duck legend. Still, to that point, our paths hadn't crossed.

At the reception, we hit it off right away. Phil had not yet consolidated his marketing genius, but the core concept of the Nike brand was already in place: passion for sport. Wherever Phil sees evidence of that deep, true passion—and he has an unerring instinct for it—he finds a way to nurture it. Phil sensed both my hunger for running and devotion to the U of O, and those qualities, I think, impressed him more than my world record. Despite the colossal success that Nike was about to achieve in sports ranging from basketball to tennis to golf, the company was founded by and for runners—specifically, University of Oregon runners—and Phil Knight feels a special bond with that tradition.

For my part, I sensed an energy, a commitment, and a sense of destiny in Nike that matched my own. At the time, of course, I merely thought that the company would continue to supply me with a generous salary along with good equipment, and I would provide world-class performances, along with sundry PR duties, in return. I had no way of knowing that my deep and enduring connection with Nike and Phil Knight would only begin after my career as an elite runner was finished.

———

For now, though, I was just getting started—or so I thought. With the marathon world record under my belt after just two races, I shifted my focus back to the somewhat shorter distances: the 10,000- and 5000-meter races on the track and the 10-K cross-country distance. I never dwelled on the past; I only thought about the future. One WR was great; two or three would be better. In my mind, I wasn't being cocky, greedy, or unrealistic. Again, I was merely being scientific and heeding the numbers. I wasn't that far off the records now: The WR for the 10 was 27:22, and I had run 27:25; the WR for the 5 was 13:06 and I had run 13:11. There were only a couple guys in the world faster than me. I was in the top-five all-time for both distances. I knew I had developed an excellent kick; I could finish a race of any distance from the 5000 meters to the marathon faster than just about any of my competitors. That kick was my insurance policy. It was the physical and psychological savings account I could always draw on at the end of a race. Again, it was a matter of toughness and wanting it more.

At bottom, the ability to kick depends on your willingness to run your fastest at the very point when every cue your body and mind put out commands you to slow down; i.e., at the point of exhaustion, you must summon the will for maximum performance. Training the body is a relatively straightforward enterprise. In workouts, you simulate the conditions of a kick. Say your goal is to finish a race by running the final lap in 60 seconds. You prepare by running a series of lap-length repeats in 58 seconds, so that the stress of the actual race feels as comfortable as possible.

Training the mind is more complex and also more important. You have to train yourself to accept more and more pain. In each speed workout, you're going a little farther, a little harder than you thought possible. These intense, kick-building sessions might occur just twice a week, but you're preparing for them every day, and not just while you work out. You're preparing every moment, waking and sleeping. You have to do that day after day. I never took a break. I didn't trust myself—maybe I didn't trust God—enough to take the shortest break, because that toughness, that edge, that kick, was the only thing separating me from a hundred other runners. And running, in turn, was in my mind the only thing that distinguished me as a man.

Looking back, I can see that running both cured my insecurity and fed it. Put another way, as long as I was running well—always moving ahead, always honing my kick, always running faster—I was able to function well during those windows of time not directly related to the sport. On December 21, 1981, Molly Morton and I got married at Ascension Episcopal Chapel in Portland, near where Molly grew up and went to high school. Rudy Chapa was my best man, and my parents and siblings came out from Massachusetts for the big event. (We had a joint Episcopal-Catholic ceremony so my father was satisfied.) After a brief honeymoon in the Bahamas, we went straight back home to Eugene so I could resume training, which provided our livelihood. Eugene was the center of the running universe. Molly and I knew the town and felt comfortable there.

We quickly became an effective team. Molly had a good head for finances and from the start managed our money, which we were blessed to have. Then, as now, the vast majority of professional distance runners live a starving-artist existence, cobbling together the semblance of a middle-class living from shoe contracts and prize winnings. Most of them have to supplement their income with part-time jobs—clerking in a running-shoe store is often the employment of choice. Meanwhile, the athletes at the top of the pile, where I was, make a comfortable income, but hardly lavish compared to professionals in the mainstream sports. I earned around $250,000 base salary from Nike—substantial money in 1981—with bonuses for big wins and national and world records. The money was welcome, but I can honestly say it was never my prime motivator.

Like the guys from earlier eras, I would have run for nothing. The fact that I enjoyed major success early in my career and made a decent salary from the start of my professional years led to a fair amount of jealousy on the part of other runners. Also, I told people what I thought—often more brusquely than necessary—and mostly trained on my own. I can understand why people regarded me as aloof and arrogant. But the people closest to me—Molly, Bill Dellinger, Rudy, and the other guys I ran with at the U of O—knew otherwise. And certainly, I knew otherwise.

———

As the high-tide year of 1981 drew to a close—the year I got married, graduated from college, set a world record, and began my professional career—the Olympic Games again started to exert their pull. The 1984 Games shaped up as especially significant because they would be held in Los Angeles, the first summer games on American soil since 1932, when LA was also the venue. I was already the prohibitive favorite to win the gold medal in the marathon. That would be my priority, and all of my training, racing, and other planning for the next 2 years would fall into place around it.

The 10,000 meters was an important part of that plan. Training hard for that shorter distance would improve my surging and kicking during the marathon, but it was also important in its own right. The greatest all-around distance runners in history—Paavo Nurmi, Emil Zátopek, Lasse Virén, Frank Shorter—ran both events in the Olympics. It's a difficult double, but feasible because the 10,000 is always held on the first day of track competition and the marathon on the final day, about 2 weeks later. That gave the runner barely enough time to recover. I resolved not only to compete in both Olympic races but also to join Zátopek as the only runners to win gold medals in each event. My preparation would begin now, in the early months of 1982.

First on my agenda was the '82 world cross-country championships, which would be held in March in Rome. Although a popular sport in Europe, where major meets often draw thousands of spectators, and a staple of US high school and college athletic programs, open-division cross-country running is somewhat of a cult activity in America, but I always enjoyed it. Running over hills, down rocky trails, and through streams returns you to the primal roots of the sport and also toughens you for racing on the track and roads. I finished second at the world meet in Rome, recalling the third-place performance at world cross that Bill Rodgers had logged before his first Boston Marathon win in 1975. When I got back to the States, I looked at the calendar and realized that the time had come for me to run Boston, too. Every serious marathoner has to make the pilgrimage to Boston, despite its eccentricities, deficiencies, and excesses, sometime during his career. Like every other Boston qualifier, I would receive neither travel expenses, appearance fee, nor prize money. But Nike would pay my tab, and if I won—when I won—the company would pay me a $5,000 bonus. Other big marathons offered me 10 times that much in appearance fees, but I wanted to win Boston. I was on my way.

———

There is no footrace on earth quite like the Boston Marathon, which at the time was a fascinating—and sometimes maddening—combination of tradition, excellence, and stubbornness. Boston then prided itself on being a strictly amateur race, unsullied by the prize money and shoe contracts and agents that were transforming the sport as it moved into a long-overdue professionalism. At the same time, the Boston Marathon took itself extremely seriously. Of course, it had earned the right. The marathon started in 1897, the year after the first modern Olympic Games, and for decades Boston was basically the only road race in America. As the monk scribes kept the word alive in the Middle Ages until the flowering of the Renaissance, so the Boston Marathon had kept the flame of distance running burning until the 1970s and the combustion of the running boom.

As a kid, I knew the race as a fixture of the local calendar, a ritual like the Red Sox's opening day at Fenway Park. Then came that electrifying moment at the '75 marathon, when I saw my GBTC teammate Bill Rodgers, and suddenly I had a personal stake in the event. I went straight from being largely ignorant of the Boston Marathon to being a contender.

I never was simply a fan of the race, nor did I care much about its extensive lore. I did not believe that Heartbreak Hill contained any mystical powers, nor did I look forward to the traditional bowl of beef stew dished out to all finishers. I wasn't interested in any of that. As was the case with the New York City Marathon, I was determined to bend Boston to my will.

The Boston Marathon is held on the Monday following Patriots' Day, most often the third Monday in April. Ten days earlier, on a Saturday, a track meet was scheduled for Hayward Field, with the 10,000-meter open to professionals. The time span between the two races would be roughly the same as at the Olympics. In Eugene in 1982, I decided, I would simulate the feat that I planned for the '84 Games. Instead of tapering for the Boston Marathon, cutting back on the volume and speed of my training, which was the orthodox practice, I would rev up for a world-class effort on the track. It would be a bold gamble, but nothing I couldn't handle, and nothing that other great runners hadn't pulled off before. If I wanted to count myself in their company, I would have to do likewise. I would race the 10,000 in Eugene and come back a little less than 2 weeks later at the marathon in Boston.

I wasn't going to make any predictions to the press, but my private plan was to shoot for a WR in both races. I was capable, and to aim for anything less wouldn't be true. To get a world-class time in the 10, however, I needed some world-class competition to push me. The meet promoter, in effect, subbed out assembling the 10,000 field to me. This represented my first foray into the business side of the sport. A local car dealership put up a couple grand for appearance fees, which I could offer to the runners of my choice. I immediately thought of Henry Rono. In fact, I didn't think of anybody else.

———

I felt as if I'd known Henry Rono for my whole life. All through college, we'd hammered at each other, with Henry almost always getting the best of our battles. Along with Rudy Chapa, Henry was the most physically talented runner I'd ever seen. He was phenomenally versatile, at one time holding an absurd four WRs simultaneously, from the 3000 up to the 10,000. He was also fearsomely tough; if Rono decided to bring his A game to a race, there was no beating him. But Henry, unfortunately, was also extremely troubled, dealing with alcoholism (which he would later openly discuss) and other destructive appetites. By 1982, he had lost much of his talent and appeared on the downside of his career. Still, on any given day, he was capable of summoning his former greatness and running as well as anyone in the world. That's the kind of effort I hoped to get out of him for the 10,000-meter race at Hayward.

Henry agreed to the appearance fee I offered. I bought him an airline ticket from the San Francisco Bay Area, where he was based at the time, but he didn't show up for the flight. I called him, and he said he'd changed his mind and wouldn't run. I knew that he was still on a small Nike contract, so I made up a story about Nike cutting him off if he didn't show. Henry reluctantly agreed to run, although I had to call a sportswriter friend of mine in California to get him on the airplane. Rono arrived in Eugene looking bloated and at least 10 pounds overweight. I could still detect that fierce glint in his eye, however, and when race day came, he didn't disappoint.

Between the weather and the Kenyan, I had my hands more than full. April can be a cruel month in the Willamette Valley, and that Saturday was particularly nasty, with a cold, persistent rain and wind. Rono and I separated from the pack midway through the race and hammered it out one-on-one the rest of the way. Henry set a sub-28-minute pace, furiously trying to break me. I hung on his shoulder, covering each of his surges. The Hayward crowd loved it, and their rhythmic clapping grew louder with each lap. I couldn't rely on my kick in this race; I had superior closing speed for a marathoner, but my kick couldn't compare to that of a world-class track runner like Rono. I had to separate from Henry with a surge before the final few hundred meters, then hope to hold him off at the end.

But my left hamstring started to twinge. I briefly considered throt-
tling back and saving myself for the marathon, which was only 9 days away.
But I'd trained myself to always push through pain; to regard pain as an
invitation rather than a warning. Also, such efforts had become my trade-
mark. There was no way I could back down here at Hayward, in front of
my home crowd, against my old rival, in a match race that I had promoted.

When the bell sounded, signaling the last of 26 laps, I pushed the
pedal to the floor, inching by Rono on the final turn and gaining a step
lead heading down the stretch. The crowd went wild, their screams
reverberating off the wooden bleachers. The rain lashed my face and
chest and hot jolts of pain thrummed through my hamstring. I ran into
that pain, ran through it, letting the pain dissolve in the white heat of the
race. But I could not shake Henry Rono.

Over the final 100 meters, tapping a vein of hunger and pride and
fear and need that was at least as deep as my own, Henry pulled even with
me, then a half step ahead. Henry hit the finish line in 27:29.90, winning
by the width of his jiggling belly, according to the sportswriters, while I
finished in 27:30. I failed to win, but in wretched conditions I had logged
one of the fastest times in history, one fast enough to win a gold medal in
Los Angeles. So the first stage of my experiment had proved successful.
Bill Bowerman, who was in the stands that day, called my battle with
Henry Rono the greatest race he'd ever seen at Hayward Field.

———

Now only a week remained before Boston. My hamstring was tender
after my unexpectedly epic struggle with Rono. Common sense dictated
that I take an easy or minimal week of training, but by Wednesday, I was
back on the track knocking out 200-meter repeats. I wasn't trying to
destroy or sabotage myself, nor was I consciously disrespecting the marathon in general or the Boston Marathon in particular. I simply contin-

ued to follow the system that had worked so well for me, the essence of which was this: I regarded my past performance as a floor rather than a ceiling. I had to perpetually demand more from myself.

My first two marathons had come relatively easily, and I'd improved my times in both races. Therefore, my goals for Boston were to run faster—i.e., to better my own world record—and to approach the race as part of my overall track-oriented training rather than as something apart. I aimed to give the marathon its due but to avoid psyching myself out by imbuing the distance with mystical powers. I had it all figured out, in other words; at the age of 23, I thought I knew more about the marathon than Bill Squires had learned in a lifetime of study. My mentality may have seemed soaked in hubris, but now I realize I was scared. I didn't trust myself enough to slow down, even for a day or two. If I relaxed, I might lose the magic. People would see me for who I really was—a shy Cuban kid trying to live up to his father. If I slowed down, I might see myself for who I was.

———

As a professional athlete, I recognized that talking to the media was an important part of my job, a way to promote my sport and my sponsor's brand. I knew how big the marathon was to the Boston media and that the triumphant homecoming of a local boy who'd broken the world record made a great story. But I was also aware that I'd developed a persona as a cold, cocky customer, aloof and imperious, different than the spacey but affable Bill Rodgers, the older hometown hero. This didn't particularly bother me, but at the same time I didn't want to fan any flames.

I wasn't going to change. If a reporter asked me a question, I would tell him or her what I thought. Better, therefore, to limit the number of questions. I called my father, who would be picking up Molly and me at Logan Airport on the Thursday night before the race, and gave him specific instructions: no reporters at the airport. I repeated the message and had him say it back to me. I wanted to relax and get a good night's sleep at home in my old bed before the Friday-morning press conference.

I remember that cross-country flight as particularly long and difficult. I had a lot on my mind. Molly was 3 months pregnant. My hamstring twinged and I couldn't get comfortable in the seat. I have never been a good or deep sleeper, and now I seethed in that nervous, overtrained state that you associate with thoroughbred race horses. I tossed and fidgeted all through the flight, and as we taxied to the gate, all I wanted was peace and quiet and some solid sleep. Instead, Molly and I walked out into a blast of cameras, lights, and microphones. A swarm of reporters came at me as if I were Larry Bird. I saw my father standing against the wall, beaming, and I knew he was behind all this.

My first impulse was to shove through this jungle snarling "no comment," but I took a breath and told myself to be a pro. I consented to a few brief questions. The cameras started whirring, the reporters opened their notebooks.

"Are you going to win, Alberto?"

"Anything can happen in a marathon, but I don't think you can argue with the numbers. I'm the fastest man in the race."

"How about Rodgers?"

"Bill is a great runner, a great champion. You can never disregard him, especially here at Boston." I left the rest unsaid: that Rodgers was 34 years old now, that I'd beaten him decisively in New York City, and that he'd lost a step.

"How about Beardsley?" They were asking about Dick Beardsley, an American runner who was riding a hot streak. Beardsley had recently tied for first at the London Marathon and had logged a sub-2:10 in winning Grandma's Marathon in Duluth, Minnesota, the previous autumn. Also, Beardsley had recently started working with Bill Squires, my old coach and the maestro of the Boston Marathon. But Beardsley was strictly a road runner, and a marathon specialist at that. His 10-K PR barely cracked 30 minutes.

"I'm the fastest runner in the race," I repeated to the reporters, not bragging, not dissembling, only responding honestly.

The TV crews dispersed, and Molly, my father, and I walked through the terminal with my close friend and longtime supporter Joe Concannon, the veteran sportswriter for the *Boston Globe*, who'd been covering the Boston Marathon for decades. Joe asked some follow-up questions about my returning home, and we parted company with him at the entrance to the parking garage. I waited until we were inside my dad's car before I unloaded on him.

"I told you no reporters at the airport and look what happens!" I snarled. "Every journalist in town was there!"

"I only told Joe Concannon!" my father shot back. "How would I know he'd blab about it to all his pals?"

And then we were into it, screaming at each other in vintage Salazar fashion all the way out to Wayland. But this wasn't like the incident with the state trooper on the turnpike after the '81 New York City Marathon. Because it affected my preparation for a critical race, I couldn't laugh this off as a minor transgression. Our argument continued to rage, with Molly sitting silent and miserable in the backseat. It got so bad that instead of going home, I demanded that my father drive Molly and me to a local hotel to spend the night.

When I finally collapsed into bed, however, I discovered that the sheets were covered with ants. I spent the next half hour cursing and smashing bugs with my shoe. The calm, measured homecoming that I'd plotted so carefully had devolved into a fiasco. As it turned out, the night only formed prologue for the trials to come.

———

The days preceding the race on Monday passed in somewhat weird, schizoid fashion, with my roles alternating between that of celebrity athlete and son returning to the hearth. I was the center of attention at a downtown Boston press conference, but I ate my prerace pancakes at Mel's Commonwealth Cafe in Wayland, where I had worked busing tables as a teenager. I appeared at marketing functions for Nike, but I got a ride to the marathon starting line in nearby Hopkinton from my parents' next-door neighbor, Norm Potochoney.

Once I arrived at the line, my focus was total. I was locked in; what I didn't completely realize until later, however, was how totally my competitors, especially Beardsley, were locked in on me. My world-record run in October along with the subsequent media attention, had painted a big X on my back. I didn't mind the pressure. In my mind, it worked to my advantage. A lot of guys saw me at the line, and the race was over before it had begun. By contrast, I only thought about what I wanted to accomplish.

But my status also worked to my rivals' advantage. I had attained the level where a Dick Beardsley could focus exclusively on me, and that in turn simplified his race plan. At the elite starting area, Dick, a friendly Minnesota farm boy whom I barely knew (I recalled that he had run in the '80 New York City Marathon and had tangled legs with Bill Rodgers, knocking Bill to the ground), approached to shake my hand. I took his hand coolly. Not that I was unfriendly or trying to play a mind game—at least not consciously. I was merely getting into my zone, putting on my game face. I just wanted to focus on my race plan. I always got wound up before competing. Molly and others close to me knew to give me a wide berth. I remember watching the classic film *Raging Bull* and feeling a strong kinship with the Jake La Motta character, played by Robert De Niro. I shared something of the fighter's singleminded rage, that violent sense of mission. I wasn't much for small talk in the moments before a marathon.

Especially this marathon. I was eager to get out on a new course because so far the only marathon I'd run had been New York. These very roads, moreover, were where I'd come of age as a runner. This was where I had grown up. As I stepped to the line, however, I realized that I would have to adjust my expectations. I had come in planning on another world record, but it was an unseasonably bright, warm day, with temperatures expected to reach the mid-70s by midafternoon. I'd have to let go of the WR scenario. Over the next 26.2 miles, a lot of my preconceptions would be overturned.

The first mile out of Hopkinton is a steep downhill, and we started fast. I fell in with the lead pack. The hamstring I'd injured in the 10,000-meter race in Eugene still felt compromised. But when you run on this high a level, you're always dinged up. You learn to run when you're hurting. I was concerned about my leg, but not overly worried. The sun was warm, and a light breeze blew in our faces, wicking the sweat. This would be my first warm-weather marathon. The weather had been cool at New York City the previous 2 years, and a mouthful of water here and there had been sufficient. This marathon would be different. This race would escalate in a manner remarkably similar to last week's shoot-out with Henry Rono, albeit in diametrically opposite weather conditions. The 1982 Boston Marathon would be remembered as a Duel in the Sun.

———

Because Squires had been my coach, I knew what he'd probably told Beardsley, and I had a pretty good idea of how Dick would approach the race. Squires was a great proponent of varying your pace, keeping your opponents guessing, and throwing in precisely timed surges that would separate you from the pack. Squires also had intimate knowledge of the Boston Marathon's point-to-point course, especially the famous hills rising between miles 17 and 22—the rolling, strength-sapping stretch of miles that culminated in the legendary Heartbreak Hill. I knew that Beardsley would try to break away on the hills. I heard that he'd been training all winter down in Atlanta, on hills similar to the ones here in Boston. Finally, I knew that Squires and Beardsley knew that my closing speed was far superior to Dick's; if he hadn't burned me off before the last mile or so, he had no prayer of winning. But the truth was, I hadn't really given Beardsley, or any of the other runners, that much of a thought. If I focused on executing my own race plan, there was no way I could lose. At least, that's what the numbers told me.

I followed the scheme that had served me well in my first two marathons. I tucked into the middle of the lead pack, biding my time, letting guys bolt ahead, knowing they'd eventually flame out and come back to the pack, conserving my energy for the real racing, which wouldn't begin for a long while. The marathon is mostly a matter of patience. I would tell Kara Goucher that 27 years later when I returned to Boston as her coach. "Try to imagine some disaster hitting the Boston area, so that the marathon only covered 6 miles instead of 26.2," I said, "If the race were only 6 miles long, would you try to lead from the front? Of course not. So why would you try to lead early when you're running the full marathon distance?"

Kara is an intelligent, perceptive young woman. But I think of the power of the marathon as having something akin to the power of the Pacific Ocean along the Oregon coast. No matter how often people are warned about the danger of the surf, each year a few tourists walk on the beach and are swept out to sea by a rogue wave. Kara surged too early at the 2009 Boston, and her impatience probably cost her victory.

In the early and middle stages of the '82 Boston, however, I remained disciplined. The hamstring I'd tweaked in my race against Rono sent an occasional throb, but it was nothing I couldn't handle. The unseasonable warmth was a factor, and much would later be made of the fact that I drank sparingly during the race, only ingesting a few cups of water. With 20-20 hindsight, I know that was a mistake. I should have drunk more, but again, I was repeating the practice that had served me so well in my first two marathons. With the exception of Beardsley, who drank liberally, accepting cups of water from spectators, taking a sip, and then dumping the remainder over the painter's cap shielding his head, I don't think I drank significantly less than other runners in the lead pack. All I had to do was stick near the front, remain patient, and choose my spot to pull away.

———

At the 17-mile mark—the beginning of the hills—the lead pack had dwindled to two: Beardsley and me. Dick stepped to the lead and the racing began. He would surge for a quarter-mile or half-mile, then back off, trying to gap me. I just stayed right on his shoulder. Then I would offer a similar ante, surging for 30 or 40 seconds. It was an idea I'd gotten from watching the Australian marathoner Derek Clayton, whose marathon WR I had bettered: Go hard for 200 meters, then ease up; a little later, surge again, but this time for 400 meters, catching your opponent off guard. But Beardsley always kept a step ahead of me. We blasted along at a sub-2:10 pace. Due to the heat, this probably wouldn't be a world-record day, but our time would likely be world class. The sun was at our backs, and he could watch my shadow move on the pavement.

All I knew of Beardsley at the time was that he was from Minnesota and had a background in dairy farming. He was under contract with New Balance, making his living as a journeyman road racer, competing almost every weekend, and running frequent marathons. Now, as the late miles unreeled, as Heartbreak Hill came and went, as the crowds grew thicker and louder as we approached downtown Boston, and as Dick stubbornly hung on a half step ahead of me, I saw that I'd underestimated him. He showed no signs of breaking. He still ran with a light, fluid stride; a more efficient stride than mine. The crowd roared, and even though most of the cheers were for me, the hometown boy, I could tell that Beardsley also drew strength from the din. Everybody in Boston that day realized they were witnessing something special: two men going at each other with the intensity and ferocity of heavyweight fighters.

Dick ran the race of a lifetime, pushing the world record holder, whom he'd been keying on all winter. Meanwhile, I drew my strength from an opposite source: from my conviction that today was just one of many in my career; that it was my destiny to win; that it was impossible for me to lose. The numbers didn't lie—they couldn't lie. I was still the fastest man in the race. In my mind, I was toying with Beardsley—testing him. When the time came to put him away, I had no doubt I was up to it.

As it turned out, Beardsley hung on like a bulldog until the end, until we took the course's final turn and I finally broke in front of him. There was a lot of confusion on the course, way too many cops on motorcycles, and later people would say that the motorcycles inadvertently cut off Beardsley and blocked him from catching up with me. That may be so, but I'd plotted my finishing move well before the motorcycles closed in, and even if Dick had rallied to catch me, I'm convinced there was no way he could have stayed with me.

As I settled into the turn, I assumed there was about a half-mile to go, giving me ample space to pull away with my kick and win by a margin of 7 or 8 seconds. But I had miscalculated. The finish line was only 200 meters away, and now Dick had recovered from the motorcycles and was back on my shoulder. Instead of a smooth, gradual acceleration through the finish, the moment called for an all-out, balls-to-the-wall sprint. So that's how I responded. I bore down, maintained my lead, and hit the line in 2:08:49, just 2 seconds ahead of Dick Beardsley, who had run a phenomenally smart, brave race that had tested me—and depleted me—more than I ever could have imagined. He and I had barely crossed the line, but everybody around Boston was already calling our race a classic.

———

Not until I crossed the line did I fully realize the degree of my dehydration. In the course of the race, I had lost 10 pounds of water weight (and my normal racing weight was only 143 pounds). I intravenously received 4 liters of fluids in the medical tent. I wasn't suffering nearly the distress that afflicted me at Falmouth, but the effort had staggered me. By the time I left the tent, however, I felt much better. At the awards ceremony, Jock Semple, the longtime race organizer, placed a laurel garland on my head and handed me the winner's trophy. I pulled Dick Beardsley up on the stage to share the moment. In many ways, the day had proved more triumphant for him than for me. His heroic underdog effort had instantly endeared him to the people of Boston and the international running community.

The day formed the high-water mark of Dick's competitive career. After that '82 Boston, he never logged another world-class marathon performance. A few months later, he suffered a debilitating Achilles injury, and by 1988 he had retired from professional running and was back in Minnesota, operating a dairy farm. Beardsley and I had minimal contact until 1989, when Dick suffered the terrible tractor accident that nearly killed him. That ordeal, followed by two car accidents and surgeries, led to his addiction to prescription painkillers, which also nearly killed him. Along with many others in the national running community, I sent him a check to help cover his medical expenses.

Dick would eventually pull out of his downward spiral. Beardsley would later make the '82 Boston Marathon—the Duel in the Sun—one of the set pieces of the powerfully moving talks he gives around the country in his role as motivational speaker. Our race that day defined him. It brought the various themes of his life together.

By contrast, I rarely give that race a thought. The same holds true for all of my important marathons and races. As years pass, my competitive career turns increasingly distant and abstract; at times, it seems like somebody else ran those endless miles. In and of themselves, my racing performances aren't very important. Certainly, compared to the contributions of others, running around a track faster than a rival, or running from point A to point B ahead of another man, doesn't amount to much. To the degree that those races pointed me toward a deeper faith, however, or inspired others to evaluate their lives in a more meaningful light, they have value. I had been gradually building toward that insight for years, but my near-death experience in 2007 drove it home indelibly. At the same time, my 14 minutes deepened my commitment to coaching and confirmed my devotion to this thing to which I've given my life.

At the time of the '82 Boston, however, running and racing were all I could think about. My performance there had cemented my standing as the world's foremost distance runner. I had met my goal of running a world-class 10,000-meter race and a world-class marathon within a single 2-week period, and I could look forward to doubling at those events in the upcoming Olympics with confidence. I conveniently ignored the fact that both races had proven far more difficult and draining than I'd expected.

Whether I chose to acknowledge it or not, my Duel in the Sun with Dick Beardsley formed a watershed. For the first time in a marathon, I felt the enormous weight of the imponderable; the brute, impersonal power of forces beyond my control. I recalled the prophecy of Bill Rodgers at mile 10 of my first New York City Marathon, when, full of youthful strength and confidence, I had asked him what was so difficult about the distance.

"Don't worry, Rookie," Bill had said. "Your day will come."

My day had arrived. My demons were starting to stir.

————

The following summer, I returned to the track and to Europe. I retained the goal of setting world records in the 5000 and 10,000 meters, but I knew that my specialty, the event for which I'd be remembered, remained the marathon. I had now run three marathons, each distinctly auspicious, each contributing to my growing legend. In my first race, I had run the fastest debut marathon ever, predicting a sub-2:10 victory and following through. In my second marathon, competing in the media capital of the world, I had forecast a world record and had made good on that prediction. And in my third race, I'd engaged with another American in an epic battle in the marathon's most hallowed venue and had prevailed in that race as well. Three marquee marathons, three ringing victories.

Now, as I prepared to return to New York City for a third time, I was considered all but invincible. I had supplanted Bill Rodgers, my friend and role model, as the master of this supremely difficult event that increasing numbers of citizen-athletes were undertaking, but one that remained an exotic mystery to the average American sports fan. During the ABC telecast of the '82 New York City Marathon, commentators compared the marathon to a yoga discipline, suggesting that I submitted myself to arcane practices that allowed me to endure the ineffable pain of my pursuit.

The marathon was new and magic during those years, Americans were on top of the wave, and I stood at the pinnacle. Timing is everything. Today, I'll be at a party and people will ask me how many Olympic medals I won. They are mildly shocked when I reply, "None."

Compared to Frank Shorter, who won a gold medal in the marathon at the '72 Munich Olympics and a silver in '76 at Montreal, or Joan Benoit, who won gold in '84 in Los Angeles, or Bill Rodgers, who won four Bostons and four New York Citys, my accomplishments were minor. But I had caught a bolt. I was on a roll at the precise time when people around the nation and world focused on the marathon. I was just 23 years old. The world assumed my roll would continue for a long, long time.

Through the summer of '82 I slogged through injuries that seemed

nagging rather than serious; the hamstring issue I'd incurred the previous spring in my 10,000 against Rono still dogged me, and I was also
coping with a stress fracture of a metatarsal bone in my foot. Still, on the
track circuit in Europe, I was able to log American records in the 10 and
5, and I came into New York in October confident of another victory. I
also arrived at the marathon as a newly minted father; Molly gave birth
to Antonio—Tony—on August 28, 1982. A strong field had gathered in
New York, including Dick Beardsley. The weather conditions were favorable, with temperatures at the start in the high 40s. I would not have to
cope with the sapping heat of Boston. Again the race was nationally televised. Marty Liquori, the former great miler, provided the color com-
mentary for Jim McKay, the renowned voice of ABC's *Wide World of
Sports*. More sharply than ever, the spotlight and cameras aimed at me.

This year, I decided on slightly different race tactics. Instead of
hanging in the back of the lead pack, I took the lead from the start. The
other guys were keying on me anyway, so I put myself out there from
the opening miles. At the midway point, a flotilla of a dozen runners
floated in my wake, including contenders such as Beardsley and Rodolfo
Gómez, whom I'd battled during the '81 marathon. (If you watch clips of
the '82 race on YouTube, you'll be struck by the total absence of Africans;
a few more years would pass before athletes from that continent dominated the elite race.) Despite the big lead pack, we went out fast, hitting
the halfway point at 1:04:16, just 6 seconds slower than the '81 pace.

Everybody hoped for a repeat of the Duel in the Sun, for Beardsley
and me to engage in another American mano a mano battle, but that wasn't
to be. Shortly beyond the 13-mile mark, Dick dropped away from the
pack, a victim of his sore Achilles. When I distanced myself from the pack
with a surge at around 18 miles, Gómez joined me. Rodolfo was a seasoned
campaigner and extremely tough; he trained on a 15,000-foot volcano near
Mexico City, living for weeks at a time in a hut without running water. He
possessed formidable closing speed. Gómez locked in on me in Upper

Manhattan and we traded punches for the next 6 miles, all the way through Harlem and into Central Park. I threw down several 4:30-mile surges, but Rodolfo covered every one. The crowds overwhelmingly supported me, the two-time defending champion, the American, although Gómez seemed a harbinger of the foreign domination to come.

I kept trying to put him away with repeated surges, but as we worked south through the park, Gómez still ran beside me. Beardsley wasn't there, but it looked like we'd reprise a nail-biting, Boston-style finish. Unlike the Boston Marathon finish area, however, I was intimately familiar with the final stretch of the New York City course. If you look at a clip of the telecast, you might notice the unshakable confidence with which I ran. Nothing separated Gómez and me but will; I had that unshakable confidence that I was the tougher man, that I wanted it more.

About 600 meters from the finish, we briefly left the pavement and ran through a patch of dirt, which the police motorcycles and pace truck had kicked up into a mini-dust storm. There I buried the dagger, emerging from the dust cloud with a three-stride lead that I stretched to a 4-second gap at the finish. I hit the line in 2:09:29, logging my third consecutive victory at New York City.

I saw no reason why I couldn't notch three more wins in succession; I couldn't see why I should lose a marathon anywhere. No one witnessing the race live, or watching it on TV around the nation, could ever imagine that this would be my final victory in a marathon, that I'd never again display my toughness and dominance in a 26.2-mile race, or that 27 years would pass before the next American man won New York City.

———

Now I searched for fresh challenges and new experiences that would prepare me for achieving the goal that would complement my world record: an Olympic gold medal in the marathon. In the spring of '83, rather than returning to Boston, I decided to run the marathon in Rotterdam, where Rob de Castella of Australia and Carlos Lopes of Portugal, my two likely chief rivals for the Olympic marathon, were entered. While training for Rotterdam, I suffered a groin-muscle strain that should have convinced me to scratch. Instead, as was my custom, I ran through the pain, logging a 2:10 performance good for fifth place.

To compensate for the pain that dogged me all through the race, I altered my stride to the extent that I wore the outer edge of the soles of one of my racing flats all the way down to the spongy midsole. This was my first "loss" in a marathon, but because it was due to injury, and because I'd responded bravely and resourcefully to adversity, the defeat didn't ruffle my self-confidence. But then, after Rotterdam, I started suffering recurrent and intense colds, sore throats, and respiratory infections. As was the case with the groin injury, I trained through these illnesses. In June 1983, I came down with a severe sore throat just 3 days before the national track-and-field championships, which were held in Indianapolis. I competed anyway, of course, winning the 10,000 with a strong 27:57 performance, which qualified me for the inaugural world track-and-field championships later that summer in Helsinki, Finland.

There, finally, my excesses caught up with me. Feeling sick and sluggish, coughing my head off, I finished dead last in the 10,000-meters finals. I couldn't race Falmouth in August because of a nasty case of bronchitis. I felt wiped out for months. Still, in December, I traveled to the venerable Fukuoka Marathon in Japan, where I again finished fifth, albeit in a world-class time of 2:09:21. Also during that mixed-bag year, I was able to twice lower my own American 10-K road record, logging times of 28:02 and 28:01. But I was never able to approach the training levels I'd maintained from 1980 through 1982, and my performances reflected that fact.

Years later, in 1994, I took my son Tony to be tested for exercise-induced asthma. The doctor asked to test me as well, and it turned out that I suffered from the condition, which was the likely underlying cause for the cycle of infections and malaise that began in 1982. Indeed, asthma ran in our family. My father suffered from it to the extent that when he was a teenager, my grandparents sent him to Arizona to escape the heat and humidity in Cuba. In the early 1980s, however, there wasn't much awareness regarding asthma. I couldn't figure out why I was always sick. In an attempt to escape infections, we built a bedroom for me over the garage, suspecting that I might be picking up germs from our baby son.

You'd think I would've been intensely disturbed by this series of setbacks and subpar performances, particularly after my long, heady streak of success, and given my total dependence on the sport for meaning and identity. But that wasn't the case. I didn't feel devastated or defeated. I maintained total faith in myself and my destiny, reasoning that these were merely minor, transitory roadblocks. I had already proved myself with my four signature marathons. I didn't hate myself, as I had during rough patches earlier in my career, because I'd been running through sickness and injury. No competition for the next year and a half would be crucial in and of itself, but only as it contributed to my larger goal.

I was going to win the Olympic gold medal in the marathon. There was no doubt in my mind.

———

I returned home to Eugene, where Tony had turned 1 and Molly was pregnant with Alex, our second child. Despite the injuries and illnesses, I never took any significant time off from training. That was beyond my frame of reference. Competitionwise, I just wanted to put 1983 behind me and focus on the all-important Olympic year to come. The US marathon trials were in Buffalo, New York, in May. I merely had to finish in the top three to make the team, so I raced conservatively, finishing second to Pete Pfitzinger in 2:11.44.

A few months earlier, in March, I had competed in the world cross-country championships, held that year in the United States in the Meadowlands in New Jersey. Our baby was due at about the same time. Molly went into labor during my final preparations for the race, and Alex was born the day before the championships. I stayed in Oregon until the last possible moment, then caught a red-eye flight and arrived in New Jersey about 4 hours before the race. Fred Lebow put me up for a short nap at his place in the city. A couple hours later, he woke me up to run. I finished seventh but twisted my knee in the process, an injury that would dog me for the rest of the year.

That summer, I engaged in heat-specific training to prepare for the steamy conditions awaiting marathoners in Los Angeles in August. My knee hurt, and workouts were not going well. I kept plugging, kept thinking my luck was about to turn. Instead, things got worse; I developed a stress fracture in a metatarsal bone in my foot. After a ton of cross-training, the fracture resolved, and I traveled to Europe and ran a 27:59 10,000. Breaking 28 minutes in the midst of dealing with injuries and focusing on the marathon seemed like an encouraging sign. But during that race, while compensating for my knee injury, I strained my right hamstring.

Dealing now with three significant injuries, along with chronic respiratory infections, I reluctantly abandoned the idea of doubling in the 10 and marathon and concentrated solely on the marathon. For further heat acclimatization, I traveled down to Houston and continued putting in the miles. I called my own shots to a degree that would be unimaginable today. Athletics West did not employ a team physician, and I was largely figuring out my own treatment. Of all of my difficulties, the knee injury was the most troubling and would have the most lasting impact. I should have stayed off that knee. I continued to doggedly pound on it, however, and gradually the integrity of the tendons became compromised.

As the Games loomed, I knew I had fallen far from the peak I'd attained 2 years earlier, but the expectations of others remained high. Nike developed a running apparel line that centered upon me as its marketing engine; when I won my expected gold medal, the company's executives assumed sales would skyrocket. During my 18 months of stagnation and decline, no other US distance runner had emerged to challenge my dominance. These would be an American Games, the marathon had evolved into a signature American event, and I was the marquee male American marathoner. None of my injuries or ailments, by themselves, had proved debilitating; none had unequivocally put me on the shelf or kept me from training. Knowledgeable people in the sport knew I was vulnerable, but to the average fan I was still the man, the prohibitive favorite in any marathon I entered.

I continued to envision myself winning, and yet at the same time I realized that great performances grew out of great training. My training, by my standards, had been spotty and frustrating. It might have been better if I had suffered something like a busted femur or ACL tear. Then, at least, my path would have been laid out for me. During the years ahead, in fact, I would frequently long for such a severe injury, not because I was masochistic, but because I craved a clear sign of God's plan.

On the evening of August 12, 1984, I ran the Olympic marathon on fumes and magical thinking. Up until the crack of the starter's pistol, I thought that somehow, some way, I would rally to pull off a transcendent performance. I still thought I might fulfill my nation's expectations. No American prayed more fervently for me to come through than my father. In retaliation for the US boycott of the 1980 Moscow Olympics, the Eastern Bloc nations, including Cuba, boycotted the Los Angeles Games. So my father couldn't look forward to any glorious patriotic triumph like the one I'd delivered in 1975 (9 years earlier, but it felt like a lifetime had elapsed), when I won the 5000 meters at the junior US–USSR track meet in Nebraska. My father knew, however, that Fidel Castro was a rabid sports fan. Even if Cubans weren't competing, Castro might tune in on the Olympic telecast. When I led the field into the Los Angeles Memorial Coliseum on the Games' final night, with 90,000 spectators standing and roaring, Castro would recognize my name and remember my father.

As badly as I wanted to give my father this moment, I could not deliver. The numbers didn't lie. My race reflected the quality of my training. Carlos Lopes of Portugal claimed the gold medal. Pete Pfitzinger, my American teammate, again finished ahead of me. I finished an exhausted, dispiriting 15th in 2:14:19, more than 6 minutes slower than my world-record run in 1981.

———

My lost year of 1984 included another dark episode. That same summer in which I vainly cast about for a solution to my injury woes, an event occurred that I barely marked at the time, but which foreshadowed my 14 minutes. On July 20, 1984, Jim Fixx, author of the bestseller *The Complete Book of Running*, collapsed and died from a massive heart attack while out on a training run in Vermont. He was only 52 years old. Fixx's death stunned the nation, which still labored under the misconception that Dr. Bassler and others had seeded at the start of the running boom in the early 1970s: that marathon training provided fail-safe protection against heart attacks, especially fatal ones. Indeed, it was then thought that distance running might actually reverse plaque buildup in the arteries.

Now one of the foremost apostles of the running boom had died of a heart attack, challenging, in dramatic fashion, every one of those notions. Of course, I cared little about the fate of a middle-aged citizen-runner, particularly when I learned that before he started running in his mid-thirties, Fixx smoked two packs of cigarettes a day, drank heavily, and was 50 pounds overweight. His past and his genes caught up with him, I assumed with a shrug. Jim Fixx and I occupied different planets. I was 24 and, my Olympic disappointment notwithstanding, knew I would live forever.

———

I told myself that defeat was only temporary. In fact, I refused to call it defeat. I was just 24, after all, and not even close to the peak of my career. I took heart from the fact that Carlos Lopes had just won the Olympic marathon at age 37. I simply needed to fix the glitches in my knee and hamstring. I regarded my problems as mechanical and therefore didn't doubt my talent or general approach. I refused to entertain the notion that my physical breakdown could be attributed to almost a decade of running over the redline; of interpreting pain as an invitation rather than a warning. Up until 1984, I had defined myself as a runner whose purpose in life was to better his PRs. Now, as 1985 dawned, I defined myself as a runner whose purpose in life was to resolve his injuries as quickly as possible.

The level of commitment—of obsession—remained the same, and my ultimate goal hadn't changed: to establish beyond doubt that I was the greatest marathoner who ever lived. I couldn't make that claim, however, until I won an Olympic gold medal. I would just have to wait 4 more years and punch that ticket at the Seoul Games. Such is the saving nature of the elite athlete's mentality: On the one hand, defeat tortures you, but on the other hand, with the next contest looming, you bury your disappointment as if it never happened. I approached my injuries in a pragmatic fashion. I consulted with number of leading orthopedic specialists on the West Coast and decided to have surgery performed by a prominent orthopedic surgeon in Southern California.

The doctor assured me that he could fix both my problems in the same operation. My knee condition was a relatively straightforward case of tendinitis, he said, and could be alleviated by scraping away accrued scar tissue. The underlying cause of my hamstring issue, he said, was constriction in the sheath of fatty tissue encasing the muscle. The sheath was pinching my hamstring. He was confident that he could surgically release the constriction, allowing me to again run pain free.

This was just the sort of clear-cut diagnosis that I ached to hear. After a year of inconclusive tests, conflicting opinions, and futile treatments, I was hungry for a resolution. The doctor's unambiguous diagnosis also satisfied my proclivity for order, systems, and scientific certainty; a proclivity, perhaps, that balances my deep faith in the unseen realms.

I had the surgery—my first running-related operation—down in Orange County in January 1985. I spent the winter and spring rehabbing and then entered my first post-op competition in June, a 3000-meter race on the track. On the second lap, I felt a sharp pain in the supposedly repaired hamstring. I virtually limped the rest of the race, finishing dead last. It was the same hamstring I'd first injured in April 1982 in the 10,000 against Rono. That race, that glorious spring, was growing increasingly distant, the golden season of a different athlete. The hamstring issue persisted into a chronic problem that worsened. The doctor told me not to worry; he would go back in and repeat the surgical procedure, and then I'd be good to go.

I underwent the second surgery and then slowly but hopefully resumed training, but the pain returned. I entered an exhaustive, comprehensive rehab program with Dr. Stan James, a respected orthopedist in Eugene, who determined that the middle muscle in the group of hamstring muscles wasn't firing at all. The doctor had apparently severed a nerve during surgery. As a result, my right hamstring was only functioning at about 70 percent of normal. I never recovered full function. In fact, if you look at my hamstring today, you can see a slight indentation of the tendon.

I traveled to Australia to consult with the staff at the Australian Institute of Sport, which had some of the top sports medicine experts in the world. There I was able to restore my hamstring to about 90 percent of full function. Parenthetically, the staff at the institute also measured my cardiac output—the volume of blood my heart pumped with each cycle—and determined that it was greater than any athlete they had tested. "You'll never have to worry about cardiovascular disease," I recall the researchers telling me. At the time, of course, my heart was the least of my worries. My knee and hamstring difficulties had seriously messed up my stride, and I needed to get it back.

Meanwhile, my overall fatigue and malaise continued, along with a seemingly endless series of heavy colds and respiratory infections. Doctors offered various theories about the underlying cause, the most prominent being that my Duel in the Sun against Beardsley in Boston, during which I'd ingested just two cups of water the entire race, had thrown my endocrine system out of whack. Perhaps there was something to that, but I think that the roots lay in my undiagnosed exercise-induced asthma— the same condition that afflicted both my father and son. The severe case of bronchitis I incurred just before the '83 world championships, I think, might have provoked the latent asthma out of dormancy. The explanation seems plausible now, but at the time I just felt chronically sick and tired. I lurched from doctor to doctor, trying to figure out what was wrong.

Vitamins? I took a thousand vitamin pills. One doc would tell me my adrenaline levels were too low, while another said they were actually too high; my adrenal output was continually elevated, this theory went. When called upon to produce more adrenaline during a race or hard workout, my body couldn't supply the extra juice. A third doctor thought that other endocrine levels had been compromised and for some reason my immune system was shot. Everybody had a theory, but no one had an answer. I was young and impatient and couldn't accept the possibility that there may not be an answer. But I was also an optimist with great faith in doctors and mainstream medicine. I became fixated on finding a cure, a scientific explanation. Why couldn't modern medicine, with all its power and insight, determine my problem? Why couldn't one of these wise, learned physicians repair me? One moment I would fall into despair, and the next I'd exult, certain that a cure was at hand. I had turned 27, but that was still young, wasn't it?

———

The '88 Olympics were on the horizon, but I could no longer break 29 minutes for the 10,000 and was only in 2:14 shape for the marathon. My lung function was only 90 percent of a normal person's, and I was competing against professional athletes whose lungs operated at 130 percent of normal. There was no defining, single injury; I just kept running slower and slower. In the space of a few years, everything had changed. Many of the changes were positive: I was the father of two wonderful, healthy boys; Molly and I were happy together; my fame had spread around the world—but the big change seemed calamitous: For some inexplicable reason—or constellation of reasons—I had gone backward as an athlete.

Inwardly, meanwhile, nothing had changed. Despite fulfilling my roles as father, husband, and provider, I continued to define myself as a runner and to judge my worth by how well I performed. Running meant everything to me. I had not yet completed my mission, not yet honored my pledge, not yet distinguished myself indelibly in the Salazar line, and had not yet definitively proven my toughness. I felt derailed on the destiny line. I felt driven to know God but no longer seemed blessed to God's purpose. It was a strange, spectral time. I didn't even know how unhappy I was.

I remained under contract with Nike, but because of my lackluster performances, the company had cut my pay. I would have to find some other way to earn income. We continued to make our home in Eugene, and I showed up for work every day; i.e., I would train on Pre's Trail through Alton Baker Park, along the Amazon Trail near our neighborhood in south Eugene, on the track at Hayward Field, up along the slopes of Spencer Butte, and out by the Bowerman spread on Coburg Road. I went to Ducks football games at Autzen Stadium near the Willamette trailheads and attended basketball games at ancient cacophonous McArthur Court. Eugene was Track Town USA, and I was royalty there. I stayed in Eugene not for the attention—the glitz and glamour of stardom still left me cold—but because the town remained the best place to run in America, and that was what I did. Now that I needed to make money outside of the sport, I had options. Back in college, I had often fantasized with my buddies about opening a sports bar—what college boy doesn't entertain such fantasies?—and a friend of mine, Cordy Jensen, kept an eye out for opportunities (Cordy talked to Prefontaine about buying a bar just before Pre's fatal car crash in '75). Cordy learned that the Oregon Electric Station, a big restaurant occupying part of the old Eugene passenger railroad station in the heart of downtown, was up for sale at a good price. He said he would manage the place; all I had to do was put up part of the money and show my face there regularly.

I agreed to the deal, and in 1987, I went into the bar and restaurant business. This seemed like a good arrangement because my days would be free to train. I hadn't given up on running; I would never give up. I never got completely down on myself. I sought the medical solution to my malaise. I did not yet see God's hand in my decline. I was no longer so young, but it seemed like I had time.

———

I didn't compete in the 1988 Olympic trials, neither in the marathon nor the 10,000 meters on the track. As time passed and my symptoms continued to dog me, as I traveled from specialist to specialist, my search now expanding beyond traditional medicine to include practitioners ranging from herbalists to experts at the Stanford Center for Sleep Sciences and Medicine, I increasingly lived in a twilight zone between outward contentment and inner turmoil. I spent my mornings and afternoons training (or visiting doctors) and then would go to the restaurant for the dinner rush. My role was to greet patrons, seat them in the bar or dining room, and be a presence. I was good at this job, like I seemed to be good at most things; i.e., I appeared to be competent, engaged, and focused. But that was just a front. My true self was a limping wraith who floundered on the trails and tracks that I used to blast over. My true self was that hesitant, hungry Cuban-American kid who was desperate to please and escape his father and who'd latched onto running as the vehicle for this purpose. My true self was the terrified child who'd watched the little boy get fished from the bottom of Salters Pond and who prayed to the Holy Mother for courage at the hour of his death.

I didn't talk to anybody about my inner chaos. I didn't talk to Molly, to Rudy, to Dellinger, or to my brothers or father. I didn't have the vocabulary. A man, especially a Cuban man, was supposed to deal with trials and difficulties on his own. A man was supposed to put up results rather than analyze and bemoan his failures—he was supposed to focus on his next race and on providing for his family. Molly knew I was hurting; she was always there for me. I knew how lucky I was to have her. I knew that by almost every conceivable measure, I was a stupendously lucky man. My family was great, the restaurant was a success, and in a few short years I had achieved more than most athletes could dream of in a lifetime.

I consider myself a pretty rational person. Rationally, I knew that my injuries and illnesses weren't the end of the world. I knew that I should be thankful for my blessings. My family, my faith, my business, and my community should have been more than enough to distract me from my poor running performance. Maybe I was too rational, too much of a moral person. I felt like I should be grateful, but I wasn't. I had been

Left: My brother José poses for me with a drawn bow; seconds later he accidentally released the arrow. I heard the point whiz by my neck. The slightest alteration in God's plan, and I would have died that day. *(Photo courtesy of Alberto Salazar)*

Below: My father José *(front row, center)* with a group of Cuban Americans training for the Bay of Pigs invasion in the Florida Everglades. *(Photo courtesy of José Salazar)*

Above: The young Salazar family at Salters Pond: from left, father José, dog Mambi (named after the Mambisa guerillas who fought against Spain in Cuba's war of independence), sister Maria Cristina, brother José, me *(center, crouching)*, mother Marta, and brother Ricardo. *(Photos above and left courtesy of Alberto Salazar)*

Left: That's me as a freshman during a meet at Wayland High School, showing signs of raw talent but with a lot to learn.

Above: "The Rookie" with Bill Rodgers *(right)*, after a weekend race with the Greater Boston Track Club when I was in high school. *(Photo courtesy of Alberto Salazar)*

Above: As a high school senior, I place 5th in 1976 World Junior Cross Country Championships in Chepstow, Wales, on a bloody cold day. *(Photo by Mark Shearman)*

Right: My brother Ricardo, a Navy pilot, shows me the cockpit controls of an F-14 Tomcat jet fighter at Naval Air Station Oceana, Virginia Beach. (1982) *(Photo courtesy of the Wayland-Weston [Mass.] Town Crier)*

Rudy Chapa *(left)* and I were best buds at the University of Oregon. *(Photos above and opposite courtesy of Alberto Salazar)*

Renowned Washington State runner Henry Rono trails me during a cross-country race at the University of Oregon.

I prepared only 5 weeks for my first New York Marathon. I didn't read any training manuals. I had run Falmouth to the point of death, and I hadn't been afraid. I was 22. What did I have to fear now? I knew I was the toughest runner in the race. *(Photos by Leo Kulinski, Jr., right, and David Madison, below)*

Above: Dick Beardsley, Bill Rodgers, me, and Ed Mendoza *(left to right),* leading the pack near the midpoint of the 1982 Boston Marathon. Soon it would be just Dick and me in the Duel in the Sun. *(Photo by Steven E. Sutton/Duomo)*

Boston's finest escort me to the medical tent moments after the dramatic battle with Dick Beardsley (in painter's cap) in the Boston Marathon that became known as the Duel in the Sun. *(Photo by Frank O'Brien/*The Boston Globe/*Getty Images)*

Left: The grueling 56-mile Comrades Marathon between Durban and Pietermaritzburg, South Africa, in 1994, was my last victory before leaving competition. *(Photo courtesy of* Runner's World*)*

Below: Just days after my heart attack, we're all smiles at Providence St. Vincent Medical Center: from left, Tony, me, Molly, Alex, and Maria. *(Photo courtesy of Alberto Salazar)*

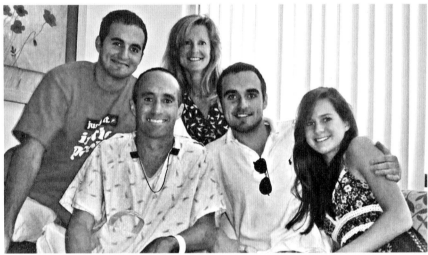

Right: I feel blessed to continue in the sport as part of the Nike Oregon Project, and to work with my friend and longtime protégé Galen Rupp, the American record holder in the 10,000 meters. *(Getty Images)*

vouchsafed this purpose in life, and I appeared to be booting it. I felt guilty for feeling ungrateful. I felt bad about feeling bad.

Through all this, I kept running. Instead of offering me a lifeline—a source of routine, order, and structure, the role that the sport plays in the life of the most plodding jogger—running now formed my cross to bear. Running used to be the one place in the world where I really felt at home—it was my refuge, my school, my therapy couch. Now the sport gave me no joy, and yet I couldn't stop running. I hadn't found anything to take the sport's place. The uncertainty, the daily immersion in limbo, hurt worse that the poor performances. I started to pray—self-serving, uncentered prayers. Instead of praying for a cure, I prayed for a sign.

Lord, please let me know if I should continue. Are you telling me to stop, or if I stopped now would I be turning away from you? Lord, show me your will, let me see it clearly, one way or the other.

Thus I prayed, but God withheld a reply, at least the kind that I wanted. The response was more grayness and doubt, more twisting in a shifting wind. As I went about my rounds, my prayers fragged off into fantasy and reverie. What if I were in bad car wreck, not bad enough to kill or paralyze me, but sufficient to fracture a leg, giving me a literal and figurative break? Then I would have to stop running, I would finally be lifted out of limbo. Lacking such a sign, I couldn't quit; I never quit. And from praying for a sign it was a short jump over the redline to fantasizing about a catastrophe. I passed my days reeling back and forth between wishing for a car wreck and maintaining a blind wild faith that salvation—the magic healing pill or procedure—waited in my next trip to a doctor's office.

And through it all, I kept running. I might take a day off here or there, but in general I kept myself firmly yoked to my rack. My workouts turned slower and slower, more and more of a chore, while my emotional distance from my family widened, and my black reveries—my daydreams of a definitive catastrophe—grew longer. I don't know if I ever harbored truly suicidal thoughts, but certainly I flirted with them. I don't know if my state of mind during this period qualified as clinical depression, but it certainly felt that way. Indeed, depression, like faith, valor, the hunger for sacrifice, loyalty, passion, and a predisposition for asthma and cardio-vascular disease, ran back in my family for generations. I had inherited everything else from my father, most notably a sense of rage and a sense of destiny, so why shouldn't I get depression as well?

—————

And now my father reenters my story. He had been there throughout, of course, the figure and the presence driving me. My father took enormous pride in my accomplishments. He always pushed me to excel—to fulfill the glorious destiny laid out for me by dint of my Salazar blood. In a few important ways, however, my dad differed from the typical overbearing father so common in the lives of accomplished athletes.

My father never claimed credit for my success. He never sought vicarious glory, and (except for minor instances such as the one with the state trooper and the speeding ticket) he never sought financial gain from my fame. He still worked for the construction company. He and my mother still lived in the house on Snake Brook Road in Wayland. Away from work, my father still devoted himself to the church and to the end-less campaign for a free Cuba. He hadn't stopped goading me to uphold the family honor, but never in the spirit of self-aggrandizement. Mainly, he pestered me to employ my celebrity, such as it was, as a platform for proselytizing the Catholic faith. He thought I could be a major magnet drawing young people to the church, a role I had little interest in filling. If I could serve as a positive influence being who I was, by the way I went about my business, fine. But I wasn't going to wear my faith on my sleeve or put myself forward as a role model. Not that, sunk in my physical and emotional trough, people looked up to me anyway.

During these years, I hadn't separated from the church—I attended

Mass and confession and had baptized Tony and Alex—but I didn't make a show of my faith and did not overtly evangelize. I had become a garden-variety churchgoer, observing the outward forms of belief, going through the motions, but with less and less emotion and conviction with each passing year, and with deeper immersion in the drama of my life and that of my family's. My father kept bugging me about my faith, not my running. He remained a stubborn, contentious pain in the ass—if anything, he grew more opinionated—but he never stopped loving or respecting me, and I felt the same toward him.

———

For several months, my father had been sending me tracts and literature dealing with a Balkan village called Medjugorje in what was then the nation of Yugoslavia. They were seemingly wild, often inchoate documents telling of apparitions of the Holy Mother appearing to a group of six children, printed on cheap paper with smudged print and murky pictures. I would deposit them straight in the trash with barely a glance and not give them another thought. The days passed in bland gray similarity, unmarked by the bursts of breakthrough brilliance that characterized my early life: that spring and summer of 1975, for instance, when I witnessed the Boston Marathon and tied the junior world record; or that summer of 1978, when I touched a bolt at the Falmouth Road Race and God spared my life, confirming my toughness and destiny.

Now, weeks and months would go by with no progress. This was the flip side of that transcendent coin, the price I paid for running over the redline. No one knew my secret purgatory or could imagine what effort I expended to appear normal and functional, to slog through the gray Oregon days. My father's evangelical dispatches only seemed to underscore my emptiness now that running had lost its magic.

My mother and father had made pilgrimage to Medjugorje in 1984,

3 years after the original apparition had appeared to the children. My father came home raving about the place, claiming that a miracle had occurred, that he'd climbed a hill overlooking the town and the chain of his rosary beads had changed from silver to gold. I listened with one ear to the wild story, which my father told with his usual tone combining tiresome lecturing with infectious, almost boyish enthusiasm. I relegated his claims to a mental trash bin similar to the actual one in which I'd deposited the paper tracts regarding the town. The fact that my sober, even-tempered mother corroborated the rosary bead story gave me pause, but not enough to seriously examine the Medjugorje phenomenon or imagine that it could mean anything to me. The charismatic arm of the Catholic Church has a long and vibrant history—manifested dramatically in apparition sites such as Lourdes in France and Fatima in Portugal—but I never had much interest. I kept pitching the tracts and clippings into the trash.

I don't know what caused me to read a tract one day instead of trashing it, anymore than I'd know 20 years later what caused one of the foremost emergency medicine physicians in the state of Oregon to sign up to coach at a football camp on the Nike campus just a 50-yard sprint away from the spot where I collapsed on the last day of June 2007.

Was I especially bored or depressed that day in Eugene? Had I just come home from a particularly slogging, dispiriting workout? Had I discovered one of the dish washers smoking a joint in the men's room at my restaurant and had to fire him? I can't recall. All I can remember is that one day I started reading one of the tracts, and the words jumped out as if written in fire. Peace, faith, conversion, prayer, fasting, return to the Son. I looked at the photos of the children. Each word printed in that pamphlet resonated with me. The setting and circumstances of the story might be exotic and extraordinary, but the message was so simple that a child could understand it. And perhaps only a child could have delivered it.

———

Some background on Medjugorje: It was a mountain village, close to the border of present-day Croatia, in the present-day state of Bosnia and Herzegovina; ethnically, it was mostly Croat (Roman Catholic) rather than Serb (Muslim). That area of southeastern Europe had been contested for centuries. It was bloody, haunted ground, dark and mysterious, province of medieval vampires and the site of a mass killing by Nazi sympathizers early in World War II.

On the afternoon of June 24, 1981, the six kids, who were in their early teens, went on a picnic. They climbed a hill overlooking the village and met a beautiful, shining woman whom they immediately recognized as the Holy Mother—she was called Gospa in the local language. The woman told the children not to be afraid. She said that God was with them, and that through them God called for a return to the fundamentals of the faith: peace, faith, conversion, prayer, fasting. The next day the kids returned to the spot, and so, they reported, did the Gospa.

She returned every day for weeks and then started showing once a week, on Thursdays. Only the children saw her. They never wavered or varied in their testimonies, nor did they seek gain from their visions. The Gospa expanded on the five themes but never strayed from them. The teachings rang true, and pilgrims started flocking to the town. *Blessed are those who have not seen and yet believe*, the Gospa said through the children.

The message drew a following, and within a few years Medjugorje had grown into one of most popular Catholic pilgrimage sites in the world—right up there with Lourdes and Fatima. Each year, more than 1 million people visit the parish to hear the teachings straight from the kids, who have grown into middle-aged adults. Since 1981, more than 30 million pilgrims have visited Medjugorje, where minor miracles are said to occur routinely and the spirit walks on a steady schedule.

———

I pored over the tracts and pamphlets in Eugene, Oregon, during the spring of 1986, in between my unyielding runs and my shifts at the restaurant, where I handed out menus and welcomed recruits of the Ducks athletic program—defensive tackles from Klamath Falls, high hurdlers from Sacramento. I studied Gospa's messages, which she delivered to the children on a weekly basis. I was struck by the fact that the messages delivered no radically new material, nor did they promise magical results. Peace is the first virtue, confirmed by the Holy Mother in one of the world's more violent places. Then comes faith, in an earthly realm increasingly enlightened—and reduced—by science and technology. Then conversion, occurring not just once as in the common Protestant understanding but continually, renewed through the act of confession of sins. Next comes prayer—prayer unceasing, "solidifying the equilibrium of the individual and provoking the response of faith in others." And finally fasting, or an expression of self-denial, "based on the truth that whoever is not in the possession of the self is in some way enslaved."

That was pretty much it. These were the same fundamentals of the faith that had been drilled into me by the sisters of my childhood—beginning, perhaps, with those nuns stunned by my rage at the summer camp in Michigan when I was 5 or 6 years old. The fundamentals I ostensibly followed as a paterfamilias parishioner but which in practice, in the flesh, I avoided or shirked. Instead, I prayed to the false god of running, blind to the light that I knew I should be thankful for, but only in my mind, and not in my heart.

Delivered anew by the Holy Mother in the Balkans through six innocent children, the fundamental truths, the bedrock dictates of the faith, struck me with the force of an electrical charge. I was gone like the first time I'd seen Molly Morton step out on Hayward Field during her long-ago freshman year; gone like in the thunderclap moment when Bill

Rodgers ran past me en route to his Boston Marathon win in 1975. Now I'd been hammered by a force transcending and encompassing those earlier watershed moments. I had no choice but to accept it.

———

I accepted it, but my first thought wasn't to make my own pilgrimage to Yugoslavia. Instead, I decided to test the precepts right where I was. If peace, faith, conversion, prayer, and fasting held sway in an obscure village in the Balkans, they should work just as well in the Willamette Valley of Oregon. Or rather, to reflect my new way of thinking, I should be able to serve those ideals as well at home as in a foreign setting. So I went to work, focusing on the third of Gospa's fundamentals, prayer. I began to pray in the place most natural to me: on the run.

(Disclaimer: I am not trying to portray myself as a religious expert here, any more than I tried to make a political point when describing my father's relationship with Castro; I'm simply relating my own experiences and interpretations.)

Each day on my morning run, often along the Amazon Trail, I would recite Hail Marys or repeat the mysteries of the rosary. It took a while to get into the rhythm, and at first my attention rarely locked into the words I voiced, but after a while my prayers fell into pace with my stride. I alternated these rote Catholic prayers with more free-form dialogues in which I'd unburden my heart and mind and strive for a more personal connection with God. Away from the track and trail, I recommitted to attending Mass and confession, and one day a week I abstained from meat according to the injunction to fast.

Day by day, I prayed. I prayed as I ran, as I waited in my car at red lights. During the dead afternoon hours at the restaurant before the dinner rush, in those slow silent moments in which I formerly sat at the bar, watching the dust motes swim in the pale Eugene sunshine and daydreaming about a dismembering car wreck: In these moments, I tried my best to pray. From these efforts, and from studying the tracts and pamphlets related to Medjugorje, I realized that I didn't have to be perfect in prayer. For me, this was a revolutionary insight. I was a perfectionist in most things, and an absolute perfectionist in the pursuit that mattered most—my running. If I failed to execute a workout or race exactly the way that I'd planned—if my concentration flagged or if I gave in to weariness or distraction or some other temptation—I felt like I'd wasted my time.

But now I understood that God accepted and loved me as I was: distracted, selfish, confused, fearful, lazy. If I brought all I had at any given moment to my prayer, it would have value. The logic of rote prayers, it seems to me, assumes a fair amount of spacing out and inattention. The essence of the prayer still goes out into the world and inward to your heart and psyche. So I kept plugging, inspired by the presence of Gospa in the Balkan village but not fixated on the apparition and not praying for another miracle to jump-start my life. This line of prayer and thought eventually led to a more powerful insight: Instead of a curse, perhaps my decline was actually a blessing, a development to welcome rather than deny or despise. Maybe my ineffable but debilitating malaise was as much a part of God's plan as my becoming a great runner in the first place.

───────

My running had been all for myself, and I had put God away in a little corner. I fooled myself into thinking I was doing God's will. What if I had it backward? I saw that in my previous prayer life, I had shied away from true, deep dialogue. Now, as I ran, I focused on the mysteries of the rosary. These prayers are keyed to the various parts of Jesus' life. As you pray them, you're basically reciting a condensed biography of Jesus and reflecting on how that can guide your own life. There are four sets of mysteries, with five mysteries in each set. It's really quite structured. The church gives you a concrete, detailed plan. Not to trivialize it, but to put the concept in terms that I feel comfortable with, it's like a coach writing a workout schedule. It's up to the runner to follow it. And, like a workout plan, the benefits accrue the deeper you commit to it. As I repeated the mysteries, for instance, I realized that they weren't describing an event out of history that occurred 2,000 years ago but a dynamic process that was going on inside me right now. I was thrilled by this insight. For the first time in months—in years—I felt fully alive.

This period of prayer and interior growth ensued over a period of a month or two. After my morning run, I'd go to the restaurant to help with the lunch business. In midafternoon, I'd leave for another workout, and then return to the restaurant from 6:00 to 8:00 for the dinner rush. The job of maître d'/floor manager didn't exactly suit my introverted runner's personality, but I learned to be good at it. By far most of my customers were cool, and many took genuine pleasure in meeting me. Occasionally, a mean drunk would taunt me, saying "You're washed up, Salazar, you're a has-been," but they were few and far between.

Our place was popular among both townspeople and the campus community. We had a contract to cater the luxury boxes during football games at Autzen Stadium. Coaches and players on the U of O sports teams would host recruits at our restaurant. I made a point of meeting the recruits; I was still something of a star in the Ducks' firmament. One day in the late '80s, a group of Oregon football players brought a high school prospect in for dinner. I stopped by the table and shook hands all around. It turned out that one of Oregon players, a linebacker, would eventually become an emergency-room physician. In June 2007, that same man, Dr. G. M. "Doug" Douglass, would volunteer to coach at a high school football camp held on the Nike campus. On June 30, 2007, when I collapsed on the far end of the field, it would be Dr. Douglass who came to my rescue.

Neither one of us had an inkling at the time, of course. But angel wings were beating all around in the spring of 1986, and after the Medjugorje bolt hit, I finally started to notice them.

———

Finally, at the end of the spring, I decided I was ready for my pilgrimage to Medjugorje. I'd be lying if I said that in some part of my mind I didn't long for a miracle; for God to fire the magic bullet that would cure me, allow me to run like my old self, remove the invisible weight from my shoulders (the Seoul Olympics were still a few years away, plenty of time to prepare!).

But I did not expect a miracle, nor did I pray for one. I had the sense that my miracle had already happened and that traveling to Medjugorje might simply seal the deal. The whole family went—Molly, who had joined the Catholic Church shortly after our marriage; Tony and Alex, 5 and 4, respectively; and myself.

As soon as you get into Medjugorje, you're enveloped in this special atmosphere, a sense of serenity and electricity combined. The six children were there, giving their messages on a rotating schedule. If there was anything phony or self-serving about their witnessing, it would've shown right away. The kids were too unsophisticated and the town was too remote for them to be pulling off any sort of scam. Also, the children and the religious people weren't trying to make a penny from their witnessing. In fact, they had suffered by reporting what they'd experienced.

Yugoslavia was positioned behind the Iron Curtain. It was considerably more liberal than the other Eastern Bloc nations, but atheism was the official line. The communist regime did everything possible to repress the Medjugorje phenomenon, including jailing the parish priests and intimidating the children and their families. But the kids didn't scare. They kept steadily and quietly serving in their role of Gospa's messenger.

Molly, the boys, and I fell into the rhythm of the pilgrimage. We attended daily Mass at the central cathedral and went to hear the Mother's teachings as witnessed by the children and translated into English by one of the priests. It wasn't just my parents who reported small miracles such as chains turning color; other pilgrims reported similar occurrences and visions. I met Father Slavko Barbaric, the resident priest who promulgated the Medjugorje teachings around the world. He asked if he could interview me for the newsletter later on in the week, and I said sure. I wasn't disappointed at all in the village. I felt the presence of the spirit, and however it chose to work through me, however I could serve, was fine by me.

I had brought along my gear and got out for daily runs on the roads outside of town, but my stride remained the same plodding exercise that it was back home. Physically, I didn't feel any different. Inside, however, everything was changing.

On one of our first nights at the inn, riffing on what seemed like my father's ravings about his rosary chain turning gold, Molly and I joked that maybe my chain would turn, too. I had bought the rosary beads in town as a souvenir. It wasn't expensive or anything special, just the standard beads, meant to help you keep track as you prayed the mysteries of the rosary, on a chain of silver gray. I put the beads on our dresser and we laughed and went to bed. The next morning, the beads and the chain, of course, appeared exactly the same as the night before. So that night, we didn't even bother to joke or give the beads a thought.

When I reached for them the next morning, however, the chain had turned from silver to gold.

Molly and I looked at each other. I took the chain into the bathroom to study it under brighter light. Yep, that sucker was gold. I washed the chain carefully in the sink, thinking that some sort of oxidation had worked on it overnight, or some sort of weird dust peculiar to the Balkans had worked into the surface of the metal. The chain was still gold. I carried it throughout the day, pulling it out of my pocket every few minutes to see if the genie had gone back in the bottle. The chain was still gold, and it remained gold the next morning. I wasn't ready to call this a miracle, but I knew it was a sign.

The conversion experience that had begun several months before in Eugene, building quietly as I prayed and ran on the wood-chip trails along the Willamette River, burst into bloom here in the rugged mountains of Yugoslavia. I felt free and at peace, but mostly I felt grateful: for Molly, my children, my parents, and the rest of my family; for all that I'd achieved during my running career and for all the amazing places it had taken me; and grateful, finally, for the mysterious injuries and malaise that had blighted my running in the years when I should have been at my peak. Indeed, being grateful—accepting God's will—regarding my trouble made possible my gratefulness for all the happier things. I saw clearly that my affliction, such as it was, was my purpose. And I didn't merely think my way to this insight. It wasn't something I thought I ought to feel. This knowledge, this faith, permeated every cell in my body.

———

My interview came around with Father Barbaric. He was a lean, scholarly looking man of around 40, with a gentle and encouraging manner. He spoke several languages and had already written about 10 books and many magazine articles about the faith in general and the Medjugorje apparitions in particular. Even by the standards of that village, he radiated goodness, simplicity, and grace. We had no way of knowing it at the time, of course, but besides being joined by faith, we also shared a silent curse: Despite our respective lack of risk factors, we would both suffer massive heart attacks in our prime. I would survive my cardiac event, but Father Barbaric wasn't so lucky—or blessed in the same manner.

On an autumn afternoon in 2000, he led a group of pilgrims on a climb to a cross on a hill overlooking Medjugorje, a ritual that kept him in seemingly excellent physical condition at age 54. The group finished their prayers and started down the trail when, without warning, Father Barbaric collapsed. Despite the priest's extraordinary faith and service, God did not spare Father Barbaric in the manner that he would spare me 7 years later on the Nike campus. A skilled emergency physician was not among the pilgrims walking on the Medjugorje trail that day. Father Barbaric died from his heart attack, performing his chosen work, while in direct service to God and man. His supporters are currently petitioning the Vatican for his beatification.

But as I sat with Father Barbaric in his study, all of that was years in the future. I poured out my heart to the priest, treating our conversation more as a confession than an interview. I told the father that running had been my god. I had placed my sport at the center of my life and everything else, including faith and family, remained on the periphery. I described my obsession with winning, my impatience and coldness with people outside the sport, and the rudeness I often displayed to my employees at the restaurant. I told of the ruthlessness with which I pursued my goal of becoming the greatest marathoner in the world, and the gnawing emptiness I felt once I'd achieved it. I described the awards ceremony following the Boston Marathon.

"They placed a laurel wreath around my head," I told the priest, "but a few weeks later, when I got the wreath out to show to a friend, the leaves had already faded."

I talked about the desolation I felt when my running turned on me, and then about finding the light through the events at Medjugorje. I told the priest about the happiness I saw radiating from the children who'd communed with the Gospa; a happiness that had nothing to do with ego, status, or worldly gain. That was the kind of happiness I sought and was beginning to feel now.

Just that day, I had been out running in the hills outside Medjugorje, I said. The road was narrow, laid against a steep hillside, with room for barely one car or horse-drawn cart to pass. As I rounded a bend on my run, a car came blasting toward me. The driver could have slowed the car or steered away from me, but instead he hurtled on, his speed undiminished, as if he were aiming at me. At the last moment, I dived into a ditch along the roadway.

"If that had happened just a few weeks ago, I would have been enraged," I told the priest. "I would have thrown a rock at the car; I would have cursed horribly. I would've let the incident ruin the rest of my day. I probably would have run home and taken my anger out on my wife and sons. But today, I didn't get mad at all. I forgave the driver in the manner that God has forgiven me for my sins. I didn't curse. I just got up and finished my run."

Father Barbaric looked at me sympathetically, encouragingly, with the hint of a smile. I realized how insignificant my troubles must seem compared to those of other pilgrims who had sat in this chair; people suffering from pain, disease, poverty, and loss; people who had committed terrible crimes, and those who were victims; people persecuted by their government; people facing death. And yet the father didn't condescend to me, nor regard my issues as trivial. He assured that God had vouchsafed me a gift with my running, that my performances had inspired a great many people, and that by husbanding this gift I was fulfilling God's purpose.

"Seek God's will as you continue to run," Father Barbaric counseled me. "The pursuit is worthy of your highest effort."

———

We went home to Oregon. I came back glowing with purpose and bursting with energy, but realized that keeping the flame burning apart from the special atmosphere of Medjugorje would require sustained, concentrated effort.

I resumed my regimen of prayer. I recommitted to attending Mass and confession and to fasting on Wednesdays and Fridays by abstaining from meat. And, of course, I continued to run, because the sport was the vehicle of my prayer, and because running, despite all the ways I'd abused it, distorted its importance, and ultimately suffered from it, remained my vocation, my craft, and my livelihood. It was no different than nursing or plumbing or cooking is for other people trying to work out their destinies.

I returned to Pre's Trail, the Amazon Trail, and the track at Hayward Field. I resumed the rigorous course of a professional, Olympic-level athlete: long runs and speedwork, strength training and stretching, chiropractic and massage therapy. I let go praying for a miracle, or even for clarity. And yet at the bottom of my heart—in some stubborn, almost animal-like part of my brain—I hoped for a miracle. Even after the girl you loved back in high school cut you loose, even after you've moved on and moved far away, you never stop illogically and masochistically hoping that she might miraculously come to her senses, recognize your true worth, and come back to you. But, of course, she doesn't come back, and my running hadn't improved.

Compared to my old self, I still felt like I was running underwater. I couldn't break 30 minutes for the 10-K, and a marathon was beyond considering. The 1988 Olympics were also out of the question. I would just have to accept the fact that God wanted me to keep churning in limbo and to celebrate each unmiraculous day as it came. I also resumed working 25 hours a week at my restaurant. The inner man might be new, but the outward man remained the same.

———

The next question was, would I share my new light with others or try to hide it? When God has given you a sign, are you going to be ashamed of it? Despite my deep slump over the past several years, I remained a star in the national and local running communities. People kept track of my movements. I knew how strange my pilgrimage to a Marian apparition site seemed to the people of Eugene, one of the most liberal—and secular—cities in the nation. The fact that I was dealing with a somewhat fringe wing of the church made people uncomfortable enough; what would they say—what would they think—if I told them the chain of my rosary beads had turned from silver to gold?

But I didn't care so much what people thought. If they thought I was crazy, so be it. It would be a blasphemy if I turned away from the light that I'd been shown. I didn't run around with a sandwich board on my chest, I didn't quit the restaurant and join a monastery, and I didn't pester all my friends and relations to go to Medjugorje—or even to go to the church, synagogue, temple, ashram, or other place of worship of their choice. But when friends and acquaintances asked about my experience, I told them. I told them everything, including the minor miracle of the rosary beads. I tried to put that episode into context, to explain that of all the things that had happened in Medjugorje, the rosary-chain deal was among the least important, but I didn't have much luck.

A sportswriter from the Eugene *Register-Guard* heard about my trip, and I consented to an interview. An article about my period of despondency and searching, and about my pilgrimage, gold-chain miracle included, soon appeared in the newspaper.

I remember a guy back at the U of O who was an evangelical Christian, a runner on our team who would wear people out with his endless proselytizing. When I saw him running down the trail toward me, I would look the other way, do anything I could to avoid him. Now I sensed people avoiding me the same way. The idea that your relationship with the spirit should form the core of your life—that your job on this planet is to figure out, to the best of your ability, God's purpose for your being here—is simply a threatening concept for most people.

Had I gone off to India to see the Dalai Lama, or had I spent months at a Zen monastery in California, the people around Eugene would have thought that was cool, that I was engaged in a hip and noble spiritual quest. I could have filled an auditorium if I gave a lecture about my experiments in meditation, but I couldn't say a word about the mysteries of the rosary without people edging away from me at parties. And yet my searching—my hunger—was the same. Instead of exploring a novel manifestation of the spirit, I sought the God that my family had worshiped and honored for centuries, the God that had driven the Gareschés to their gruesome but honorable deaths and my father to live in exile.

———

It now seemed certain that the Salazar era in American distance running was finished. If you're seriously injured for 3 to 6 months, you can still mount a viable comeback, but my period had now stretched to 18 months. I couldn't run like before, but now the uncertainty was gone. I settled into my life as a father, husband, and businessman, trying to serve God in my unexceptional daily life. From 1987 to 1991, I continued to train under my professional Nike contract, although the sport wasn't all consuming as before. I didn't rule out a return to elite competition, but until I got a handle on my health, I had to consider other options. In my early thirties, I finally had to grow up and accept a life of trade-offs and compromises.

At the same time, I had this reinfusion of faith, this new sense of meaning derived from my pilgrimage. How would I enact my belief? How could I translate the bright, pure truth I'd glimpsed in the Balkans into the practical dictates of earning a living, raising a family, participating as a member of a community? My father, of course, was thrilled by my rediscovery of the church and urged me to leverage my fame as an athlete to become a sort of full-time evangelist, recruiting people into the faith. I had no interest in this role. I understood a Christian's duty to witness. I accepted any invitation to talk to youth or sports groups or anybody else who was interested in my experiences. But I didn't push myself on people or present myself as any kind of expert or role model in spiritual matters.

I was no mystic, contemplative or ascetic. I was trying to build a rich prayer life, and I'd had a number of dramatic encounters with the spirit, but I had no monklike ambitions, and I knew I wasn't a visionary. I'm a literal, practical person. When I pray in a nonrote fashion, I pray for practical help: how to deal with a person or situation, or guidance on a difficult decision. I wasn't interested in fasting in a desert cave, and as a happily married father, I wasn't about to join the priesthood. Nor did I feel called to make a radical shift in my life and career: Go coach kids in a disadvantaged inner-city setting, say, or work on an Indian mission. My job was to stay in Eugene, raise my family, operate an honest business, and run the best that I could.

I entered the 1992 Olympic marathon trials—I was 34 years old and knew this would be my last shot. I had worked hard and thought that with a lot of luck, I might be able to pull off a 2:12- or 2:13-caliber performance, much slower than in my prime, but quick enough to finish in the top three given the dramatically and mysteriously diminished capabilities of elite American runners. Since the early '80s—about the time of my third and final victory at New York—performances had been spiraling downhill. With the rise of Kenyan and Ethiopian runners, American athletes seemed to have lost all confidence and drive—a subject I will explore a little later in greater depth. Those '92 trials, however, ended as dispiritingly as all my other comeback attempts. At the 7-mile mark, a sore Achilles tendon flared up, and I was forced to drop out.

"So that's it," I thought after the race. "I am done, I'm retired." I was disappointed but hardly blown away. In fact, I was relieved. This day had

been coming for years. A chapter in my life had closed, and I was ready
to open the next one.

————

The restaurant was doing well, but I never saw that venture as a permanent or sustaining kind of enterprise. It worked as an anchor for my days
and a good source of income, but it mainly served as ballast and supplement to my running, an ideal sort of part-time job that I could perform
mostly in the evening, leaving the core of the day free for training. Now
that my competitive running career was winding down, the restaurant
business seemed less attractive. In fact, it had felt increasingly unfulfill-
ing for a long while. Running a big restaurant has its glamorous side, but
mostly it's a lot of hard work, not all of it pretty. For instance, it's a common practice to accept more dinner reservations than you have available
tables. You tell the customers they can wait in the bar, where they'll
spend a lot of money on drinks. And alcohol, with its major markup, is
where you make your big profits.

Selling alcohol bothered me in other ways. Not that I'm a prude or
teetotaler—I enjoy a beer or glass of wine as much as anybody—but I
didn't like making drinking seem glamorous or attractive for the young
adults who formed most of our clientele. I wanted to earn a living at
something more satisfying. As I looked around at my options, I remembered something that Geoff Hollister had told me in what seemed a previous lifetime—that one day I would have the opportunity to go to work
full time for Nike. That deal sweetener had convinced me to sign with
Nike rather than Adidas when both companies were competing for my
services back in 1981. It seemed like I'd never have to take Nike up on
that offer. I thought, or imagined, that I'd run brilliantly forever, amass-
ing such fame and fortune that I'd never have to work a 9-to 5-job,
occupy a cubicle, or answer voice mail.

But 11 years later, I was a different and wiser man. Also, I didn't look at a "real" job as a death sentence. I had majored in marketing at the U of O, and over the decade of my association with Nike, I had watched it develop from a shoe and apparel manufacturer into something much bigger. The products were mostly excellent, but the idea that Nike had planted in people's minds and imaginations formed its true contribution. I wanted to be part of that, and not merely as one of the company's sponsored athletes.

I contacted Hollister and let him know I wanted to take him up on his offer and work full time for the company. I thought I had a lot to offer, and not just in terms of my name and erstwhile fame. I had my marketing degree, and now I'd rung up years of experience as an entrepreneur. I understood the business of professional sports, especially as it pertained to world-class athletes. I had extensive contacts in the worlds of track and field and distance running. Moreover, after spending my entire adult life around Eugene and the University of Oregon, I understood Nike's culture and institutional history, how it had started as a partnership between two extraordinary "Men of Oregon": Bill Bowerman and Phil Knight, combining Bowerman's inspired shoe designs and Knight's genius for marketing.

Finally, and most important, I understood the deeper purpose that drove Phil as he built the company into a global giant. Nike's passion for sports wasn't merely a slogan for selling shoes. It reflected zeal, energy, and enthusiasm for life; the belief that the highest human values could be expressed through sports and play, and that those values were universal in their appeal and available to anybody, as a participant as well as a spectator.

Hollister put me in touch with Nike executives up in Portland, and I went through a round of interviews over a period of several months early in 1992. The consensus was that I'd be a perfect fit working as a liaison and recruiter for elite athletes. We practically had a handshake deal, and I traveled back down to Eugene—a 100-mile drive, a straight 2-hour shot down the green heart of the Willamette Valley on Interstate 5—and Molly and I made plans to move. A native Portlander, Molly was all for the change. Tony and Alex were in elementary school, and Maria, our youngest, was just a toddler, born after we made a second pilgrimage to Medjugorje in 1990. During that second trip, I had resolved to get out of the bar business, and Molly and I decided to have another child, whom we named in honor of the Blessed Virgin Mother.

The family was ready to move, I was pumped, but the offer from Nike never came. I anxiously phoned Hollister and asked what was up. Geoff said that the deal had stalled at the desk of Phil Knight himself.

"The problem is that he's so fond of you, Alberto," Geoff told me. "He regards you as part of the family. Phil is worried about what might happen if your job here doesn't work out. He doesn't want to jeopardize that relationship."

I promised Geoff that that wouldn't be a problem. I wouldn't fail. I would work my butt off for the company. I wouldn't cop an attitude as a famous athlete and refuse to dirty my hands on the gritty day-to-day details of the working life. I never talked directly to Phil Knight during this process, but my assurances must have satisfied him, because I was hired by Nike in May 1992. It was springtime of yet another Olympic year, the first one in 12 years that failed to pull me, the first Games since I was a teenager in which I did not have a legitimate shot to compete.

I came into Nike ready to work. I didn't feel any sense of privilege, even though a building on the brand-new Nike campus near Beaverton in suburban Portland had been named after me. Other buildings had been named after superstars such as Michael Jordan, Mike Schmidt, and Bo Jackson. I didn't feel like I was on the same level. They had earned tons more money in their sports than I had made from running. There was no economic need for them to punch the clock when their playing days were through. I didn't expect any handouts. My first assignment was to supervise the network of elite Nike-sponsored running clubs around the nation, with a related task of recruiting and signing top runners and other track-and-field athletes for sponsorship deals. If I needed to send a shipment of shoes to a club in Florida, I went down to the warehouse myself to gather the boxes. I was absolutely determined not to be perceived as a prima donna. I was going to work harder than anybody.

———

I traveled to the Olympics in Barcelona, serving Nike in various roles. I worked as a liaison for the superstar sprinter Michael Johnson, master of the 200 meters, who was considered as much a lock to win a gold medal in his event as, 8 years earlier, I'd been the odds-on favorite to win a gold medal in the marathon. My job was to drive Michael to his races at the Olympic stadium. Also, rather comically, I was assigned similar duties in conjunction with the US Olympic basketball team—the first and most famous "Dream Team" that included Nike-sponsored NBA legends such as Jordan, Charles Barkley, Karl Malone, and John Stockton.

These guys, of course, traveled in a completely different universe than most of the other US Olympians. Charles Barkley, the massive and flamboyant "Round Mound of Rebound," was staying at a beachside resort in Spain, and I was assigned to pick him up and deliver him to a press conference. Barkley's entourage included armed bodyguards, but I was in charge of delivering him safely to the Nike-sponsored event. Barkley and I got out of the limousine and were immediately engulfed by swarms of paparazzi. The tabloid reporters in Europe are wilder than anywhere else in the world; they make the New York media seem tame.

My competitive, combative juices kicked in. I forged a path through the photographers, snarling and belting and shoving, a 140-pound distance runner playing the blocking back for 250-pound Sir Charles. Once we were safely onstage, Charles turned to me. "Damn, Salazar," he said, "you marathoners really are tough guys."

Ever since then, I've taken great pleasure in telling people that I once worked as Charles Barkley's bodyguard.

———

Another episode from the Barcelona Games sticks with me, but in a more serious vein. As I mentioned, the entire world, Nike included, expected Michael Johnson to win the 200-meter gold medal. But Michael contracted a case of food poisoning just before the Games and was significantly weakened when competition began. When he finished sixth in his semifinal heat and failed to qualify for the finals, the entire world was stunned. I got the call to pick up Michael at the stadium after his devastating race. My sons Tony and Alex were with me in Barcelona, and after some thought, I decided to bring the boys along. We drove to the stadium and found Michael sitting alone on the curb in the parking lot, holding his head in his hands. He got in next to me in the front seat, and we drove in silence back to the hotel. Tony and Alex sat in the back, too scared to move or make a sound.

But the episode was a valuable experience for the boys. They learned that nothing in life is certain. They also learned that if you want something as badly as Michael wanted that gold medal, it's okay to be profoundly disappointed when you fail to achieve it. That goes against the current fashionable teaching, which holds that participation and trying hard always matter more than winning and losing. I believe that if you take away the transcendent thrill of victory, and the piercing bitterness of defeat, then you miss the essence of sports. The most important lesson the boys learned that day, however, was that you don't let defeat and disappointment stop you.

Four years later, at the Atlanta Games, Michael Johnson stormed back with one of the greatest performances in Olympic history, winning gold medals in both the 200 and 400 meters while logging a WR in the former event. His triumph in Atlanta wouldn't have been as sweet without the desolation of Barcelona.

———

One morning at the Barcelona Olympics, I went out for a run with a man named Laurent Boquillet, who headed the Nike running division in Europe. During our run, he told me about this amazing event in the nation of South Africa called the Comrades Marathon. Held each May for more than 70 years to commemorate South African veterans of World War I, Comrades, despite its name, was actually an ultramarathon, covering 56 hot, hilly miles between Durban, a city on the coast of the Indian Ocean, and Pietermaritzburg, a town in the interior of Natal (now KwaZulu-Natal) Province.

Despite its difficulty, Boquillet explained to me, thousands of South Africans ran the event each year. Part spectacle, part national holiday, part sporting event, part survival trek, Comrades was the largest and most prestigious ultramarathon in the world. From that moment, I was fascinated by the idea of Comrades Marathon, although I had no inkling that soon the race would play a pivotal role in my life.

———

I was past the point of making a Michael Johnson–style return to Olympic or world-class glory, but my passion for running was no longer tinged by hatred. I no longer fantasized about suffering a dismembering injury—a clear, unambiguous sign that I should stop torturing myself with the thing that had once provided my sole sense of meaning and satisfaction. I continued to pray during my workouts; running and praying had become intertwined, and I couldn't imagine one without the other.

Meanwhile, I found partial outlet for my competitive instincts in my role at Nike. One of my jobs was recruiting top track athletes for marketing sponsorships. The top female sprinter in the world at the time was Gail Devers, an American athlete. Gail's contract was expiring with Adidas, and she was ready to sign again with that company, which is Nike's main worldwide competitor. But before Gail signed the contract, I buttonholed her coach, Bobby Kersee, and made a sales pitch. I gave it my best persuasive shot, and it seemed like Bobby was impressed. He said he'd take the offer to Gail and let me know. About an hour later, I walked past the door to Gail's dressing room; the trash can next to it contained a pair of Adidas sprint spikes, in Gail's shoe size. Out on the track, the world's top female sprinter stepped to the starting line in a pair of Nikes. I felt terrific.

That episode reflected the importance of shoe companies in the sport, which had been building since around 1984. Prior to that time, a professional runner relied mainly on race winnings for his or her income, and even the very best athletes had to compete frequently in order to earn a living. As a result, it was harder to forego smaller races to train deliberately for a major competition such as the Olympics or Boston Marathon. Since the mid-1980s, however, shoe-company endorsement deals have supplanted prize winnings as a runner's financial staple. They form a steady baseline income that allows the athlete a chance to peak for a big event.

You hear a lot of nostalgia from certain quarters about the good old egalitarian days when you only earned what you won, which promoted a sense of camaraderie among athletes. You were all in this together, the argument went, and therefore it was easier to form friendships with rivals. Once shoe company money entered the sport, some old-timers complain, runners started feeling jealous and possessive about contracts. I don't buy that at all. I think that the new system is far superior, promoting improved performances and longer careers. Reflecting its dominant market position, Nike is by far the largest supplier of marketing contracts to runners around the world. This reflects the direct influence of Phil Knight.

Phil is a very private man who shuns publicity. Unlike many wealthy, powerful men who haven't achieved a fraction of what he has, Phil prefers to stay in the background rather than to seize the limelight. I bet that Phil Knight has anonymously donated more money to charity than any philanthropist in the world. Besides his public contributions for programs and buildings ranging from the Knight Cancer Institute at Oregon Health and Science University hospital to the Stanford Graduate School of Business to the Matthew Knight Arena (named for his son, who died tragically in a scuba diving accident in El Salvador in 2004) at the University of Oregon, Phil has funded many causes without fanfare.

He's also a good guy: low-key, unassuming, and friendly, albeit in a guarded way with strangers, since he's learned that many people crossing his path want something from him in one way or another. It's tough to win his trust and get into his inner circle, but Phil trusted Rudy Chapa and me right away. He could tell that we shared his same core passions for sports and the U of O, feelings that are rooted in the deep tradition of Oregon running. Starting with Bowerman's tenure as head coach from 1949 to 1972, a magic river ran through Eugene that transcended distance running yet always stayed connected to it. Nike was born as a running-shoe company, and Phil has never forgotten that fact.

That Nike was a homegrown Eugene company made it all the more attractive. Phil Knight had bottled the essence of Hayward Field, combining the fire of Pre and the wisdom of Bowerman. The Cold War had ended (although Castro held on to power in Cuba, and the United States maintained its economic and travel embargo), and the free-market system was ascendant. People around the world looked for a galvanizing symbol of the capitalist spirit—a concept that epitomized freedom, fun, and the pursuit of excellence—and found it in the Nike swoosh. I felt lucky to be a part of it.

———

So I settled into a new life. I no longer seemed touched by destiny, driven by the spirit and my singular family heritage to become the greatest marathoner in the world, but there were other consolations and pleasures. I liked the routine of going to work each day and promoting the growth of the sport that had given me so much. I had more time to spend with my family, and I especially enjoyed coaching Tony and Alex's sports teams. I kept running seriously, but not obsessively. I had invested too much in the sport to stop.

My Medjugorje pilgrimage had borne fruit externally as well as internally. I had become more patient with people and less prone to judge. I tried to make amends for my past obsession, looking for ways that running could heal rather than hurt. At age 35, I had evolved into a sort of hybrid between an elite professional athlete and a high-quality citizen-runner. At Nike, I functioned as a kind of minister-without-portfolio, promoting the sport on all levels. My spirituality remained central, but it wasn't the overwhelming force for me that it was for my father. If I witnessed when given the opportunity and served as a positive role model to the people around me, I felt like I was fulfilling my proper role. My life might have lacked the high pitch and thrumming excitement of my competitive days, but I told myself I was content.

———

And yet, despite all my inward and outward changes; despite my solid family life, satisfying job, and the reconciliation I had struck with my dormant running career, I still at times felt depressed. I surveyed all my blessings but couldn't rationalize my way out of feeling low. Depression (along with heart disease and asthma, volatile emotion, and transcendent faith) ran back generations on my father's side, perhaps related somehow to that deep religious sensibility. My mother's Spanish heritage was similarly filled with figures whose rage often smoldered into a lingering sadness. It never occurred to me to seek treatment for depression, however. But then fate again intervened.

A man named Paul Raether was an acquaintance of mine. Paul was a physician by profession, a specialist in physiatry, but I knew him as a dedicated citizen-runner. I would often meet him on the running trails in Eugene and, later, in Portland; we had both moved from the former to the latter city around the same time. Paul had suffered a long-term running slump similar to mine. In seeking a remedy, he happened to read a study describing the effects of Prozac, the antidepressant drug that had just hit the market. Dr. Raether wondered if his running malaise could be related to the same brain-chemical imbalances that Prozac addressed. He tried the medication himself and within weeks was running better than he had in years. Paul contacted me and suggested that I might give Prozac a try.

Paul couldn't explain the exact connection between the medication, a selective serotonin reuptake inhibitor (SSRI), and running, but he theorized that the fundamental mechanism of Prozac and similar drugs yielded unforeseen, or "off-label," benefits. Prozac therapy presupposes that depression is, at root, a physiological problem, a matter of brain chemistry, not your life story. The idea that prevailing sadness could be pinpointed in your brain, and that it was essentially unconnected to your outward circumstances, appealed to me. It explained why, despite all the good things in my life, I often felt so blue (this concept also seems to support some of the theories behind the near-death experience; maybe the mind and the brain are separate in the way that achievement and happiness are disconnected—at least for some people).

Dr. Raether wrote me a prescription, and I gave the stuff a shot. I did not have high hopes. Every purported cure that I'd tried for my various—and interrelated—physical and psychological issues had fizzled in the decade since my last significant triumph at the New York City Marathon. More than 10 years after my malaise had first manifested, in fact, I still didn't even know what my problem was. Prozac? Sure, why not. My top-level running career was finished anyway. I wasn't taking the stuff to get faster. I just wanted to lift the cloud.

Paul Raether was right. Prozac worked. I had been watching the world on a black-and-white TV, and all at once it appeared in color. I never knew how sad I'd been until I started to feel happy. Had Prozac done nothing more than color my world, I would have been grateful. But to my amazement, the drug had the same effect on my running as it had had on Paul's. With a few molecules of brain chemicals rejiggered, the deep, underlying fatigue and malaise that had been leeching me for years dramatically eased. I felt like I could breathe again, like I was 10 pounds lighter. I went out and hammered an 8-mile interval workout faster than I had since 1984. I'd been running my mile repeats at a relatively pedestrian 5:00 pace. No matter what I tried, I could go no faster. But within 2 weeks of starting on Prozac, I hit those miles at a 4:45 pace.

Suddenly, it seemed like I could run to full capacity again, but at age 35 that capacity had diminished from my prime. It wasn't sufficient to return me to the Olympic level. It occurred to me that while I was no longer capable of running 26 miles at a 5-minute-per-mile pace, I might be able to run even farther at a 6-minute pace. That sort of effort, I reckoned, would put me in contention for a victory at the Comrades Marathon, the ultramarathon in South Africa that Laurent Boquillet had told me about at the Barcelona Olympics.

Comrades also appealed to the spiritual, emotional side of my nature. You didn't run Comrades for money (at the time, there wasn't any prize money). On a global, mainstream level, compared to the Olympics or the Boston Marathon, there wasn't much prestige attached to the event. If I decided to run Comrades, it would be for other reasons. I would run it in honor of the new power in my life. I would run it in a key of faith and gratitude.

———

As I was deciding whether to commit to Comrades, I had to contend with yet another controversy. Word had gotten out that I had used Prozac, and the gossip engines started up full throttle. That was a disadvantage of my living in Oregon, a hotbed for the sport that could sometimes seem like a petri dish. The controversy also arose from my proclivity for responding honestly when people asked me a question.

Back in '81, when journalists asked if I was going to set a WR at the New York City Marathon, I hadn't resorted to false modesty or platitudes; I said that if I raced the way that I'd trained, and barring the unforeseen, then a world record was likely. Similarly, when I came back from my first pilgrimage to Medjugorje and people asked, often smirking, if I'd witnessed a miracle, I unapologetically told them the story of the rosary beads. Now, when journalists asked me of the rumor about my using Prozac was true, I said sure it was true. I had nothing to hide and nothing to be ashamed of. I've always been open about what I do.

I took Prozac only for a few months, until my moods felt better stabilized and I'd solidly broken the cycle of fatigue and illness that had dogged me for more than a decade (I have not used an antidepressant since). But the SSRI class of antidepressants were a new thing in the early '90s, and people didn't understand them. That a famous athlete would take the stuff raised eyebrows. At the time, depression bore a stigma. In the popular imagination, it was a condition suffered by neurotics or other marginally functional individuals. Coming at it from the other side, other people suspected that Prozac was some sort of performance enhancer akin to the blood-doping drug erythropoietin (EPO), and that my self-described "depression" was nothing more than an excuse for me to juice.

But the fact is that Prozac-style medications actually inhibit athletic performance and have never appeared on the World Anti-Doping Agency's list of banned substances. The larger truth is that despite my respective obsessions on winning and finding a cure, and despite the fact that the use of performance-enhancing drugs (PEDs) had spread into an epidemic among the world's endurance athletes in the early '90s, I have never doped.

That fact will disappoint many conspiracy theorists, and the chatroom rats will scoff. To be fair, I might have brought on some of their suspicions myself, with my longtime obsession on winning and my relentless search for a medical solution to my problems. During the late 1980s, while in the depths of my malaise, I visited the clinic of Dr. Robert Voy, former head of the US Olympic Committee's Sports Medicine Division. Dr. Voy was famous for his fight against the use of PEDs and had recently resigned from his USOC post because he felt the USOC wasn't supporting his recommendations to fight the problem adequately. Thinking that my condition stemmed from an endocrine imbalance brought on by heat exhaustion during my Duel in the Sun with Beardsley, Dr. Voy suggested certain medications and advised me to seek permission from the USOC before taking them. USOC officials responded that I could use those medicines under a doctor's supervision, but while doing so, I could not compete. So during the time I followed the prescribed treatment for a period of several months, I continued to train, but did not race. In short, instead of trying to circumvent the rules, I scrupulously adhered to them and sought the advice of the foremost anti-drug crusader of the time. But I made the mistake of telling some runners in Eugene, and it quickly metastasized into gossip that I was illicitly using PEDs. In writing this chapter, I called Dr. Voy to seek his permission to write the above and he gladly granted me that permission.

A few years later, along with many other prominent, honest athletes, I ordered a legal, zinc-based food supplement from a distributor in California named Victor Conte, who operated a then-legitimate business called the Bay Area Laboratory Cooperative, or BALCO. When the BALCO doping scandal broke in 2003, engulfing superstar athletes such as Barry Bonds and Marion Jones, my name appeared on the master list of the firm's customers (including such redoubtable figures as former great miler and then US congressman, Jim Ryun). I was never suspected of wrongdoing in the case, but some people attributed guilt to this tenuous association. Finally, the suspicions arose from the simple fact that I had reached the top of a sport that, since the Eastern Bloc steroid era of the 1970s, had been inextricably bound up with the use of performance-enhancing drugs.

During my competitive career, I was never even offered a performance enhancer. It never occurred to me to cheat. Doping ran against every precept I'd been raised by. My father would have disowned me had I juiced. Had Bowerman or Dellinger suspected that a Duck athlete was using, he would've gotten the bum's rush out of Eugene. By the same token, if Phil Knight were to harbor even the faintest suspicion that I promoted or condoned doping for a team of runners based under his nose on the Nike campus, he would shut down the Oregon Project in a heartbeat and toss me to the wolves, a punishment I would richly deserve. How could the benefits of juicing be worth a fraction of the risk? What marketing advantage could compare to the colossal disaster of a doping scandal?

Other programs and coaches had a different philosophy. Beginning in the late '90s, after I'd retired from competition, the red-cell booster erythropoietin, or EPO, phenomenally effective and, at the time, virtually undetectable, became the drug of choice among doping endurance athletes, and it was no coincidence that around that point the distance-running records began to plummet. With the exception of a couple national-class athletes, however, I'm convinced that few, if any, elite American runners partook of PEDs. With our extensive out-of-competition testing system, in which athletes are randomly tested at any time and place throughout the year, it's just too difficult to get away with juicing.

Also, the incentive to dope is lacking for American runners, the great majority of whom are college educated and cognizant of the long-term health risks involved with PED abuse. I refuse to point my finger at individuals, but runners from Eastern Europe, North Africa, and other nations lack these strictures, most prominently out-of-competition testing. For decades, elite US runners have lined up beside opponents who are neither more talented nor better prepared but who because of PEDs enjoy an edge of 3 to 4 percent, which is just about impossible for an honest athlete to overcome. But the cold, hard fact is that we have to find a way to overcome.

Doping plants a seed of doubt in the minds of honest athletes, which, in my opinion, stands among the most insidious effects of the junk. By speculating that the guy next to you is cheating, you give yourself an excuse to lose. You take yourself off the hook. In a related way, that dynamic holds for competing against athletes from Kenya, Ethiopia, and other East African nations. Due to the Africans' long dominance of distance running and their famous behavioral and genetic advantages, US runners simply don't believe that they're capable of beating East Africans. That's the great challenge—and great fun—that I've accepted as a coach: doing everything within legal and moral limits to compensate for those pharmaceutical and genetic advantages.

The other lasting harm of the doping age is the cynicism of the public. After the Marion Jones disgrace, it's virtually impossible for the average fan to believe in the honesty of an elite US track-and-field athlete. I understand the mistrust, and I know that it's impossible to prove a negative. One thing I can promise, however: The Oregon Project athletes are clean. When Galen Rupp, Dathan Ritzenhein, or Mo Farah step to the starting line at the Olympics, world championships, or any other competition around the world, you can root for them with confidence. Your trust will not be betrayed.

———

Such were the Prozac-related issues I was dealing with. However, after being subjected to gossip and innuendo for so long—and after being dismissed as a semiwingnut due to my religious faith—I'd developed a pretty thick skin. Moreover, if I could encourage even a few people to seek help for their depression rather than covering it up in shame, I didn't care what was being whispered behind my back. The one criticism that did give me pause was that taking an antidepressant somehow contradicted my religious beliefs. "How can Salazar profess to be this big Christian while at the same time be taking an antidepressant? Why doesn't his faith in God make him happy?"

I failed to see a contradiction. I think that the divide between science and religion is in most ways false. How can God, who has granted humans the rationality that produces science, be antiscience? Jesus healed the sick and suffering. So how can a medicine contradict Christ's teachings?

Some of the abuse I received aimed pretty low. The annual Hood to Coast Relay goes from the top of Mount Hood in the Cascades to the town of Seaside on the Oregon coast; the eight- to 12-person teams ride in vans along the 200-mile route. At the '94 edition of the race, I led an elite Nike team against an elite team from Adidas. Emblazoned on the side of one of the Adidas vehicles was a sign reading: "We Don't Run on Prozac." Our Nike team soundly beat Adidas on the relay, a victory that tasted especially sweet.

Rather than making me dependent on meds, or on other forces outside myself, my experience with Prozac reinforced the enduring truth that you can't hide from your problems. You certainly can't hide from depression. I tried to hide behind running for more than 20 years, and it ultimately made me miserable. I learned that depression has no correlation with toughness. Mentally, I was as tough as they came, but that didn't stop me from feeling low.

Now I know I'll go through tough periods and be able to come out the other side. But I won't make it unless I'm honest with myself and accept help from other people. Through the agency of Prozac, I was granted a physical and psychological renewal corresponding to the spiritual reawakening I'd experienced 8 years earlier, before and during my pilgrimage to Medjugorje. The Comrades Marathon, I decided, would be another part of this renewal.

———

I begin checking out Comrades in detail at the beginning of 1994. The race occupies a special place in the world running community. It's a white whale, a monstrosity, and just about impossible to get your head around. Although not quite as venerable as the Boston Marathon, Comrades might feature even more legend and tradition. The race began in 1921 to honor South Africans who had served in the First World War. Vic Clapham, the founder, sought a test to approximate the 1,700-mile forced march across Eastern Africa that he and other soldiers had endured, and he struck upon the idea of a 56-mile journey between Pietermaritzburg and Durban in what was then Natal Province.

The route bisects some of the most rugged and beautiful country in South Africa. The terrain is hilly and difficult, and the race changes directions each year to vary the torture that the runners endure; one year the course goes "down" from Pietermaritzburg to Durban, and the next year it goes "up" in the opposite direction (although the net elevation gain and loss are similar in both directions). Also like Boston, Comrades' course is distinguished by a series of taxing hills with memorable names: Cowies, Fields, Bothas, Inchanga, and Polly Shortts. The founders conceived Comrades as an event to endure rather than race.

Woven deep into the fabric of colonial, and later apartheid, South Africa, Comrades through most of its history was the province of a handful of leather-jerky-tough South Africans of British and Afrikaner background, cheered on by their white countrymen on the nation's Empire Day at the end of May. But with the rise of the modern running movement that started in the USA around the time of Frank Shorter's 1972 gold medal—and that spread partly through my own contributions—Comrades grew and evolved. Runners learned how to race the distance instead of merely survive it. Citizen-athletes entered in larger numbers, and organizers established a cutoff time of 12 hours; runners who came in after were denied one of the coveted finisher's medals. Comrades referred to a harder, less merciful era, which was a significant part of its allure.

By the 1980s, thousands of South Africans ran Comrades each year, qualifying by completing a standard 26.2-mile marathon; through many of the apartheid years, Comrades was one of the few South African institutions open to all races. The '94 edition of Comrades would be held on May 31—an "up" year through the Valley of a Thousand Hills, past the grass-thatched circular huts of Zulu villages, and up and down steep sunburnt ravines. No American runner had ever won Comrades; few Americans had even attempted it. But I was going all in. I would be running to win.

No other runner in the race could approach my pedigree—former marathon world record holder, champion of the Boston and New York City marathons. On the other hand, I had never attempted an ultra before—the farthest distance I'd ever run was the standard marathon distance, and on least one occasion that had nearly ruined me. How could I race for twice as long? How much had my fitness diminished during my lost decade? Though these doubts nagged me, I felt compelled to respond to the challenge. Training for and running Comrades would bring together all the conflicting and convergent themes that had governed my life. I would commit this race to God's grace.

———

I set out to train for this monster, to try to harpoon the white whale. Nike fully supported the mission and gave me the time and resources to prepare. I was only semiretired as an athlete, and part of my job was to appear at relatively high-profile events such as Comrades. Nike's South Africa division got wind of the development and started thumping the tub in that country.

I basically had 12 weeks to get ready. My regimen wouldn't be all that different from standard marathon training—there are only so many hours in a day, so many miles in your legs—but there were a few new wrinkles.

I would have to learn to ingest fluids and calories while running continuous 6-minute miles. My weekly long run, never exceeding 20 miles during standard marathon training, would stretch to 30 miles. To spare my joints the pounding, I would log half of my miles indoors on the treadmill and as much of the remainder as possible on unpaved trails.

I gave equal attention to my spiritual preparation. My mantra was the rosary and its mysteries, the condensed story of Christ's sinless life, a way to inform my own sinful, imperfect life. But the Bible teaches that God expects imperfection. The fear of being imperfect, of falling short of the ideal you've constructed in your own head, often keeps you from trying. People say they have no time to pray, but you've always got time: while waiting for a traffic light to change; while moving laundry from the washer to the dryer; and in my case, while running on a treadmill in my basement with a fan blowing in my face and ESPN pulsing silently on a TV across the room, training to run a 56-mile footrace on the far side of the world. Fifteen minutes of distracted prayer is better than no prayer at all.

While my motivation and some of my methods for running had changed, the expectations of others remained the same. Everybody—at least everybody who cared at all about a broken-down old distance runner entering a difficult race in a faraway, largely unknown country— assumed that I would win Comrades. As was the case earlier in my career, I was open about my goals; I thought I could do very well. But the Comrades community in South Africa, possessive of their race and its reputation, remained skeptical. There was no way an American could come out to Africa and nail Comrades on the first try, they said.

As they had around my first marathon, which now seemed like it had happened a century ago, people were talking about the ineffable, mystical properties of a distance race. Again I tried to approach it objectively. It sounded like I was bragging, but I was only being honest: I was capable of running at a level that would bring home a win. The media in South Africa had a field day with that. I tried to deflect the attention to my deeper purpose for running, to celebrate and share my faith, but even that came out wrong in some venues. I was portrayed as a religious zealot claiming a direct line to God, and that my way was the only way to the spirit.

In my previous career, I would have been outraged at how my words and image were being distorted, but now I simply shrugged and went about my business. I couldn't control what other people thought. Nike was tolerant of my religious beliefs, and anybody who knew me understood what I was trying to accomplish.

———

The truth was I had nothing but respect for Comrades. I read the stories of great runners falling to pieces when they reached Polly Shortts hill at about the 50-mile mark (Polly Shortts—named for a pioneer farmer in the region—might sound silly and childlike, but I knew otherwise). Comrades presented a terrific, intriguing challenge. Except for Boston '82 and the Olympic race in Los Angeles, my marathons had been cool-weather affairs, and I hadn't worried much about fluid intake. Nor had I ever concerned myself with taking in calories during a race or workout. I had to train myself to eat and drink in a manner that would replenish my glycogen and fluid stores without slowing me down. I experimented with gel packs of carbo goo that got me through 35-mile training runs in relative comfort.

On Sundays, for my long runs, I would head out from our house high in the west hills of Portland, which Molly and I chose in part due to its proximity to the excellent running trails of the city's Forest Park. To simulate the heat and discomfort I'd face in South Africa, I wore a weighted vest. I would meet two friends, coworkers from Nike training for a standard marathon, and the three of us would run from 17 to 20 miles through the park. Then I'd say so long to those guys, run 4 miles uphill to my house, and from there set out on an additional 15-mile loop, praying the mysteries of the rosary to honor God and get me through. I would grow so weary that my leg muscles quivered. I never fell below a sub-7-minute pace because I needed to maintain a 6:15 pace at Comrades to have a shot at winning.

The entire 35-mile workout would take me around 4 hours. As I set out early in the morning, I often waved to a neighbor who was out gardening. When I staggered back home in the afternoon, I'd see the same neighbor, out on another round of gardening. He would look at me, smile, and shake his head.

"Don't you ever have to go to work?" he would say.

————

Despite the enormous effort, I was encouraged by my progress and deeply excited about both my physical and spiritual prospects. There's a huge difference between running more or less indefinitely at a 6:15 pace instead of a 5-minute pace, as was required during a world-class marathon. At that relatively sedate former pace, my asthma wasn't a problem, nor was processing oxygen; I never entered anaerobic debt. Instead, the limiting factors were glycogen depletion—keeping sufficient glucose supplied to the muscles—and the accrued pounding on joints. My long Sunday training runs beat me up so badly that Monday and Tuesday were very easy days. On Wednesday, I'd do some easy strides, and on Friday, I'd log another hard effort consisting of long intervals; 10-mile runs at a 5:30 minute pace, or 8 x 1-mile at 5-minute pace.

Thus I built the combination of stamina and speed required to succeed under the harsh demands of Comrades.

As was the case 8 years earlier, in the months before I took my pilgrimage to Medjugorje, I felt like I was on a mental and spiritual roll, achieving breakthroughs and striking new insights. These states don't happen by accident, and I wasn't magically tapped into some divine wavelength. I worked hard at prayer and kept an open heart and mind through the barren stretches. I hungered for what God provided on the trails training for Comrades, and I didn't know any other place to find it.

I also enjoyed the running. This training experiment built upon all the endurance, speed, and savvy I'd developed over 20 years, yet it was also a departure from anything I'd done before. Running is both science and art, and I worked both spheres in a new combination, incorporating everything I'd learned from all my coaches and mentors. Men like Bowerman,

Squires, and Dellinger didn't focus on the scientific aspects; their approach was more intuitive, although at the same time it was physiologically sound. The building blocks of speed and endurance are simple but can be applied in infinite combinations and variations of emphasis.

Now, for the first time in 10 years, I was playing with the equivalent of a full deck. I wasn't nursing a major injury or trying to compensate for a pervasive malaise. I was having fun again. If Comrades represented a culmination of the various themes of my life up to that point, it also formed a return to the beginning. Some days, I felt like a kid again, outside the house near Salters Pond, trying to beat my previous best time for running around the block, timing myself on my brother Ricardo's stopwatch.

And so in late May 1994, near the close of an Oregon rainy season and after months of intense inner and outer work, I boarded a plane in Portland, bound with Molly for South Africa.

———

I had been to Kenya, but never to South Africa. The moment we stepped off the plane in Johannesburg after the 36-hour journey, I felt the electric atmosphere. This would be the first edition of Comrades since the fall of the apartheid government and the rise of democratic rule under Nelson Mandela and the African National Congress. A general air of euphoria prevailed. After decades of isolation and shame, the nation was reconnecting to the outside world, and my arrival was a small testament to the change. Indeed, there seemed many parallels between the respective histories of South Africa and Cuba, and as we came into Johannesburg, I imagined that this would be what Havana would feel like if and when the Castro regime ended.

Molly and I received a warm, almost celebrity-style welcome, but one laced with a cool undercurrent. The national media portrayed me as "guaranteeing" a victory. Many South Africans resented my seeming arrogance regarding an event that citizens of all colors held as a symbol of national pride.

We arrived 4 or 5 days before the race. Willie Mtolo, one of South Africa's Olympic-level marathoners and a Nike-sponsored athlete, hosted us at his native Zulu village in KwaZulu-Natal Province. The villagers staged a dance in our honor—women shaking and ululating, big drums pounding bass in a clearing among circular thatched cottages, Africa the way we collectively dream it—and Molly and I felt like visiting dignitaries. The entire nation buzzed about Comrades. It was like the Super Bowl and World Series combined. We would pull into a service station and the guy pumping gas would know who I was and give me his opinion about how to approach the event.

When we arrived in Durban, however, where the '94 ultramarathon would start, reporters gave me a hostile reception. "Why do you think you can do this?" they demanded, referring to Comrades' daunting challenges. "You're in for a big surprise, Yank," they warned me.

The journalists took umbrage at what they perceived as a cocky American disrespecting their sacred race. By my lights, of course, I was just being open and confident. In fact, honoring the ordeal ahead, I changed my usual habit and took 2 days off from running; normally, I never missed a day. The intake of calories and fluids remained my biggest worry. It didn't matter how thoroughly I'd trained if I couldn't fuel my muscles or hydrate. I would certainly bonk by the time I got to Polly Shortts, the hill on which so many other fine runners had been reduced to a tortured walk.

My rivals, most notably the renowned Bruce Fordyce, a nine-time Comrades winner, had long experience acclimating their systems to the demands of pounding 6-minute miles while assimilating food and drink. I only had 3 months of training in cool, gray Oregon, and I had never endured the fire of an ultramarathon-distance race. I had done well on my diet of carbo-goo gel packs and water, however. Getting water out on the race course wouldn't be a problem, and officials assured me that there would be aid stations posted every few miles offering my precious gel. Even so, I hired a local Nike employee to organize a team of seconds to deliver my own supply of gel as a backup.

———

Despite all the turmoil, strangeness, and uncertainty, I slept well the night before the race. I was eager to get on with it, to see what the imponderable day ahead might bring. The air was cool, almost chilly, in the predawn darkness. During much of my training, especially the long runs, I'd worn a heart rate monitor to ration my pace and ensure that I was neither slacking off nor pushing too hard. The digital numbers of the monitor display formed a kind of security blanket that I planned to wear throughout the 56-mile race. But at the last moment, I decided to leave the monitor behind, choosing art over science for today's long, long run.

I kissed Molly, who would travel the course in a car driven by my backup team, and fell into the movement toward the 5:00 a.m. start. Walking through the predawn darkness of Durban reminded me of moving through the streets of Medjugorje toward evening prayers on Provko Hill; I felt the same sense of collective, migratory power. But the starting line itself was a portrait of chaos. There were 13,500 starters, as many as at the New York City Marathon during the early '80s, but, unlike New York, there wasn't much organization. I asked how to get to the elite section of the starting line, and people pointed in six different directions. The spectral atmosphere intensified with the traditional Comrades start, a recording of a Zulu gold-mining chant followed by a guy imitating a rooster crow. And then, finally, we were off.

I fell into a pack of runners who looked like the leaders. Similar to my first three marathons, my plan was to tuck in at the back of the lead pack and patiently let the race unreel, husbanding my energy for the hard, late miles. Two South Africans, Bruce Fordyce and Nick Bester, would form my chief competition, but they were nowhere in sight. So I simply ran, hitting out the first in a seemingly eternal series of 6:15 miles, which, barring the unforeseen, would deliver me to the finish in Pietermaritzburg about 5½ hours later.

I hadn't even gone 3 miles when, amid the darkness and confusion, a spectator yelled to me, "Looking good, Yank! You're in the lead!"

Which was exactly where I did *not* want to be. Moreover, I was far in the lead, by a good 200 yards. "Too fast, too fast," I warned myself. But I'd already committed to that pace, which felt comfortable, so I just kept rolling. Now it started to get light. I was running with the rising sun at my back, which infused the hills of KwaZulu-Natal Province. We had left the city and passed into the countryside. The air remained cool, but I knew that the African sun, even at the start of winter in the Southern Hemisphere, would cut like a stiletto as the day wore on. Five miles, 10, 15, 20: I hit out my pace with metronomic regularity, maintaining my lead.

Just ahead of me, on the press truck, the South African reporters did not look impressed. I knew what they were telling each other: The arrogant Yank Salazar had gone out way too fast and would be staggering like a pathetic drunk when the killer hills rose later in the day. "Stagger my butt," I thought; I felt strong. But I registered an ominous sign—the aid stations appeared far less frequently than advertised and offered none of the promised gel packs. An alternate brand of carbo-replacement goo was available, but my system was accustomed to a certain gel and a change at midrace could prove disastrous. Trying the unfamiliar stuff wasn't worth the risk.

My private support crew, meanwhile, was having trouble fighting through the traffic. I had seen them only once during the race's first half, and we'd planned on three meetings. This did not bode well for the race's later stages. Beyond 2 or 3 hours of running, your glycogen levels zero out and you start burning fat, not nearly as efficient a way of delivering energy to your muscles as burning carbohydrates. Eventually, your liver receives no more sugar to convert into glycogen, and you bonk—i.e., you hit "the wall" of total-body exhaustion that every standard-distance marathoner knows so well; I shuddered to think how thick and high the wall would prove in an ultramarathon. Had this snafu with my support team and supplies occurred a few years earlier, I would have thrown a tantrum and wasted even more precious energy cursing out my crew and my fate. But now I kept my cool. I would deal with the crisis when it arose, I told myself, and continued to hit my rhythm.

The bonk descended, with a capital "B," at 25 miles, just short of the standard marathon mark and a few miles shy of the Comrades halfway point. One moment I was clicking along at my 6:15 pace, and the next I just wanted to lie down in the shade. There was no particular source of pain, just an overall iron-clad exhaustion. The idea that more than 26 miles of running lay ahead of me seemed laughable. I had gone from feeling so good to feeling utterly miserable in the blink of an eye. But I still had my big lead. I could neither see nor sense a runner closing behind me. Ahead of me, the press truck ground on with its cadre of scowling sportswriters, who apparently would soon get what they wanted: the spectacle of the famous Yank marathoner staggering like a high school kid after downing his first six-pack. I think I even walked four or five steps.

And then I started to pray; or rather, a prayer rose from somewhere inside me. *Lord, there is no way for me to do this unless you want me to. It's in your hands.*

I started to run again, concentrating very intently on my form. I still felt terrible. I just tried to relax and keep up my form. The numbers didn't lie. With no calories coming in, no raw material for my liver to process into glycogen, there was no way for me to run more than a few more miles. *It's in your hands. . . . It's in your hands. . . .*

Minutes and kilometers crept by. My body still seemed to be running 6:15 miles, but in my mind, I wanted to lie down on the side of the road and sleep. I passed Zulu villagers ululating and women walking in bright dresses with enormous loads on their heads. There was nobody running behind me. I held my pace. No water station, no gel packs, no private support crew. Somehow, I covered another 5 miles. But up ahead in the press truck, the sharks smelled blood. "Fordyce is coming for you, Yank!"

In your hands, in your hands . . . I started to pray the mysteries of the rosary. The life of Christ condensed and codified. Suddenly, I was back in Portland, back on Leif Erickson Drive on the hills above downtown. The air was cool and moist, the trillium blooming as the early Oregon spring came on. Instead of suffering over the hot, pitiless African highway, I was running free and easy under a green cover of Douglas fir, my pace meted by my heart rate monitor and powered by my prayers. *Hail Mary, full of grace.*

My support vehicle appeared, Molly in the back, looking sweet and cool and lovely. If I could just lie down with her in back for a few minutes . . . but if I lay down with Molly, I wouldn't be able to go back to Nike. I wouldn't be able to look Phil Knight in the eye. I cursed myself for choosing this inferno, this adventure of almost absurd pain and difficulty. And then I prayed. *In your hands, in your hands. Our Father, who art in heaven* . . . If I lay down with Molly, then I couldn't say the mysteries, couldn't complete the cycle. Reciting each mystery takes 20 to 25 minutes. Five events in each mystery. The assumption, the glorification, the sorrow. *Hail Mary, full of grace.*

———

From mile 26 on, it was a death march, harder by far than anything I'd ever attempted. Harder than my New York City triumphs, harder than the Duel in the Sun with Beardsley at Boston, even harder than that hot, humiliating marathon at the Los Angeles Olympics. The temperature spiked into the mid-80s as we neared the city of Pietermaritzburg. And now the hills loomed—Cowie's, Fields, Botha and the final two with their exotic, chilling names: Inchanga and Polly Shortts. Hills to make a mockery of Boston's Heartbreak.

I continued to pray the rosary, repeating the familiar words and phrases as if I were drowning, and they formed a life raft. I prayed just under my breath, but apparently the words were audible, or at least the fact that I was praying became evident, because a new tide of sympathy surged from the spectators lining the route, especially the Zulu tribespeople who might have had an added sympathy for the spirit. Also, my prayers must have softened the xenophobic reporters on the truck ahead; as Pietermaritzburg approached, they stopped taunting me and began to encourage me.

"Looking good, Salazar! Come on, Alberto, you can do it!"

———

I entered the hills still holding my lead. The hills themselves were no more difficult than the bonked miles I'd already logged. It was all a seamless, weltering chute of pain and color and clamor. The final miles through the city of Pietermaritzburg, with a population around 230,000, struck me as endless. Pietermaritzburg seemed bigger than New York City, as big as the world.

There were many turns to get to the finish at the city's rugby stadium, and this felt patently unfair. Negotiating these turns required every ounce of my attention, because my balance was precarious. I could not allow myself to fall; I was quite sure I wouldn't be able to stand back up. I feared falling down more than losing.

I did not fall. Somehow, I stayed upright, keeping the pace I had established a lifetime ago during the dark, cool miles leaving Durban. I crossed the line and did not so much collapse as disintegrate. My winning time was 5:38:39. There was no physical explanation for running more than 26 miles at 6:15 pace while ingesting virtually no calories. The only possible explanation was that I had taken my ego and will completely out of the equation and put the race in God's hands.

I have always been reluctant to paste a label on my experience with the rosary beads in Medjugorje. But as a lifelong elite-level distance runner and coach, I can unequivocally declare that my Comrades victory was a miracle.

PART 3

AN AMAZING THING about human nature—at least this human's nature: the sheer, confounding, self-defeating stubbornness with which we repeat the same mistakes. Everything can change on one level, you can strike blazing new insights, your life can completely alter internally, and yet the same hairy face stares back at you in the bathroom mirror each morning. As time passes after a life-altering event, you find yourself settling into the same grooves and exhibiting the same strengths, weaknesses, and blind spots. But at least you're a degree more aware of those blind spots. You've gained some distance and perspective, and perhaps you've moved a mile down the road toward a kind of wisdom.

My 14 minutes, for example. In the weeks following my release from the hospital and my return to the world, I felt like everything had changed. It was like the transformation that had happened after I started taking Prozac back in 1994, but multiplied a hundred times. Each passing moment seemed vivid and spectacular, even the apparently ordinary ones.

I stayed in the hospital for 9 days after my heart attack. Doctors implanted an internal defibrillator—a hotel-bar-of-soap size lump in my chest, a compact electro-wonder box primed to start buzzing if my heart spasms into arrhythmia again—and Dr. Caulfield installed a stent—a meshlike device that augments bloodflow—in my right coronary artery. My runners came to visit—Kara and Adam and Galen. Molly and Maria and the boys were always there, of course, and Rudy visited several times. Once, I opened my eyes and saw Phil Knight sitting beside my bed. On the night of July 4, Molly and the kids came to my room. They moved chairs around the window and we watched a fireworks display light up the night sky above Portland.

I especially appreciated the presence of Maria, my daughter, whom I thought of often during my lucid moments. I felt guilty about not spending more time with her. During their key formative years, I had paid a lot of attention to my boys, Tony and Alex. I had coached their youth-league teams, supervised their training, and never missed a game when they started playing on the high school and college levels. By contrast, Molly had been Maria's main parent connection. As I grew increasingly immersed in my coaching career, and in the boys' athletic careers, Molly took up the slack with our daughter.

"You need to tune in more with Maria," Molly would tell me. "Turn around, and she's going to be a grown woman."

I knew that Molly was right, but I'd kept putting off the commitment. I kept finding excuses for missing Maria's equestrian competitions and other activities and events. That was going to change, I resolved. A lot of things would change. From here on out, I would be a kinder and more sympathetic man. I would make amends for past slights and settle unresolved conflicts. And I would start by reconnecting with my daughter.

Through most of my time in the hospital, however, I inhabited a sort of twilight zone. I was both there and not there; for a long while, I couldn't fully register what had happened to me. I was under the influence of a number of strong medications and focused mostly on the next visit from my cardiologist or an adjustment of my tubes by an attending nurse. When my attention drifted from these details, it fastened on training plans for my runners. Galen, Kara, and Adam had cycled out of their rest phase after the national championships in Indianapolis and had started to prepare for the world championships in Osaka, Japan, in August, the most important meet of the year. It didn't matter if their coach was in the hospital. The clock was ticking. Their competitors around the world were hard at work. So I discussed workouts with my runners, my three main people. I also talked to Phil Knight about Galen's future. If I'm not around anymore, I said, I wanted Galen to find a good coach.

Phil knew how much Galen meant to me. He told me not to worry.

During those 9 days, my family, friends, Providence St. Vincent's hospital, and Nike all shielded me from outside attention, which was sizable. It wasn't as if Phil Knight himself, or one of Nike's iconic athletes like Tiger or Lance, had collapsed, but I was still famous in the running community and was moderately known in the mainstream, especially around Portland. Given my past as a world-class distance runner, and the absence of risk factors, it was amazing that I'd suffered a crushing cardiac arrest and more amazing still that I'd survived clinical death. By the day of my release, I was aware of the miraculous nature of my experience and knew that the public hoped to learn more about it. I was intellectually grateful for my spared life in the manner that I'd been intellectually grateful for my overall blessings during the dark period of my competitive career. It took a dramatic pilgrimage to Medjugorje to bring me to my senses during that earlier crisis. Now, to absorb the full impact of my 14 minutes, all it took was sitting on the couch with Molly.

It happened on my first night home from the hospital. Molly and I settled into the couch in the family room. I flipped on the TV, she plumped the pillows, and the dogs settled around our feet.. All at once, with the weight of a collapsing roof, it hit me that I was alive—I was alive! I was present, without pain or loss of self, to experience this ordinary yet wondrous moment. This wasn't a mentally framed idea but a jolt of deep knowing. For days and weeks afterward, I moved in that sphere of moment-by-moment awareness as I met with my benefactors from the football camp and the EMT crew; as I talked to reporters from local and national media; as I resumed working with Kara, Adam, and Galen, tending to their world-championship dreams.

I recall, for instance, driving from Eugene to Portland to see Galen, my first trip out of town after my collapse. He was living in an apartment in Eugene while attending the U of O, but I still coached him. During Galen's college years, I spent untold hours on Interstate 5 between the two cities, often enduring epic traffic jams. I was not the most patient driver. During a 5-mile crawl through the suburbs south of Portland, my blood typically boiled.

On my first post-virtual-death trip down to Eugene, I was socketed deep in gridlock. I would be late, way late, to supervise a key interval session with Galen down at Hayward, and there were no days—no moments—to waste before Osaka. All this stress just rolled right off me. Road rage? Never heard of it. On this beautiful day that God had made, with no pain in my body and the summer sun shining, how could I be the least upset that a stretch of freeway happened to be clogged? Later that day, on the drive back to Portland, Galen and I stopped at a 7-Eleven for Slurpees. When I sucked at the sugary, icy confection, the flavor burst upon my tongue with a sweetness and intensity that nearly made me weep.

You tell yourself you're never going to get impatient or angry again, and that you're going to savor every Slurpee for the rest of your life. You tell yourself that you're going to change the way you do business. You're not going to fret, obsess, or overcommit to your job.

For a while, you stick to this resolution. You adopt a new general attitude, letting the little stuff slide. You grow more tolerant and try to atone for past mistakes and offenses. When a talented young runner from the Midwest calls, asking to join the Nike Oregon Project, you respectfully tell him no. But over time . . . over time, the glow gradually fades. One day, a few years later, you find yourself sitting on I-5, deep in gridlock, burning gas and time, and you're hammering your smartphone with e-mails to five different athletes on five different training schedules. When Mo Farah calls from Great Britain asking you to coach him you say yes, adding another layer of intense commitment. When you suck at a Slurpee, it just makes your teeth ache. When you finally make it home,

the couch and TV that, 9 days after your virtual death, vibrated with
transcendent presence, have lost their pixie dust. The couch needs vacu-
uming, and you can't find anything good on cable. (The exception to this
trend was my resolution regarding Maria; that never faded.)

———

After Comrades, I arrived back in Portland feeling the divine hand. It
seemed clear that God intended me to be an ultramarathoner, to win
races all around the world and thereby spread the truth of the spirit. *Here
we go, Lord, give me the ball and get out of my way.* Nike made a nice little
fuss over my accomplishment, and people within the running community were impressed. But for the average American sports fan paying any
attention at all, Comrades seemed like a bizarre, fringe event, and the
fact that I'd won it appeared to form yet another emblem of my eccentric-
ity. First chains turning gold, then Prozac, and now a 56-mile footrace
across South Africa. What was I going to do next, run across America
wearing a hair shirt??

But again, I didn't care what most people thought—I cared less all
the time. I just charged off in the direction I saw God pointing me, and
I promptly stepped in a hole. A real hole, a literal hole, one in the solid
ground. A few months after Comrades, I was in Washington, DC, on
Nike business and went out for a run. Afterward, I was doing some
bounding drills—leaping in the air, coming down hard—and one foot
landed in a hole. I went down like I was shot; I had torn a tendon in my
foot. A year of rehab ensued, along with orthotics and cross-training and
endless visits to docs with their conflicting opinions. Other injuries
sprouted off the trunk of the tendon problem. To repair the original
injury, a surgeon stripped a tendon from my toes to put my ankle back
together. It was a painful, complicated mess that, after 2 years, left me
with a weird shuffling gait. I basically ran with a limp. Finally, even I

admitted the inevitable, the undeniable, and, at age 38 called it quits on my competitive career.

———

I still ran, but only for health and fitness, and I turned my focus to family and career. The '90s were boom years for Nike (most years are boom years for Nike). The company consolidated its mystique with the "Just Do It" motto and with the apotheosis of Michael Jordan, Tiger Woods, and Lance Armstrong. I continued in my role in the sports marketing department, servicing the top track-and-field athletes who had Nike contracts. I felt happy and fulfilled with the job. Unfortunately, it was a down period for elite American distance running. The decline that had begun in the mid-'80s had intensified, reaching such a nadir that only one US man even qualified by time to run the 2000 Olympic marathon, and the lone American female qualifier was a full-time physician living in Anchorage, Alaska, who did most of her training on a treadmill. Bob Kennedy finished sixth in the '96 Games in the 5000, but that was pretty much it. Only a handful of American men were running under 2:10 for the marathon. It was all Kenyan, as far as the eye could see, along with Ethiopians rising and a few athletes from Morocco.

Some major prize and appearance money had come into the sport of road racing, especially the big-city marathons. Instead of accepting scholarships to US universities, as Henry Rono and other top Africans had done in the '70s, the talented Africans now went directly to the pro road circuit. For the East African runners, the sport has always been about earning a living. When they make enough to buy a farm or invest in an apartment building, many of these splendid athletes simply stop running and go home.

I started to dabble in coaching, writing workouts in my spare time for Nike-sponsored national-class distance runners. I also helped coach my sons' sports teams. Neither boy took an interest in running; Tony excelled in football and baseball and Alex developed into a fine soccer player. They were far more balanced, well-rounded individuals than I had been as a boy. They did not descend into black funks of despair if their team happened to lose a game, and looking back, I'm glad they didn't become runners. Overseeing their early development, moreover, I decided that my boys would also be more athletically balanced than I had been. I got the idea from studying the case of Valery Borzov, the great Soviet sprinter of the 1970s. I wanted Tony and Alex to have fundamentally sound athletic skills that could be applied to any sport. Thus they would both maximize performance and, more important, avoid the incessant, debilitating injuries that dogged my career.

When they were still quite young, a few years short of puberty, I started both boys on a comprehensive training regimen that would develop their underlying athletic foundation. I'm not talking about skill training in a specific sport—how to slide into second base or place a corner kick—but the universal athletic skills: quickness, coordination, power, and explosiveness. In the United States, it's much easier to find the former than the latter, but, after some searching, I located a young man named Matt James who worked as a trainer at a Nautilus fitness center near Portland. A former college football player, Matt was helping to pioneer a system called SAQ, an acronym for speed-agility-quickness that he offered as a supplement to strength training.

The program employed specific exercises tailored to an individual athlete's physiology, temperament, and goals. Rather than a tag-on afterthought at the end of a sports practice, SAQ formed its own separate workout performed two or three times a week. Tony, Alex, and later Maria blossomed under Matt's training. Tony developed into a star high-school football player who eventually played for the U of O; Alex became an All-American soccer player at the University of Portland, who played professionally for a year after college; and Maria became a national-class equestrian competitor, excelling in the sport at the University of Georgia. From Matt's program, they developed the agility, speed, and explosiveness that have served them throughout their sports careers.

I thought it was time to challenge some long-held assumptions about sports and athletes. The common wisdom is that kids are apportioned athletic talent at birth—you either have it or you don't. The "natural athletes" are the ones we watch on Friday night at high school stadiums and eventually, perhaps, on Sunday afternoon on TV, while the rest are condemned to be citizen-athletes at best or mere spectators at worst. But I believed that the so-called natural athletic attributes—quickness, agility, coordination, etc.—could be taught to anybody. And anybody could improve. The kid with average inherent ability could become a good athlete, and the talented kid could excel. Moreover, the younger you start this type of comprehensive, full-body training, the better.

This philosophy had produced extravagant success, albeit in a rigid, grim, often corrupt manner, in East Germany and the Soviet Union, and I thought it could work, in a more relaxed, sustainable fashion, in the States. I encouraged Matt James to leave Nautilus and hang his own shingle, and soon, along with my sons, he was training young athletes from around the Portland metro region. A seed started spinning in my brain: Couldn't distance runners also benefit from this work? Shouldn't this training be common to all sports?

The seed lay dormant as I focused on my kids' development and my career at Nike. I enjoyed my limited coaching, advising a runner named Marc Davis. I also coached my good friend Mary Slaney, the American middle-distance legend, at the end of her career. But I had no burning ambition to coach. I certainly didn't feel called to the profession the way I'd felt called to my competitive career. I had come to terms with all that I'd accomplished—and with the ways I'd fallen short of my dreams. I still felt committed to the sport, but I was no longer a kid who defined himself by it.

———

At the start of the 2000–2001 school year, Tony's senior year, he transferred from Jesuit High School, in the Portland suburbs, to Central
Catholic, a parochial high school in the city. I met with the school's athletic director, who asked if I'd be interested in coaching the school's
cross-country team, which had suffered a period of decline. At first I said
no—I was busy at the office, coaching was a big daily commitment,
etc.—but then thought better of it. Central Catholic had accepted Tony
at the last minute, and this would be my way of thanking the school.
Also, I was intrigued; perhaps the SAQ seed could be planted here. Nike
gave the okay, so each autumn day from 2000 to 2004, I would leave the
office near Beaverton by 2:30 in the afternoon and drive into town for
cross-country practice.

From the first practice, I incorporated the full-body, fundamental
athletic training into our workouts. It meant extra time and effort, and
for kids of limited ability—by far the majority of our squad—the payoff
was far from immediate. But I was blessed with a great group of young
people who bought into my experiment. I immensely enjoyed working
with high school kids, and the feeling seemed to be mutual.

And then fate again shoved the wheel. Portland in many ways
remains a small town with tight networks. It turned out that Jim Rilatt,
Central's soccer coach, also coached my son Alex's club soccer team. Jim
asked me if I would suggest some endurance training for the Central
squad. I proposed that instead of having his players jog 2 miles at the end
of practice, as was the rule for most teams, that the Central boys run
200-meter intervals, perhaps 10 or 12 at a time, which built the kind of
endurance specific to soccer (the same principle I had learned from Bill
Squires at the Greater Boston Track Club). Jim gave it a try. A week or so
into the season, he stopped me on the way to practice.

"Thanks for the tip, Alberto," he said. "I think the kids are responding to it. Makes a lot more sense than grinding laps. Hey, by the way, this one freshman kid, maybe you should take a look at him for cross-country. He's running those 200s in 30 to 31 seconds each. The other guys can barely see him, he's so far ahead."

Thirty seconds is an outlandishly fast time for an untrained athlete in that type of workout; it was a great time for a trained runner. "Jim, you must be timing him wrong," I said. "Or else you measured the distance incorrectly."

"I know how long 200 meters is," Jim said. "And I know how to punch a stopwatch. This kid is something special, Alberto."

Jim was right. This kid was something special. The boy's name was Galen Rupp. This skinny, blond 14-year-old already had a fluid, effortless stride that reminded me of Rudy Chapa's in his prime. I learned that Galen's mother had been a two-time Oregon state high school cross-country champion. So he had the genes. He was a fine athlete, good enough to make the varsity soccer team as a freshman in one of the region's best programs. Jim told me that Galen wouldn't be starting that season, so he'd "lend" the boy to me for some cross-country races. Galen ran two 5-K races for us. Without any specific cross-country training, he logged times in the 16:40 range, making him the top runner on the Central Catholic team and the best frosh runner in our conference. At the close of the fall sports season, Galen accepted my invitation to train him for the National Junior Olympic cross-country championships, which would take place in Nevada in December. After just 4 weeks of training, Galen finished second in the nation in the 13-to-14 age-group.

Galen Rupp was indeed something special. Here was a naturally talented runner whose future appeared limitless. I felt that same sense of discovery—that same sense of knowing—as I had when watching Bill Rodgers win the '75 Boston Marathon. To realize his potential, however, Galen would need more help than I required when I was starting out. Thirty years earlier, sheer will and endless high-quality miles had been sufficient to get me to the top. Now the global competition was far more intense. Now, if you wanted to be world class, you couldn't get away with an awkward, unschooled running stride. You couldn't train by running alone—unless you happened to have grown up in the Rift Valley of East Africa and had already loped 10,000 miles by the time you were 14.

I thought that if he acquired the fundamental base of athletic training that SAQ offered, Galen might become the American runner who could one day challenge the Africans. Starting this early, working with him over a period of years, I could help build him into an athlete capable of winning an Olympic gold medal or a Boston Marathon. In Galen, I saw a runner looking fluid and smooth, who appeared to be competitive and tough. I sensed that he might possess the psychological makeup of a great athlete: the hatred of losing balanced by the pragmatic ability to learn from inevitable losses; the strength of mind to persevere through injuries, setbacks, dry spells, and losing streaks and through seasons of flat improvement and even the occasional lost season (although, with a solid, balanced athletic-training foundation, injuries would be minimal; there'd be no lost seasons). I didn't see the whole package yet with Galen, but I recognized potential greatness.

———

On a Monday in April in 2001—Patriots' Day back in Massachusetts—I stopped in the auspiciously named Boston Deli on the Nike campus for lunch. That year's edition of the Boston Marathon played on the TV, and I sat down with Nike president Tom Clarke to watch. When the top US male finisher crossed the line in sixth place, the announcer sounded almost as excited as Jim McKay calling my WR run at New York City in 1981. Tom and I looked at each other.

"Wow," Tom said. "Have we gotten that bad, that we're celebrating finishing sixth?"

"We can do better," I replied. And then I heard myself saying, "I could coach Americans to be competitive again."

I told Tom about my coaching experiment at Central Catholic. I explained how I was interested in first building athletes, and then distance runners. I described my analytic approach to the sport, studying details like stride mechanics and emphasizing the strength, flexibility, and explosiveness training that enhanced an athlete's stride. I could apply the same principles to elite runners, I told Tom.

"If I could systematically work with a small group of top Americans, I could deliver a runner capable of winning the Boston Marathon," I said. "We wouldn't have to celebrate finishing sixth anymore."

"Let's go for it, Alberto," Tom said.

Thus was born the Nike Oregon Project. Over the next few weeks, I hammered out details with Tom and other Nike executives. I recruited postcollegiate US distance runners to join the project, including Dan Browne, one of the top Americans at the marathon and 10,000 meters, a West Point graduate and Portland native. Meanwhile, I continued to coach Central Catholic. Galen Rupp trained with both of my groups.

I explained to Phil and Tom that I wanted to start the Oregon Project with the best available professional runners, but ultimately, Galen was going to be the star. I pointed out that he possessed the small markers of distance-running talent; the fact that he landed on the balls of his feet rather than his heels, for instance. I told Phil and Tom that I wanted to give Galen the same experience with the Oregon Project that I had had with the Greater Boston Track Club: the chance to simultaneously compete for his high school and train with national- and world-class runners; to pay his dues through a long apprenticeship in which the victories and glory would be scant, at least at first.

But Galen's case differed from mine in a few important ways. First, Galen had far more natural talent. He was quicker and more powerful. Those attributes translated into an efficient, elastic running stride that would allow him to excel on the track as well as in the marathon and likely spare him debilitating injuries. Second, I started coaching Galen when he was 14, 2 years younger than the age that I started working with Squires. Those 2 adolescent years were crucial in terms of physical and psychological development. Third, Galen would have a far richer and more varied experience working with the Oregon Project than I had with the GBTC. Squires's club provided the best training in the world at the time, but it was almost strictly confined to running. I wanted to build the total athlete, the total person, in a sustainable, incremental fashion, drawing upon the wealth of sports medicine and training advances that had been made since the 1970s.

I told Phil Knight about my hopes for Galen, and Phil agreed with my long-term strategy. (He had taken a similar long-term approach to supporting University of Oregon athletic programs.) I didn't make Galen or his family any promises. I emphasized that we needed to stick with the program through the long march. I told him he'd have to be mentally tough, that his career wouldn't progress in a long rising line. I guaranteed that we'd encounter detours and setbacks. Galen simply nodded and went to work.

In the summer after his sophomore year, he logged a breakthrough 8:58 performance at a 2-mile race. During his senior season at Central Catholic, he swept the individual major state distance titles, winning in cross-country and in both the 1500 and 3000 on the track. In the fall of his senior year, he finished second in the national high school cross-country championships. Central Catholic won a state team title and Galen led the way, but the group's success hinged on the commitment and dedication of each runner on the team, a tradition that has continued at Central Catholic and that has produced scores of young women and men with an abiding commitment to the sport. The four seasons I spent coaching high school cross-country were among the most enjoyable and rewarding of my life.

———

Meanwhile, the elite, professional-level Oregon Project evolved more slowly. I began by visiting some of the best sprint and middle-distance coaches in the United States, men such as Brooks Johnson, the former Stanford head coach, and Tom Tellez, who helped develop the legendary American sprinter Carl Lewis. I picked their brains regarding stride mechanics (the precise manner in which a runner moves over the ground). The prevailing wisdom was that the distance runner and the sprinter were totally different animals. The sprinters were the "athletes," and the nonathletes who couldn't make it as sprinters became distance runners. Reams of data and analysis went into the sprinter's stride and technique, while virtually zero was invested in the form of a distance runner. The distance runner, it was assumed, was stuck with her "natural" stride, and there was nothing a coach could do to change it.

While this model held some validity—the scenario, of course, described my own competitive career—it was also based on untested assumptions. Who said that stride couldn't be taught? What research showed that distance running was a less "athletic" activity than sprinting? How much more could I have accomplished, for instance, if a coach had cleaned up my notoriously ungainly running form and maximized my strength, agility, and coordination? I posed these questions to the nation's leading sprint coaches, and they all gave roughly the same replies. Running fast was running fast, no matter what the distance. An efficient form would serve the distance runner as well as the sprinter. The mechanics of the sprinter's stride resembled the optimal distance runner's stride more than it differed from it.

I examined the strides of the dominant African distance runners such as Haile Gebrselassie of Ethiopia; they ran with breathtaking efficiency, power, and grace. From the way they carried their heads to the position of their footstrikes, each fiber of their bodies was biomechanically attuned to the act of running. If the key skills that came "naturally" to a young African runner couldn't be taught to his American counterpart, what was I doing in the coaching business?

———

I returned to Portland and began to systematically inculcate these skills and attributes into a select group of American runners. It wasn't like I started with a bunch of klutzes. These were good runners who I aimed to elevate to the next level using every legal and ethical tool at my disposal. I was drawn to science and technology, and in the early years, perhaps, I overplayed my hand in this regard. The most famous example was the "Altitude House," where most of the runners lived during the first year of the project. This was a house in a Portland neighborhood equipped with an air-filtering system that simulated high-altitude oxygen levels. Combined with hard training, living and sleeping in these reduced-oxygen rooms boosted the runner's hemoglobin levels and oxygen-processing capacity; in effect, it provided the benefits of altitude living at sea level.

The idea was sound, but the execution proved unwieldy. A reporter from *Wired* magazine visited and wrote a subsequent article portraying me as a Dr. Frankenstein–type character and my athletes as guinea pigs for my dark experiments. But the Altitude House was merely a tool, and one not nearly as important as others. Why didn't the reporter describe our innovative plyometric drills or the weight room where runners logged their daily strength training, or sit in on a sports psychology session, or just come watch us run?

Several years later, I decided to shut down the Altitude House and provide Oregon Project athletes with altitude-simulating units they could install in their bedrooms at home. Other technologies I explored, such as blood testing and the antigravity treadmill, were similarly distorted by the media. The stories depicted me as a gadget-obsessed eccentric playing with expensive toys bought with Nike money. This false image might have been forgiven, and even celebrated, if the project had quickly produced a stable of winners. But alas, such was not the case. With the exception of Dan Browne, no Oregon Project runner in the early years advanced to a world-class level.

I never doubted the wisdom of my incremental, long-term approach, nor did Phil Knight, Tom Clarke, and the rest of Nike's leadership. While technology was important, the real focus was on fashioning a comprehensive, exhaustive system that built—or rebuilt—an elite distance runner from the ground up, that left no stone unturned, no detail unaddressed. I knew we were making progress, but we had little to show for it. Phil took a personal interest in the project. When I voiced discouragement at our meager early results, Phil pointed out that that was why our group was called a "project" rather than a "team." He was as hungry to win as I was—it's hard to imagine anyone more competitive than Phil Knight—but he reminded me that such was the Nike style. One of the key units of the company, he pointed out, was a lab in which designers envisioned products that were wildly unmarketable but that seeded Nike's future.

I always felt reassured by these sessions with Phil or Tom. In fact, the trust Phil has shown in me and his patient, generous investment in the Oregon Project have fueled my motivations for coaching. Still, I wanted desperately to succeed on the world-class level. As the 2004 Olympics passed with only a single Oregon Project athlete, Dan Browne, competing, I realized that I would have to start with faster horses; "A level" talent instead of "B level" talent. There was no way to make a 25-year-old with a relatively pedestrian 28:30 10-K PR into a sub-2:08 marathoner by age 27. The only true A level talent I coached was Galen Rupp, and he was still in high school.

At that point, early in 2005, John Capriotti, my immediate boss at Nike running, put me in touch with Kara and Adam Goucher.

———

Kara and Adam: American running's hard-luck couple, a husband and wife who had met at the University of Colorado, where both won individual NCAA championships and exhibited tremendous talent, and where both were laid low by a seemingly never-ending series of debilitating injuries. In the recent US Olympic trials, Adam, battling injury, had failed to earn a spot in the 5000, and Kara hadn't been healthy enough to compete. Desperate for a change in fortune and scenery, they left Mark Wetmore, their longtime coach in Boulder, and moved to Portland to join the Oregon Project.

I explained my philosophy to the couple: harder overall work, although not necessarily more running mileage. We would get to the root cause of their physical problems, revamping their strides and revising their training regimen into a system that, over time, would yield both faster races and fewer injuries. They would have to be patient and be willing to let go of old habits and learn new ones. Most important, they would have to trust me. In return, I would give them virtually undivided attention and complete honesty. As opposed to a university coach such as Wetmore who oversaw scores of runners, I coached only five or six in the select Oregon Project.

I remember picking up Adam and Kara at the airport on their first visit to Portland, when he and Kara were deciding whether to move. I was driving. We didn't know each other well; we had met briefly at a few track meets over the years. "Maybe you've heard stories about me," I said to Adam. "Maybe you've heard that I'm some sort of wild man and zealot concerning religion. Well, my faith is important to me, and I'll gladly discuss it if you want me to, but I'm never going to try to sell you on it. I'm never going to be the one to bring it up."

As much as anything, that sort of directness sold the Gouchers. At that point, Kara had been injured and sidelined for so long that she had almost given up the sport, mostly playing a support role for her husband. Training primarily on soft surfaces, and building his strength in the gym, Adam quickly got healthy. In his first season with the project, he logged a 27:40 10-K PR, and over the next few years, from 2005 through 2007, he returned as one of the top-ranked Americans in the 5000 and 10,000 meters.

Kara progressed more slowly. During her first few months in Portland, I didn't let her run much and only on soft surfaces or an AlterG treadmill. It was winter, dark and rainy for weeks on end, and at first Kara seemed uncertain. But over time, we developed a close rapport. I started feeding her workouts in which she could achieve a level of success, and once she regained confidence in her health, she just took off. A heel-striker, Kara's strength lies in the longer distances. By 2007, she had established herself as the top female US 10,000-meter runner and was starting to eye the marathon.

The Gouchers' renaissance, along with Galen's steady progress, validated my training ideas and gave the Oregon Project credibility in the national and international running communities. By this time, most people realized that our philosophy was based on heart, grit, and intelligence rather than gadgets. We worked as hard as any track athletes in the world. People were shocked when, after a major race, Galen or Kara or Adam would engage in a workout. Sometimes the interval session or tempo run would take more out of them than the race.

After track meets in Europe, we are invariably the last athletes to leave the stadium; I've often had to beg the maintenance crews to leave a few lights on for us so we could finish our workouts. But all that effort built great chemistry and solidarity. Some of my favorite moments as a coach occur in Park City, Utah, where we go to train at altitude in the weeks before a major competition. Away from the city, away from distractions, all we do is train and hang out.

During the Oregon Project sojourns to Utah in the mid-2000s, the group grew very tight; Kara Goucher treated Galen like a younger brother. I definitely felt very good about the Oregon Project in June 2007, when we broke camp at Park City and headed for the US national track-and-field championships in Indianapolis.

————

I slept soundly on the flight across the country from Eugene. Twenty-five years had gone by since the night Molly and I flew into Logan Airport before the Boston Marathon. I hadn't slept well on that flight because of the pain in the hamstring I'd injured in my match race against Henry Rono and because of the overall frenzied obsession I brought to my calling. Now, a quarter century later, there was no pain in my body. A few weeks earlier, I'd seen my doctor for a thorough checkup. I stood 6 foot 1 and weighed 158 pounds, 14 pounds over my prime racing weight, but much of the gain was due to the increased muscle mass I'd built through my recent focus on weight training. I measured 4.9 percent body fat, less than half the average for a man my age, and my blood pressure read a rock-steady 125/75 (albeit with the help of medication I took to control a genetic predisposition toward elevated BP). I had a total cholesterol level of 175, with favorable HDL/LDL ratios. My doc proclaimed me surpassingly fit, especially by the standards of a 48-year-old American man.

Meanwhile, in the 25 years since my Boston Marathon victory, the first running boom had faded, and now another and much larger boom was rising. In the 1970s and '80s, no one entered the sport on a competitive basis unless they were dead serious; unless they lost toenails and hammered 20-mile runs on Saturday mornings with their like-minded pals; unless their goal in life was to log a sub-3-hour marathon and qualify for Boston; unless they crashed on a friend's floor on the night before the marathon; unless they powered through the chute of screaming

Wellesley women at the halfway mark and then confronted the hills, maybe while thinking of Dick Beardsley and me blasting along in the lead, far enough ahead of the citizens that it seemed like we came from another planet, but not so far ahead, and not so different than that devoted citizen-runner, that he couldn't imagine himself in our place.

Those days were over. The ascetic citizen-runners of the first boom were now middle-aged and raising families and immersed in careers. Nursing their old running injuries, the sprung hips and knees, they worked out on the elliptical trainer or dragged their mats to yoga class. But the trail these pioneers had blazed was now traveled by the masses. Every year around the world, hundreds of thousands of average people trained for and completed marathons. They cared relatively little about time. Quite often, they ran to raise money for a charity, and they were as likely to be women as men. America's marathons were now the province of armies of well-meaning citizens run/walking the distance in 5 hours or more, inspired not by transcendent elite American performers such as Rodgers or Prefontaine but by figures like Jeff Galloway and the Penguin, John Bingham, who reassured the masses that slow was cool, who promoted training programs that took sedentary citizens from the couch to the marathon in 6 months.

Despite this sea change, my business remained elite distance running. I was still trying to create that Great American Distance Runner, although now it wasn't going to be me. I no longer worked to fill a hole inside of me—consciously or otherwise, I wasn't trying to feed my own ego. I was no longer that insecure Cuban-American kid desperately trying to earn my father's approval while at the same time trying to escape him. And yet I worked with the same absorption and intensity. Indeed, the effort was even more consuming. Elite distance running was no longer a pursuit you could leave on the road or track at the end of day's run. Now, at run's end, the work was just beginning.

Now there were plyometric drills, core-strength-building drills, and good old-fashioned weight-lifting sessions to administer, each exercise and rep tailored to the specific needs of the individual runner. Now there were agents to deal with and racing schedules to plot; you had to balance a runner's hope of attaining a world-class effort with his (or her) need to make a living. Even with Nike providing a margin of security, we lived with this worry. In fact, Phil Knight's generosity added to my concerns; I didn't want to let him down. I wanted to make good on his investment. I wanted him to be proud of the Oregon Project.

Now there were injuries to manage, which meant hours on the AlterG treadmill or running in the pool. There were medical appointments to schedule and flights to book. Sometimes, I just had to get out there on the central lawn of the Nike campus with my orange plastic cones and lay out a path for my runners, no different than your everyday high school coach or soccer dad. And like a dad, I was always on call; I could never quite relax. When one of my runners succeeded—when Amy Begley popped a 5-K PR or Kara Goucher upset Paula Radcliffe at the Bupa Great North Run in England—I might feel good for an hour, but in the back of my mind, I'd worry. I'd worry about the ankle that Adam Goucher turned during the Shamrock Run in Portland or whether Dathan Ritzenhein's shredded foot would hold up through the Olympic trials.

Dathan's case especially concerned me. I started working with Dathan early in 2009, shortly after he'd finished ninth in the marathon at the Beijing Olympics. A heralded athlete since high school, when he'd been part of a US schoolboy cluster that included Ryan Hall and Alan Webb, Dathan had been dogged by injuries throughout his college and early professional career in Colorado. We both thought that he'd benefit from the Oregon Project's systematic, whole-body approach. He thrived during our first year together, logging an American record (AR) in the 5000 and breakthrough performances in the 10,000 and half-marathon. In 2010, in a high-stakes, highly publicized gambit, I helped Dathan revamp his stride, a strategy that we hoped would curtail his chronic foot

injuries and serve him better for the marathon. We unveiled the changes
in the glaring stage of the 2010 New York City Marathon. There, unfortunately, our hopes foundered. Dathan finished a disappointing eighth
and in the process of training for the race reinjured his foot.

Dathan easily could have blamed me for the disappointment, but instead
he agreed that the stride adjustment was a sound idea that would eventually
bear fruit. I had developed an enormous amount of respect for Dathan,
both as a man and athlete, and was determined to help him succeed.

In short, they say a mother is only as happy as her least happy child,
and the same held true for a coach—at least for this coach. Besides this
preoccupation, there was the inevitable question from journalists, the
same multipronged question asked with metronomic regularity before
the Boston Marathon in the spring and the New York City Marathon in
the fall: "Alberto, what's wrong with American distance runners? When
will a homegrown American finally beat the Africans in a prime-time
race? When will we see the next Alberto Salazar?"

All of this came at me from morning until evening, and often throughout my sleepless nights. Most of the time, I enjoyed it. It was terrific fun
to be in my position, and I realized how privileged I was to be backed by
Nike. But it seemed like I was constantly answering e-mails and talking or
texting on my cell phone or checking my voice mail, and that my only
escape from the crush came when I boarded an airplane, when the flight
attendant commanded us to power off all electronic devices. Then, finally,
for the span of the flight, I could relax, I could sleep.

———

I woke up as the plane landed at the airport in Indianapolis. Adam, Kara,
and Galen had flown in the day before. My cell phone lit up with messages
as I collected my luggage. There was a lot of gear because I had workouts
to supervise. In fact, I had to hit the ground running, as it were. After

checking in at the hotel, I would go straight to the track at Butler University to put the trio through an interval session. I exited the terminal and got whapped by an intense wave of heat and humidity. Hydration would be an issue, I thought, although we had trained for that back in Oregon. We had trained for everything; left no stone unturned. We trained for the physiological implications of heat—the consequences I had grappled with in my competitive days—and also for the psychological challenges.

For the last few years, we had our own sports psychologist on staff, a man named Darren Treasure. I'd brought Darren on a few years earlier to help Galen, who was then a sophomore at the U of O and enduring a bit of a slump—one of those dry spells I had warned him about. Galen had lost confidence as a closer. He couldn't finish a race. He would be in great position down the stretch, ready to put away the field with a blasting finishing lap, but then something would happen. Galen would freeze. Some inner brake would clamp down, one he couldn't articulate to me or even to himself, one we couldn't release during training, and one that could seriously mess with his mind if we left it untended. So I hired Darren, who was able to get Galen over the hump after just a few conversations.

I'm not sure how Darren did it, and I'm not sure I want to know. I believe in specialists. I know my limitations. Now Darren was working closely with Kara on some deep-seated self-confidence and self-worth issues. The work was paying off; lately, Kara had been giving herself permission to win, and a beast was rising. On paper, it seemed certain that Kara, Galen, and Adam would finish in the top three of their events and punch their tickets for Osaka. But you don't run races on paper. Adam was dealing with an aching knee, and Galen had been down with a heavy cold. There were so many other imponderables. Running hews to form more than other sports. You almost always race the way that you train, especially for shorter distances on the track. But at the same time, you're all alone out there with your doubts and your fears. You can't share the pain, blame, or glory with a teammate. There are so many ways to beat yourself.

I checked in at the hotel, loaded the stuff in my rental car, and followed the directions to the track on the Butler University campus. I jacked up the air-conditioning, but the humidity seemed to work through the air ducts to stupefy me. Despite my solid sleep on the plane, I felt exhausted. I decided I needed to blow out my tubes with a run. I still ran about 5 miles a day, at a 7-minute pace, and I hated to miss a day. Your daily run is one piece of business that you can almost always finish.

———

Kara, Adam, and Galen met me at the track. The school term was over, and there was nobody around. We had the track to ourselves. I'd been told that there was a nearby trail, and I sent the trio off on a half-hour warmup run. Meanwhile, I set up the cones for the interval drill and then started running my own laps around the track, figuring I'd cover about 3 miles by the time my runners returned. I ran in a tight, crabbed stride, courtesy of the long chain of injuries sprouting from stepping in that hole after Comrades more than a decade earlier. During the first quarter-mile lap, my mind teemed with the tumbling thoughts you get early in a run, before the effort and the rhythm slow down your brain and you start to see things clearly.

My thoughts ranged from details—should I make it 8 repeats today instead of 10, given the sticky heat?—to the big picture: It seemed that Kara especially was poised for a breakthrough. She was the healthiest of the Oregon Project's three contenders, and with her intelligence, fresh beauty, and ingenuous charm, I envisioned what a wonderful spokesperson she would make for the sport and all the opportunities that would come her way. I also briefly savored how far Galen had traveled from his freshman year at Central Catholic, and how his development had fostered other happy outcomes.

As Galen approached his high school graduation in 2004, it was clear that I'd been right about his talent; as much as he'd accomplished, he was just getting started. Galen, his parents, and I agreed that I would continue to coach him; our goal was long-term, consistent training. The big question was where Galen would go to college—or if he should put off school until his elite running career was finished. The US college system, with its tendency to overwork runners in order to win as a team, isn't always conducive to the development of top-tier runners. On the other hand, Galen was an excellent student with a 4.0 GPA, and he deserved the college experience.

The obvious compromise would be for him to attend the University of Oregon. I could commute down to Eugene to coach Galen, with minimal conflicts with the Ducks' schedule. There was a precedent for this arrangement: In the 1980s, the great Brazilian 800-meter runner Joaquim Cruz had attended the U of O, competing for the school's track and cross-country teams while being coached by his countryman Luiz de Oliveira. These factors, combined with the university's rich running tradition, seemed to make Galen's choice a no-brainer. The problem was, the Ducks running program had fallen on hard times, and it was partly my fault.

A few years earlier, along with other former prominent Oregon runners, I had helped select the new head coach for the Ducks track and cross-country program to follow in the hallowed line. As it turned out, the University of Oregon had started to move away from a distance-based program toward more sprinting and jumping, and I didn't think that was the ideal atmosphere for Galen. I felt he needed to train with good distance runners and advised him as such. I told this to Bill Moos, the Oregon athletic director at the time, who, conscious of the embarrassment if the most promising American runner in years, and one with such deep Oregon bloodlines, attended a rival school, begged me to reconsider.

Meanwhile, Phil Knight was having his own difficulties with his alma mater. During these years, some students were protesting labor conditions in factories that Nike and other US companies had contracted with in Asia. Phil didn't begrudge students their right to protest but he felt that U of O administrators had not dealt forthrightly regarding the issue.

This development, along with the coaching problem, had dampened Phil's enthusiasm for supporting the university. Knowing my involvement in hiring the new coach, Phil summoned me to his office. I frequently met with Phil—and still do. He takes great pleasure in following the development of the Oregon Project in general and Galen Rupp in particular. I'm careful not to abuse our relationship, and I never bother him unless there's something essential on my mind.

As I mentioned, Phil would encourage me during the project's dues-paying years and assure me I was on the right track with the long-term approach. "Alberto, not everybody's going to love you," he told me. "If you're doing something important, some people will hate you. If you don't want people to run you down, then don't achieve anything."

But now Phil was not in a consoling mood. I listed my grievances about the U of O program and explained that Galen would likely enroll in another school.

"That's quite a problem you've got there, Alberto," Phil said. His tone wasn't unkind, but he definitely had my attention. "I guess you'll just have to fix it."

I never took any overt action to undermine the coach's tenure. I just repeated to Moos that Galen wasn't coming to Oregon. Instead, he would attend the University of Portland, whose coach had readily agreed to my continuing to direct Galen's training. Moos bought out the coach's contract, and the next year, Vin Lananna, the former Dartmouth and Stanford coach, took over the job. Under Vin's expert guidance, the distance and middle-distance programs were once more ascendant, with Galen Rupp leading the charge. Galen was happy, I was happy (even though I put tons of miles on my car driving back and forth between Portland and Eugene), the university was happy, and, for the long-term good of the University of Oregon, Phil Knight was happy.

Galen joined the Ducks fold, and soon Oregon's distance-running tradition was restored. Soon after, a new athletic director was appointed, and Phil's bonds with the university were fully restored. He began giving more liberally and actively, supporting academics as well as athletics, which jump-started a long period of growth for the University of Oregon that continues to this day. I'm not saying that Galen Rupp was the reason for all this, but had he attended the University of Portland as planned, the resurgence of the U of O athletic program might have taken longer to build.

Now, in June 2007, Galen was a rising junior. He had just finished second in the 10,000 at the NCAA championships and was about to run the same distance at nationals. There was much to feel good about, but stopping to smell the roses still wasn't my long suit. Galen was getting over a heavy cold, the competition had stiffened in the 10,000 meters, and we had a lot of work to do.

Also, I had this sharp, weird pain at the back of my neck.

As I began my third lap, I rolled my head to loosen my neck but the pain was still there. Strange. I couldn't recall wrenching or bruising or in any other way injuring my neck. This must be some sort of kink that developed from sleeping in an awkward position on the plane. I kept running. I always keep running.

Four laps, five laps, six laps, seven. The pain still jabbed at my neck, the heat and humidity continued to form a suffocating blanket, and the track remained empty. The only sounds were the chuff of my breath and the chant of the cicadas. I calculated that Adam, Kara, and Galen wouldn't return to the track for another 10 minutes. I would later remember my isolation at that moment, along with the pain.

I labored on for another few laps, until the pain in my neck forced me to stop. As soon as I ceased running, however, the odd pain vanished, so I didn't give it another thought. Not for a few more days, anyway.

––––––

For the next week, I was intensely busy in Indianapolis. I felt generally exhausted, like I was moving underwater, but my neck pain—what I now know was angina—did not return.

Like most people, perhaps, I assumed that angina only referred to chest pain. I associated angina with silver-haired men suddenly clutching their hearts and fumbling to swallow a nitroglycerin tablet. But the reality is far more complex. Angina can occur when plaque in the lining of blood vessels supplying the heart ruptures. Blood clots form on the ruptured plaque, blocking bloodflow to the area of the heart fed by that artery. If the restriction continues for longer than about 15 minutes, the heart muscle becomes damaged, or infarcted. Hence the medical term for a heart attack: myocardial infarction.

You can use the metaphor of a river to explain the phenomenon. Much in the way that displaced rocks and uprooted trees form a dam blocking the flow of a river, a chunk of displaced plaque shuts off the bloodflow in an artery. The result is a searing bolt of pain arising from the sector of the heart deprived of the blood. Or you can imagine the human cardiovascular system functioning like the water pipes in your house. If you keep the pipes clear, the water flows freely and everything's fine. But the arteries feeding your heart, unfortunately, don't conform to the same logic as a plumbing system.

Some people never bother keeping their arterial pipes clean—they smoke and overindulge in fatty foods and don't exercise—but somehow their pipes stay open anyway. Blood flows to their heart, and everything's fine. Other people assiduously maintain their arterial pipes—they avoid tobacco and work out and limit their fat intake—and yet, due to genetic and other factors, their pipes clog anyway. Their blood gets plugged on the way to their hearts, and everything is most emphatically *not* okay. By the same token, the seemingly straightforward process of angina—the physiological equivalent of your basement flooding when your clogged pipes burst—turns out to be devilishly complex and deceptive.

There are two main classifications of angina: stable and unstable. Although it sounds contradictory, my neck pain was the stable kind, meaning that it occurred during out-of-the-ordinary physical effort.

Unstable angina, by contrast, often occurs when a person is at rest. Unstable angina is an almost unvarying indicator of a looming heart attack, but, as my experience illustrates, stable angina may also presage a severe heart attack or other cardiac event. To complicate matters further, while angina always originates in the blood-deprived heart muscle, it can express itself in distant regions of the body—the shoulder, arm, jaw, or, as in my case, the neck. This phenomenon is known as "referred pain," and, interestingly, doctors aren't quite sure how it works.

The most widely accepted theory has to do with something called dermatomes, which are areas of skin supplied by nerve fibers originating from a single nerve root in the spine. If your blood-deprived heart sends pain signals via the brain to the spinal nerves that connect to the dermatomes in the neck, then that's where you feel the pain. Sometimes the referred pain is preceded by the more commonly known chest pain, other times not.

If it sounds confusing, that's because it is. In a colossal understatement, experts declare that "Knowledge of the complex constellation of heart attack symptoms is deficient in the US population."

No wonder. How was I supposed to know that my pain in the neck—uncomfortable but not debilitating, unaccompanied by chest pain—was in fact a symptom of lethal heart disease? Moreover, as I mentioned at the start of this book, roughly 60 percent of fatal heart attacks—nearly two out of three—occur without warning. So on that first day in Indianapolis, when (presumably) a plug of plaque clinging to a lesion in my coronary artery broke loose, blocking the bloodflow to my heart, this blockage just as easily could have expressed itself in a massive heart attack rather than a nagging pain in my neck. And had I suffered my heart attack while running all alone on the Butler track, rather than a week later on the Nike campus, I certainly wouldn't have survived.

In other words, it was too bad that I failed to heed the warning signal of my neck pain. But it was also a miraculous stroke of fortune—the first of several over the next 10 days—that I didn't die on the spot.

———

The US nationals meet in Indianapolis went on for 5 days. Things worked out well for the Oregon Project. That year, the national championships served as a qualifier for the world championships to be held that August in Osaka, so our goal was to simply place in the top three of each event we entered. This is more stressful than it sounds. In every sport, the pressure to earn a place in an ultimate competition is greater than in the ultimate competition itself. There are so many things that can go wrong in a race, so many factors beyond your control. The first job is always not to beat yourself, and Kara, Adam, and Galen came through on that score. In the women's 10,000, Kara let Deena Kastor, a bronze medalist in the marathon at the 2004 Games, go unchallenged for the top spot while Kara took a comfortable second place. Galen followed suit in the men's 10,000, finishing second behind prerace favorite Abdi Abdirahman. In the men's 5000, Adam shook off a season's worth of nagging injuries to finish third.

Meanwhile, the punishing weather continued. I dragged through the week feeling exhausted but chalked that up to the stress and the heat. The meet concluded on a Sunday. On Monday, I flew home, feeling good about placing three distance runners in the world championships. No other training group had fared so well, and our success formed another affirmation for the Oregon Project. I arrived back in Portland to an empty house; Maria was entered in an equestrian competition in Texas, and Molly was with her. I looked forward to some peace and quiet. If I could just log some solid sleep, I thought, then the exhaustion would lift. I had some light duties scheduled—Josh Rohatinsky had just arrived from Utah to join the Oregon Project, and I wanted to help him settle— but nothing taxing. The next few days passed uneventfully. On Thursday morning, I went into my office at Nike like usual. Around midday, I started to feel tired; the same bone weariness that had dogged me in

Indianapolis. All I wanted to do was sleep. I drove home and lay down.

Around 2:00 p.m., I got up to use the bathroom. As I made this simple, rote, undemanding movement, the pain in my neck returned. But it was sharper now—it rose like a shout, and I experienced a moment of vertigo so intense that I began to black out. I managed to sit before losing consciousness. The pain—the referred pain of angina—abated, and the world came back into focus. "I must have a flu bug coming on," I thought, "and I just got up too quickly." I couldn't believe that anything was seriously wrong, but as a precaution I called Tony and Alex, who both lived nearby, and asked them to come over.

When they arrived, we talked through the situation. My near blackout had to be due to an impending flu or general weariness, we decided, and the neck pain must be caused by my moving some heavy equipment while in Indianapolis. I took some Celebrex, and an hour later I felt better. Still, I called our family physician and told her my symptoms. She asked me a long series of questions. It sounded like I was fine, she said, but she told me to come into the office the next morning, Friday, to make sure.

The next morning, at her office, she administered a thorough battery of tests but couldn't detect any serious underlying disease. That wasn't the same as a clean bill of health—coronary heart disease, or CHD, is so complex, so deceptive, so paradoxical, that a truly "clean bill" is impossible—but, based on the evidence, based on science, I appeared to be okay. (I certainly don't think my family doctor was negligent or that she had missed clear signs that might have prevented calamity; remember, while roughly 60 percent of fatal heart attacks occur without warning, approximately 40 percent occur otherwise; that means thousands of victims each year dutifully report their symptoms to their physicians and subsequently collapse and die anyway; my family and I still entrust our health to that doctor as our primary-care physician.) As a further precaution, however, my family doctor referred me to a cardiologist, who scheduled a treadmill stress test for me the following week. Finally, knowing my habits, she advised me not to run over the weekend.

My first thought, my first response to that advice: Of course I'm going to run. The former baseball slugger feels no need to step into the batting cage at age 48, and the former football wide receiver, at the same age, feels no compulsion to practice his square-out patterns, but a runner of any caliber almost never outlives the need to run. Once you get hooked—once the day comes when you suffer more by not running than by running—you're stuck with it. Your daily run becomes your solace and your refuge, the place you go to reflect, heal, and pray.

I think every committed runner prays in her own way while she's moving. It might not be the mysteries of the rosary or the Lord's Prayer. It may be a line from a book or a scrap of dialogue from a movie. It may be a song or the memory of a lover's touch or a child's smile. Something in the act of running, the heat and rhythm and dance of your stride, connects you to the spirit. It's the same for a 2:08 marathoner as for a 5:08 one. If you go too long without that connection, you grow strange to yourself.

Twelve years had passed since my last race at the Comrades Marathon. A few months earlier, honoring a Nike commitment, I had helped pace Lance Armstrong as the cycling legend ran his first New York City Marathon, but except for that and a very few other appearances, I never ran publicly. Unlike my friends Bill Rodgers and Dick Beardsley, I no longer ran marathons or competed in age-group categories, nor did I give talks on the expo circuit. Like millions of people around the world, however, I still relied on my daily run. Nearly 40 years into the modern running movement, this might be the sport's greatest contribution—the regular connection it gives to the spirit.

So it was no small thing for me to go a weekend without a run, and I was already planning my next workout. I decided to skip Friday but get out for an easy few miles the next morning, Saturday, before meeting up with the Rohatinsky brothers and Galen at the Nike campus. I planned to run my standard 5-mile route around my house in the Portland hills, the prologue miles to the brutal runs I logged while training for Comrades. But I woke up late that Saturday, the morning's first fateful movement, a seemingly inconsequential detail that, by the end of the day, accrued into my 14 minutes.

What if I had gone for a run that morning? What if I had headed out alone when the plumbing system of my heart teetered on the edge of bursting? Had I gone running that morning, I am sure, the thrombosis that felled me out at Nike would have happened on the quiet blocks of my neighborhood, with no one around to rescue me.

Instead of running, I fed the dogs and grabbed some breakfast. My cell phone rang. It was Galen, calling from his parents' house in Southeast Portland. We were scheduled to meet out at the Nike campus at 11:30, but he had gotten behind on some errands. Could we make it 12:30 instead? he asked. I said sure. We were in a lax down week after nationals, and I wasn't going to hassle him like I might later in the summer during crunch time before the worlds. That delay turned out be as crucial as my casual decision to put off my solo morning run.

I picked up Josh and Jared at their hotel around noon. The morning overcast was beginning to lift. The brothers were excited. They were two Mormon boys from Utah. Josh was just coming on board the Oregon Project after an All-American career at Brigham Young University. His younger brother Jared was about to embark on his 2-year Latter-day Saints mission, a rite of passage for young Mormons that calls upon them to spread the message of the church. In the wake of the Oregon Project, a number of other elite running groups had sprung up around the country, including the Terrence Mahon–led Mammoth Track Project in Mammoth Lakes, California, and the Hansons-Brooks Distance Project in Detroit, Michigan. Those other clubs have produced some of the best US runners of our time, including Deena Kastor, Meb Keflezighi, and Ryan Hall—and without the advantage of training on the Nike campus, which offers the best facilities and support services in the world. Some people in the American running community jealously resent the Oregon Project, and resent me, and on one level, I can understand that.

When you step onto the Nike grounds, you feel like you're entering the campus of a major university. It's about that size, and the buildings gleam with the same sort of order and promise. The famous berm—the leveelike landscaping that forms a perimeter around campus—leads some people to imagine that we do dark, secret stuff behind it: Pump runners full of designer performance-enhancing drugs, for instance, or subject them to illicit blood testing and brain-wave experiments. But, of course, that's not true. Besides the ethical issues, think about the risk-benefit ratio. Consider the enormous disgrace and damage to the Nike brand if it came out that in the heart of company headquarters, athletes were being fed illegal performance-enhancing drugs.

What is true is that something about the Nike campus demands your attention and your best effort. You have to live up to working here. It's not for everybody. Just like some ballplayers can't handle the pressure of playing for the New York Yankees, every distance runner can't handle the pressure of the Oregon Project. You're constantly under the spotlight. You don't have any excuses. All first-rate distance runners work hard; there's no half-ass way to be a good runner. But my runners work longer, harder, and—I believe—more intelligently and sustainably than any athletes on earth.

The Nike campus is also a playful place, with funky unexpected corners: the forest covering the track infield, for instance, a patch of Douglas fir and hardwood that I've cut through a thousand times while supervising speed workouts. The ideas hatched within these buildings radiate around the world, but at the same time, there's a distinctly local feel. Nike couldn't have grown out of any other ground but Oregon. Most of our Oregon Project business gets done on the track, in the gyms and pools and weight rooms of the Lance Armstrong Sports and Fitness Center and out on the central green, big as two soccer pitches, where we run intervals and tempo workouts and do plyo drills.

For all of the campus's handsome, high-tech gleam, though, the core of the project, like that of any team, consists of the emotional bonds between the athlete and the coach and among the athletes themselves. When a runner first arrives on campus, it might be the track or the machines that wow him, but that quickly fades. Pretty soon, he realizes that the chemistry is what matters, the trust that I give an athlete and that I expect in return. Trust is all that matters in any coach-athlete relationship, really. Because my long-term, science-based program often differs from more conventional training, that trust is sometimes hard to maintain.

For instance, late in 2009, the star American middle-distance runner Alan Webb joined the Oregon Project. The fastest miler in US history, Alan was in the midst of a 2-year trough of injury and subpar performances. I proposed rebuilding him from the ground up, starting with his stride and his mental approach to competition. Alan signed on, despite my warning him that he'd likely spend an entire year away from world-class competition. After some promising early work with the project, however, Alan grew impatient and wanted to run some major meets. I told him let's hit some singles and doubles before we swing for a home run, but Alan resisted. I stuck by my guns. Early in 2011, he jumped in some international races after spotty training and again ran disappointingly. Alan's belief in my strength-based training program never had a chance to form fully, and he left the project shortly thereafter. (Later in 2011, Kara and Adam Goucher also decided to leave the Oregon Project. At that point Adam was about to retire from elite competition, and Kara, at 33, felt that a fresh coaching approach would best help her earn a slot on the Olympic marathon team. We parted on good terms, and Kara joined a group coached by Jerry Schumacher, which is also based on the Nike campus.)

So some people thrive in the atmosphere of the Nike campus, and others never cotton to it. I have always felt at home on these green, sweeping grounds. Along with Salters Pond, it's the place on earth that I might know best. It only seemed fitting that my 14 minutes would pass here.

———

I drove with the Rohatinsky brothers to the parking lot across from the Lance Armstrong Center. I parked in my customary spot. My office is in the Mia Hamm Building, just off one of the main gyms. I never wanted to have an office in the Alberto Salazar Building. In fact, I rarely have been there except for its unveiling back in 1990. Galen met us in the parking lot around 12:15. I wasn't feeling that bad. There were no intimations. We walked across the perimeter road to the sidewalk leading to the interior entrance of the Lance Armstrong Center on the far end of the central green. The brothers walked ahead, but Galen and I soon passed them. We made easy small talk, discussing where to go for lunch. The cafeteria in the Mia Hamm Building was closed on Saturday. Galen was the host, this was his town, he was only 21 years old, and in a few weeks he was going to Osaka, Japan, to run for his country. He was talking about a deli in Southeast Portland. The summer sun lanced through the last of the morning clouds. Out of the corner of my eye, I saw the football camp at the far end of the field, but I barely registered it because there was always something happening on campus. I flashed on Maria and Molly in Texas, what they might be doing at this moment. Galen, the brothers, and I reached the patio outside the main entrance. Suddenly, the boys' voices seemed far away. I remember looking down at the red latticed brickwork of the patio.

The pain blazed up in my neck, a crusher, a bright hot star of pain filling my world. I knew I was going to faint. I sank to one knee. There was time neither to feel fear nor to know peace. The world went black.

———

Although we're still not sure what caused it—a plug of displaced plaque or an angry patch of scar tissue—my blood-starved heart muscle spasmed in ventricular fibrillation. Instead of pulsing in steady powerful beats, my heart began to twitch and my coronary artery backed up like a clogged kitchen pipe. The heart is an organ of marvelous complexity, simultaneously fragile and indestructible. Mine quivered wildly. The intricate system of electrochemical impulses, which can withstand the most extreme conditions and grievous injury yet remains subject to lethal breakdown with only a single mistimed neural switch, profoundly misfired.

My face turned purple. My pulse ceased. I started down a path toward death, a kingdom I never would have returned from given virtually any other joining of time and circumstance. My 14 minutes had begun.

My three young runners did what came naturally to them: They started to run, and they reached for their cell phones. Specifically, Jared sprinted for help, moving instinctively toward the end of the field, where the football camp was in progress (but it wouldn't have been happening if Galen had been on time for our meeting; the camp's first session of the week, of the day, was just getting under way; 30 minutes earlier and the field would have been empty).

Meanwhile, Galen dialed 911. What if he had forgotten to charge his phone? What if he had left it in his car and had to run around looking for a pay phone? What if cell phones hadn't been invented yet?

Every tenth of a second was critical. It was almost like a track or road race. A race was on between my flailing heart and oxygen-starved brain, whose millions of electrical neurons and currents were already starting to shut down, like the lights of a stadium after a ballgame is over and the last diehard fans straggle toward the gates.

The first symptoms of oxygen deficiency are recorded within seconds after the onset of cardiac arrest. If a viable heartbeat isn't restored, electrical activity shuts down in the brain's cerebral cortex. The longer the cardiac arrest, most often, the more severe the brain damage. The resultant loss of consciousness, reflex, and respiration is known as clinical death. Without resuscitation, your brain will typically suffer irreparable damage within 5 to 10 minutes, and you will die for real.

By the old definition of the term, in fact, I was already dead: My heart was fibrillating, I had no pulse, oxygen-bearing blood no longer suffused my tissues, and my brain was shutting down. Anytime before the 1950s, before medical science and technology developed to the point that miracles could enter the field of play, my story would have been over. Death, at that time, was still an event, an irrevocable moment, an indelible line you crossed only once.

Now death had become a process that unfolded with hurtling, unreckonable speed, but one that could be reversed. Now, if you were as fortunate or blessed as I was, you could work death instead of merely suffer it. Still, the odds remained heavily against me. Only about 8 percent of people who suffer cardiac arrest outside of a hospital survive. I had less than one chance in 10 of making it, and a much smaller chance than that of surviving without significant brain damage. And yet, even greater odds were stacked against the probability that of all the people standing on the Nike green that morning, one would be Dr. G. M. "Doug" Douglass.

———

Doug would later explain to me that despite his professional qualifications, he wasn't serving as the trainer at the football camp. Doug's regular, full-time job was as an emergency room doc at Legacy Emanuel Medical Center in Portland, one of the foremost trauma centers in Oregon, where they bring the gunshot wounds and the drug overdoses, the climbers with broken necks plucked off the slopes of Mount Hood, and the chilled semicorpses fished from the surf out at Newport. Most of his ER patients came from the hard side of life. They were the kind of people who put themselves in harm's way. Sometimes, at the end of a shift, Doug would darkly joke with his colleagues about how many coke dealers and pimps they'd put back on the street that day.

But Doug loved the action and intensity of emergency-room work.

Both his grandfather and father had been physicians, and both men had died—suddenly and prematurely—from heart attacks. Dr. George Douglass Jr., Doug's father, served as the longtime doctor for the Tigard High School football team near Portland. Knowing that cardiovascular disease ran in his family, Doug's dad took meticulous care of himself. In fact, he was a devoted distance runner. Aerobic fitness doesn't form an impermeable shield against heart disease. But at the same time, along with avoiding cigarettes and limiting fatty foods, regular aerobic exercise is the best thing you can do for your cardiovascular health.

Definitive proof comes from many sources, including a study out of Stanford University. Starting in 1984, Stanford researchers followed 538 members of a running club and 423 healthy nonrunners. They found that runners age 50 and older had significantly less heart disease than the control group. More important, nonrunners were almost twice as likely to die of cardiovascular disease; roughly 6 percent of the runners died from CHD compared to roughly 11 percent of the nonrunners.

But there's a catch. Unfortunately, when it comes to matters of life, death, and the heart, there always seems to be a catch. While regular vigorous exercise *reduces* your chances of developing cardiovascular disease, a vigorous workout *increases* your chance of dying from cardiac arrest if you've already developed heart disease that predisposes to sudden death. Most often, of course, victims of exercise-induced sudden death don't realize they've developed lethal heart disease. Dr. George Douglass was one of these unfortunate individuals. In 2000, at age 58, in great shape and reporting no symptoms of distress, Doug's dad went out for his daily run and never returned. Unknowingly "predisposed to sudden death," he collapsed and died, one of the roughly 60 percent of cardiac arrest victims who die without warning. It fell to Doug to go to the hospital and identify his father's body.

Tigard High School named its football stadium in Dr. George Douglass's memory. On that same field, before it bore his father's name,

Doug had starred as a linebacker, earning all-state honors and a scholar-
ship to the University of Oregon. One day in the late '80s, Doug, then a
starter for the Ducks, brought a recruit to my restaurant in Eugene. I
shook Doug's hand but didn't register his name, and I never gave him a
thought afterward.

Now, at age 38, Doug was volunteering at the football camp as a
favor to the director, a former Ducks teammate, who had played for a few
years in the NFL. Doug's assignment was to help coach the high school
kids who played the linebacker position. A man named Louis Barahona,
who had recently returned from a deployment as a medic with a National
Guard unit in Iraq, served as trainer for the camp. Saturday was opening
day. The SPARQ guys from Nike were out putting the kids through
some drills. SPARQ was the comprehensive system of athletic training
that had grown out of the program that Matt James had helped develop;
it was basically the same system that I used with the Oregon Project. So,
for a moment, Doug didn't have much to do. He stood by the field in his
shorts and T-shirt, a whistle hanging around his neck, enjoying the
morning sunshine and the smell of the fresh-cut lawn.

But then he saw Jared sprinting from the far end of the field, near the
entrance to the Lance Armstrong Center. The young man appeared to
be in a panic. Jared ran up to one of the SPARQ guys and pointed wildly
to the far end of the lawn. A moment later, the SPARQ guy hollered for
Dr. Douglass. Doug started jogging toward them, thinking that this was
a coaching issue, a football question. I can imagine him moving with that
rolling, easy, football player's gait, the way my brother José jogged out on
the football field at Wayland High School.

Then the SPARQ guys called for him again, their voices sharp and
urgent, flailing their arms windmill-fashion for him to hurry. Doug
broke into a dead sprint, a linebacker's get-the-QB sprint. He realized
that something bad had happened at the far end of the field. Doug continued to sprint, following the kid while assembling his game face, his

doc's face, his ER face. Louis Barahona was already there. I was down, and Louis was leaning over me.

Recently returned from Iraq, Louis had enrolled at community college using his veteran's benefits. He'd taken this volunteer camp gig to keep his skills sharp and because he liked football. A lot of paramedics returned from the Middle East wars, an oversupply of guys skilled at applying emergency techniques to fit young men who had suffered grievous wounds out in the field. You brought a different game to a 24-year-old Marine than to a 65-year-old woman in a diabetic coma. Back here in the world, a former combat medic saw a lot more 65-year-olds than 24-year-olds. Louis needed experience working with out-of-shape older patients, so what does he get? A fit younger man down in the field, resembling the kind of patient he'd ministered to in Iraq. (Louis would later tell me that, at the time of this episode, he was considering leaving the medical field; in the battlefield of Iraq and in other dangerous venues, he just saw too much death, and so much of his labor ended up being in vain. My successful outcome—my walk back from death—renewed his faith in his profession. Louis remained in emergency medicine and at the time of this writing was beginning studies in a program to train physician assistants.)

Following first responder protocol, Louis had turned me on my side to lower the chance of asphyxiation if my windpipe was blocked. I was down, but, so far, that's all Doug knew. He was getting into his zone. The action slowed down, he would later tell me, the way it did during intense moments at Legacy Emanuel ER. His vision both focused and widened. He could see the whole field of play. He noticed details. The more desperate and unraveled the situation, the calmer he grew. Doug was good at this. So good that he taught EMTs, paramedics, firefighters, and nurses techniques for treating cardiac arrest, especially CPR and defibrillation, the staples in death situations. Indeed, CPR and defibrillation were largely responsible for converting death from an event into a process. Those techniques gave practitioners—and sometimes lay bystanders—time to work inside of death.

If I could have handpicked any person in the state of Oregon to be sprinting toward me at that moment, in short, I would have chosen Dr. Douglass, a master at working the death situation. But at the same time, paradoxically, my type of crisis was brand-new to him. His trauma experience took place in a hospital emergency room, where the variables could be controlled, where all the members of his team knew their roles, and where Dr. Douglass almost never directly applied CPR, defibrillation, and other life-saving techniques. As a physician, he directed the play instead of performing in it. He had even less experience out in the field; I was only the second cardiac arrest he had encountered. Dr. Douglass had taught CPR to hundreds of medical personnel, but I would be only the second live—or semilive—patient upon whom he'd practice his craft.

Doug put his finger on my neck to check for a pulse. There wasn't one. For every minute in the field that passes without CPR, the patient's chances of survival go down 10 percent. Doug glanced up, scanning the stunned faces of the three runners. They looked so young, Doug would recall later; Galen looked like a baby.

"Did someone call 911?" Doug asked. Galen nodded. The doc pointed at Josh. "Go inside that building and find a defibrillator," he said.

Doug referred to an automatic emergency defibrillator, or AED. An AED automatically analyzes a patient's heart fibrillation and diagnoses the shock necessary to restore a viable rhythm; no clinical skill is required to use the device. Josh ran into the Lance Armstrong Center to search for one. Meanwhile, Doug and Louis carefully rolled me on my back. Doug recognized me: Alberto Salazar, the marathon champion, whom he'd met once at my restaurant in Eugene years earlier. Doug knew that my physical condition and athletic pedigree formed no guarantee against cardiovascular disease—he saw the anomalies frequently in the ER—yet he was still surprised. I looked like a classic heart attack victim, and Doug would proceed as such, but he also considered other explanations for my cardiac arrest. That a famous endurance athlete would suffer a heart attack in his forties just didn't sound right to him. (Today, 5 years later, with two coronary arteries stented and an internal defibrillator implanted in my chest, it doesn't sound right to me, either.)

About 3 to 5 minutes had elapsed since I'd gone down. However confusing the underlying cause of my cardiac arrest, the treatment was clear: My heart had to stop quivering and start working rhythmically; my pump had to get back online. The only way to do that was through defibrillation—a therapeutic shot of electricity delivered either through the paddles of the AED that Josh sought inside the building or through the machine in the ambulance that, Doug hoped, would appear any moment.

Five minutes, 6 minutes. I approached the redline beyond which recovery turned unlikely. Until a defibrillator appeared, Doug and Louis would have to perform CPR. Louis said he'd do the chest compressions; Dr. Doug would do the mouth-to-mouth. It was not an easy call. I was a mess. I was drooling and purple and blood was trickling out of my mouth. I either bit my tongue or my lip or both during my fall. The blood and spittle would have discouraged most people from attempting mouth-to-mouth, even if they knew the technique. In fact, the unsavory nature of mouth-to-mouth has caused the leading medical associations to revise its bystander CPR guidelines.

When confronted with a bloody, drooling individual sprawled in the dirt, many people flinch at the prospect of breathing into the victim's mouth, and so they don't get involved at all. Realizing this fact—and knowing that, with CPR, something is almost always better than nothing—leading medical associations now recommend chest compressions only for bystander CPR. But Dr. Douglass maintains that chest compressions and mouth-to-mouth, in combination, still deliver the best chance of bringing the patient out the other side of clinical death; of pumping just enough blood to the brain to keep the cerebral cortex functioning, to keep the pilot light from flickering out during those precious, fleeting 5 or 10 minutes in which the play of death unfolds.

So the two big men went to work, pounding the hell out of me so that I'd return to this world. Louis blasted down on my chest and rib cage, manually pumping my heart muscle. On every fifth compression, Doug bent to my bloody, spit-spattered mouth to deliver a loaner shot of oxygen, anything to feed my brain. Then Louis returned to his violent pumping. Doug again touched my neck; no pulse. They kept working, with no positive feedback, not knowing if all their expertise, all their effort, was being expended on a corpse or on an entity in which some critical mass of brain tissue remained viable.

Josh returned from the Lance Armstrong Center empty-handed. He couldn't find the AED (later, as a result of this episode, Nike staffers repositioned AEDs in prominent places campuswide). Doug again touched my neck: no pulse. My brain cells were dying and my blood was turning acidic; the complex tide of disintegration leading to irrevocable death was mounting. But Doug and Louis couldn't dwell on that. Much of the art of emergency medicine, Doug would tell me later, consists of knowing when to call it quits on a dying patient. There is little point, for instance, in traumatizing bystanders and family members by breaking the ribs of a frail 80-year-old in a long-shot attempt to resuscitate her during a cardiac arrest. Neither frail nor elderly, by contrast, I remained a worthwhile bet for resuscitation. But the seconds were hurtling by. After 5 minutes without a viable heartbeat, you start losing masses of brain cells and brain function. On the other side of the ledger was the fact that Doug bent over me, one of the most experienced ER docs in the state of Oregon. And for his partner, fate had assigned Louis, a man almost equally qualified in the art of working death.

The two men kept working. They continued to pump and inspire in that CPR rhythm and dance that seems primal, that you'd think has been around forever. But, in fact, cardiopulmonary resuscitation has only been practiced for the last few decades. Developed in the 1950s at Johns Hopkins University and first taught to the public in the 1970s, CPR alone is unlikely to restart the heart; its main purpose is to restore partial flow of oxygenated blood to the brain, delaying tissue death and providing a window for resuscitation without permanent brain damage. At this point, approximately 10 minutes had passed since my collapse.

Finally, the men heard the siren, and the ambulance from Tualatin Valley Fire and Rescue blasted into the Nike campus. Doug and Louis rose from their labors. They had saved my life, although they didn't know it at the time.

Doug ceded authority to the EMT crew, one member of whom he recognized from a training session that Doug had recently taught. I still showed no pulse. It appeared I was going to be among the 92 percent of cardiac arrest victims out in the field who don't survive. I can envision the focus and intensity of that moment, the attention to detail, the sense of life distilled. The crew applied the defibrillator paddles to my chest, but the first shock failed to jump-start my heart. This was a bad sign; the chance of resuscitation drops with each successive shock.

Defibrillation treats arrhythmia by delivering a therapeutic dose of electrical energy to the heart muscle. The shock depolarizes a critical mass of the muscle, stopping the arrhythmia and allowing normal rhythm, set by the natural pacemaker in the sinoatrial node of the heart, to resume. The first clinical use of an electrical defibrillator occurred in 1947, when a professor of surgery at Case Western Reserve University employed the device during an operation of a 14-year-old boy with a congenital heart defect. Closed-chest machines were developed in the 1950s in the Soviet Union, and AEDs and implantable defibrillators came into use in the 1980s.

After my first unsuccessful shock, the EMTs applied three more, paced 1 minute apart. Each shock briefly returned my heart muscle to "atrial fibrillation"—a nonrhythmic but less lethal form of spasming. But after each shock, I quickly reverted to the deadly ventricular fibrillation.

This went on for four cycles; around 4 minutes without a sustaining heartbeat. 14 minutes. The shock, the kick, my body flying up with the charge and then flopping back on the ground. Galen and the brothers watched, horrified, but still expecting the adults in charge to save me. Meanwhile, Louis and Doug looked on soberly, aware of the odds against me. I can see them breathing heavily, like two linebackers who've just mounted a goal line stand, watching their offense go to work; watching the first few plays—the first four shocks to my heart—fail dismally.

———

And where was I during this time? Have I ceased to exist? What is the "I"? Is it the mind? Is the mind the same as the brain? What happens when we die? What happens to the mind and consciousness during clinical death?

Research shows that from 10 to 20 percent of people resuscitated from clinical death report lucid, well-structured thoughts during the early part of clinical death. With all measurable electrical activity in the brain extinguished, all bodily and brain-stem reflexes gone, many people nonetheless report vivid, verifiable memories of the death scene.

This was the time when "I" might have floated above the patio, serenely observing the frantically laboring EMTs, the panting Doug and Louis, the shocked runners, and my own body sprawled under the defib paddles. But for whatever combination of divine and worldly reasons, I did not experience such a vision. Finally, after the fourth shock and 14 minutes after my heart had stopped, my heart remained in atrial fibrillation. A faint, fluttering pulse returned.

———

During the 8-minute ride to the hospital, however, my heart failed yet again, and EMTs had to apply four more shocks of the defibrillator;

therefore, added to my 14 Minutes out in the field, a total of at least 22 minutes passed before I developed a viable, self-sustaining heartbeat. I remember hearing a whooshing noise and the rattle of bottles and gear. What if Providence St. Vincent Hospital hadn't been so near? What if this were a weekday rather than a Saturday, with weekday traffic?

They wheeled me into the ER, where Dr. Todd Caulfield started directing the story. Having gone nearly half an hour without a self-sustaining pulse, I had entered outlier realms, approaching places from which few returned. Dr. Caulfield noted who I was. He determined that he'd treat me like just another patient. My heart rate was in the low 100s, and I was in atrial fibrillation; my heart still beat in a syncopated rhythm, but blood flowed and I was tenuously alive. My blood had turned dangerously acidic. The normal value is 7.4; according to Dr. Caulfield, cardiac-arrest patients with a value of 7.0 or below rarely survive. My level was 7.1.

Overall, my case confused Dr. Caulfield. He couldn't determine the precise underlying cause of my collapse and cardiac arrest. My right coronary artery was 70 percent occluded, which was significant blockage but by itself didn't seem enough to cause the calamity. Dr. Caulfield was amazed by the bore of my artery, which, widened by a lifetime of aerobic exercise, he likened to a "garden hose." He couldn't find evidence of a blood clot that might have plugged the flow of blood. The arrhythmia might have been caused by the old scar tissue. My EKG showed no history of rhythm problems. My collapse seemed as strange as the fact that I'd survived. In the field, I had received four shocks for ventricular fibrillation between 12:38 and 12:46 p.m. If there had been a blood clot, it might have dissolved during this period.

A few things seemed clear. I had had phenomenally good CPR out in the field, but after being down and out that long, a complete recovery was still extremely unlikely. Tony and Alex had arrived by this time, and I was able to recognize them. I was able to move my extremities. Good signs all. The bad sign: I had required external support for a heartbeat for at least 14 minutes. Once a patient hits the 10-minute mark, Dr. Caulfield would explain later, he got a "queasy feeling" regarding survival. There was all that acid in my blood. And eight jolts were a lot—a whole lot. If a patient was going to make it, one jolt of the defib usually did the trick.

Going through an incision made in my groin, Dr. Caulfield inserted a stent in my right coronary artery, which an angiogram (x-ray pictures taken through a catheter, also inserted through a small incision in my groin) showed was 70 percent blocked. Also working through a catheter, Dr. Caulfied performed angioplasty, which consists of widening the artery using tiny balloons. To hold open the artery and prevent narrowing in the future, he then inserted a stent, which is a mesh tube made out of special metal that acts as a sort of internal scaffolding for the blood vessel, roughly resembling the support beams that miners use to keep a tunnel from collapsing. Interestingly, my artery was so wide that Dr. Caulfied had to enlarge the stent by hand.

Now that I had made it to the hospital, my chances of survival had improved. Now the big question was cognition—how much brain function had I lost? Given the probability that I'd lost a great deal, Caulfield and his colleagues considered a hypothermia protocol: submerging me in an ice-water bath to slow my metabolism and reduce the demands on my cardiovascular system. You read about climbers being buried by snow avalanches for 30 minutes and making a full recovery, which is the basis for this treatment. But Dr. Caulfield watched me interact with my sons and saw me respond to commands to wiggle my fingers and toes. Had I suffered significant cognitive damage, I wouldn't have been able to perform these functions. He and his team of physicians decided against the ice-bath protocol.

"No," Dr. Caulfield said to his team. "He's going to do fine."

Dr. Caulfield made this prediction on a combination of scientific knowledge, clinical experience, and instinct. In the end, there seems to be no unequivocal scientific explanation for my escaping significant brain damage. The two most obvious factors in my favor were the superb CPR I'd received from Doug and Louis—they succeeded in keeping my brain's pilot light illuminated, supplying enough oxygen to my cerebral cortex that a critical mass of cells survived—along with my superior physical condition.

But the fact is that, just as the imponderable plays a key role in the science of distance running, it plays a similar role in the science of cardiac arrest and sudden death. Every year, on high-school football fields and basketball courts across America, teenaged athletes who are in better shape than I was that day collapse from cardiac arrest. Expert EMT crews are treating these kids within moments, and yet they still die or suffer extreme brain damage. I basically walked away from my 14 minutes unscathed, saved by an inexplicable combination of science and grace.

———

Dr. Douglass went home from the football camp that evening, and his wife asked him how his day had gone. "Eventful," he answered, and then he told her the story. He said that he'd called a colleague at Providence for an update on my condition. He found out that I had survived, but Doug knew that might prove to be a mixed blessing.

"Do you think his brain is going to be okay?" his wife asked

"I'm not optimistic," Doug said. "He was gone for such a long time."

Meanwhile, back in the hospital, I was placed in a shallow, drug-induced coma and remained only spectrally aware of life going on around me. My first memory was of awakening in the hospital room, with a crucifix and some rosary beads, along with a scapular, a sort of cloth necklace square at one end, which my father had given Alex. I remember thinking, "Where am I?" I have images of Phil Knight and Rudy Chapa being in the room at different times.

Later, I learned that Phil had called Rudy with the news that I'd been stricken. Rudy recalls an episode at the hospital when a doctor came in, checked me, then departed. A moment later, I said to Rudy, "I wonder when the doctor's going to come?" And once, sitting with Molly, I kept obsessively asking her if she had fed the dogs, which was my responsibility.

But the good news—the seemingly miraculous news—was that, except for these minor blips in my short-term memory, my cognitive function was undiminished. I recognized my friends and family and was aware of my surroundings. (Minor short-term memory loss remains the only lingering effect of my 14 minutes. I can instantly recall the time that Galen ran in a race two years ago, for instance, but recent, non-running-related memories occasionally elude me. A few years ago, for example, I was in Flagstaff, Arizona, riding in a car with Kara and Adam Goucher, looking for a place to eat dinner. "That place looks good," I said, pointing to a Mexican restaurant. Not until we were inside, seated at a table, did I recall that we'd dined at this restaurant the night before.)

I spent 10 days in the hospital. Only gradually did the awareness sift down to me that I'd probably suffered a heart attack. The people out in the blogospheres and Internet chat rooms learned of my condition before I did. I didn't fully realize what had happened to me—my anomalous "cardiac event," and my equally anomalous survival free of significant brain damage—until the night I went home and settled on the couch with Molly.

Just as Dr. Caulfield never quite reached the bottom of what caused my cardiac arrest, I couldn't justify myself to the fact of my affliction. Cardiovascular disease seemed the province of my father and grandfather, an old man's disease, an obese man's disease, a smoker's disease. I had done everything right in terms of risk factors and still I'd fallen.

Something in the human mind craves order and compulsively seeks the reason behind events. Something in *my* mind seeks the rational in direct proportion to my soul's hunger for the ineffable. Perhaps no endeavor connects the two realms—the empirical and the imponderable—in a more satisfying symbiosis than distance running. That's why I'm drawn to it, why I stuck with it through all those years when, on the surface, running only brought me grief.

But there seemed no satisfying explanation for my cardiac crisis. The sole explanation for my collapse seemed to be genetic predisposition. There was too much of the imponderable and not enough of the empirical. This seemed wrong to me. What was the point of working so hard at being healthy if genes ran the entire game? What was the point of anything?

———

I questioned God, much in the way that I questioned the spirit during my long malaise before Medjugorje. Then, too, I had left no stone unturned in seeking a medical explanation for my problems. Then, too, I bemoaned a fate that I did not seem to deserve. Then, too, I felt that I was hewing to God's plan and had suffered as a result. But then my affliction was the price I paid for my excess. This time I had not indulged in excess—I failed to see my sin. For days, I searched, confounded by what had happened, until gratitude broke through and I recognized the miracle of my survival. I wasn't the first supremely fit person to suffer a cardiac arrest, and, unfortunately, I wouldn't be the last. Jim Fixx hadn't been as lucky as me, and neither had Ryan Shay, the 28-year-old elite runner who died of cardiac arrest a few miles into the 2008 Olympic marathon trials in New York City. Almost absurdly, fatal cardiac events happen to people who would seem to be the most heart-healthy people on the planet. Dr. Caulfield has several patients suffering from advanced heart disease who are also avid marathoners and who have done everything right. Why? How?

The days passed, and finally I went home, still black and blue from where Louis had pounded on me. Molly and I sat on the couch. The dogs settled around our feet. The full weight of the truth hit me: Though I'd never understand exactly why or how it had happened, I was alive.

———

Because the marathon has developed into the world's most popular and lucrative running event, and because it was my signature distance, people constantly ask when Galen Rupp, my longtime protégé, will tackle 26.2. As of early 2012, his longest race has been a half-marathon, which he has attempted only once—an outstanding 60:30 performance, the third fastest ever by an American. I have advised Galen to hold off on the marathon, much in the way that, a generation ago, Bill Squires told me to wait. I'll advise Galen to stay away from the marathon as long as he keeps getting faster on the track. I will do everything in my power to prevent him from repeating my self-immolating mistakes.

I now know that I didn't wait nearly long enough, and that once I started running marathons at age 22, I failed to pay the distance its proper respect. I doubled in the 10,000 and the marathon in the spring of 1982. That was hubris. We have since learned that, on the highest level, you can no longer do both events. Once you run a marathon, you can't return to the track with the same consistent short-distance speed that you exhibited before running 26.2. Regardless of what I thought in my arrogant youth, the marathon is special. Its mystique is deep and legitimate.

I think about my runners constantly. Maybe even to the point of obsession. For instance, I tossed and turned one sleepless night in October 2011, consumed by thoughts of the nearly invisible hitch in Galen's running stride. I suspected that he attained an inch or two more extension pushing off his left leg than his right. To test that hypothesis, I decided, I'd conduct a low-tech experiment the next day. I would dump a load of sand on one lane of the running track, have Galen run through it at race pace, and measure the distance between his footprints. If I found a discrepancy, I would work with experts to design a combination of flexibility and strength-training exercises that would balance his stride.

The average fan—even the most avid fan—would never notice Galen's flaw. Neither would the great majority of distance-running coaches or other authorities in the sport. And if they did happen to notice that inch or two of imbalance, they would almost certainly say leave it alone. If it ain't broke, don't fix it, they'd tell me. After all, Galen set an American record in the 10,000 meters the previous September, smashing the old mark by more than 11 seconds with a 26:48 performance, thus becoming just the second non-African to run sub-27 minutes for the distance. Galen concluded the 2011 season—in fact, he had passed his entire 10-year career—without serious injury. Among male US distance runners, he stood as one of the best hopes of winning a medal in the 2012 London Olympics. So why mess with him?

My critics, I imagined, could gossip endlessly over that question. Salazar is at it again, they'd say, micromanaging and overcontrolling, trumping up this "hitch" as a pretext for employing the vast, and vastly expensive, array of technical and sports-science wizardry that Nike puts at the Oregon Project's disposal. They would scoff at my focus on stride mechanics, arguing that I ignored the forest for the trees. They would insist that running was an art rather than a science and that an athlete's stride was as singular, and as essentially unalterable, as his fingerprints. Those critics would whisper, finally, that I was trying to impose my ego on Galen's career, that I was working out my own unfinished business, and that through Galen I hoped to win the Olympic medal that I never earned myself.

To a slight degree, the criticisms have merit. I am imposing my will on Galen, but there's no hidden, egotistical agenda involved. I'm simply trying to pass along what I've learned from a lifetime in the sport and save him from repeating my mistakes. Why bother to locate and repair this semiphantom hitch? Because, for starters, at that Diamond League track meet in Brussels in which Galen set his AR, he only finished third in the race, behind Kenenisa Bekele from Ethiopia and Lucas Kimeli Rotich from Kenya. That's fine for now. At age 25, Galen is still a few years away from his peak.

Ultimately, however, third place won't be good enough. Being the world's best non-African distance runner won't be good enough. The goal is to win. More precisely, the goal to put yourself in the very best possible position to win; to do every conceivable, ethical thing in your power before letting the imponderable—the forces beyond your control—take over.

Traditionally, there have been only two ways for a distance runner to accomplish this goal. One is to dope, to cheat, which I have never considered. The other way is to camp out on the far side of the redline, to strike a pact with the devil, jack your training to unsustainable levels and hope that you squeeze out a few transcendent races before the devil takes his due in injury and illness. This latter path, of course, was the one that I followed as a young athlete and that, eventually, inevitably, brought me to grief.

Now, as a coach, I'm proposing a third way. I think you can catch up with the world's best by training smarter, by running with greater efficiency. That infinitesimal hitch in Galen's stride may cost him only 10 seconds over the course of a 6.2-mile race. But 10 seconds translates to almost 70 yards—the gap between a gold medal and relative obscurity. Equally important, if we seek to close that gap through applied sports science rather than draining, risky speedwork, Galen stands a better chance of avoiding injury. His career will last longer and bring him less heartache.

————

If my critics think I'm gilding the lily by tinkering with Galen's stride, they'd say I'm drowning the whole garden by fiddling with Mo. A Somaliaborn British citizen who joined the Oregon Project early in 2011, Mo just concluded one of the most dominant seasons in recent distance-running history, winning a gold medal in the 5000 at the world championships and a just-miss silver medal in the 10.

What could possibly be wrong with Mo's stride? Arm carriage. When he runs at race pace, his right arm swings on a horizontal arc, crossing the midline of his body. The arms should drive straight ahead, parallel to each other. If he corrected that glitch, I think, Mo could be virtually unbeatable. But fixing that problem, such as it is, might prove more complicated than addressing Galen's imbalance.

Mo and his family are still adjusting to living in the United States in general and Oregon in particular. The pressure on him is fearsome. After his breakthrough success last summer, and as London hosts the Games, Mo stands as the great British Olympic hope. The Muslim and African worlds also embrace him. As a man born in one culture who made his life in another—and as a former Olympian who once staggered under the expectations of his nation—I can relate to what Mo is going through. Maybe, regarding his arm carriage, I'll leave well enough alone—for now.

———

I notice a curious thing as I get older. The more painstaking and relentless my approach to coaching—the more obsessed I become about honoring the trust invested in me and guiding runners to the precipice, but saving them from falling over—the more relaxed I've become in other areas of my life.

My cardiovascular condition, for instance. Right after my 14 minutes, I wanted to know everything about the heart and its workings. I immersed myself in the complexities of the marvelously intricate plumbing system. I learned about the subtle connections between the heart and the brain: the electrochemical charges, the various pulsing chambers, the suffusing rhythms.

I became a lay expert out of necessity, due to a series of cardiac aftershocks. A few weeks after my release from the hospital, doctors discovered significant blockage in a second coronary artery and surgically inserted a second stent. At the 2007 world-championship meet in Osaka, I suffered from severe vertigo and had to go to the hospital emergency room. The Japanese doctors determined that my arteries were fine but that I'd experienced a sudden drop in blood pressure due to medication. A year later, at, the Beijing Olympics, I had a scare when a security guard's metal-detector wand disturbed the rhythm of my internal defibrillator, producing a searing bolt of chest pain.

During the period following my 14 minutes, meanwhile, I became something of a cardiac-arrest-survival celebrity. People layered my experience with all manner of interpretations. Detractors of endurance sports attributed my seemingly anomalous cardiac event to the harmful effects of long-term extreme marathon training. Conspiracy theorists speculated that I damaged my heart by ingesting performance-enhancing drugs. More responsible voices in the heart-health community promoted my case as an example of the need for vigilance in the absence of obvious risk factors. Some members of religious and New Age spiritual groups regarded my survival as a miraculous, quid pro quo product of my faith.

I appeared at several cardiology conferences, gave numerous interviews, and accepted invitations to speak to church groups. While I gladly contributed to the campaign against fatal cardiac arrest, I reluctantly wore the label of heart attack victim, just as I shrank from wearing my faith on my sleeve after my Medjugorje pilgrimage. I feel uncomfortable in the role of spokesman or symbol, no matter the cause. I feel I can be of most use, and affect the greatest good, by practicing my trade and taking care of the people around me.

Just as the miracle at Medjugorje returned me to the everyday fun-

damentals of my faith—prayer, confession, observing the sacraments—
the miracle of my 14 minutes reinforced the prosaic realities of good
health: avoiding smoking, regular exercise, and a low-fat diet.

For the last 3 years, I have been largely asymptomatic and have
received consistently good reports from Dr. Caulfield. I still occasionally speak to medical and church groups about my experience, and on a
personal level I continue to exercise, watch my diet, and control my
stress. But my curiosity about my condition—my hunger to know and
discuss the details—has waned. An acquaintance of mine, for instance,
has also survived a near-fatal heart attack. Whenever we meet, he
eagerly brings up the subject. I wish the fellow well, but, during the last
few years, when I see the man approach, I tend to look the other way.

And now, when Dr. Caulfield offers to show me my latest CT scans
or readouts from a stress test, I most often decline. It just feels like a little
too much information. I prefer trusting the details to God and my medical team.

———

Similarly, I have grown more relaxed—or perhaps more humble—
regarding my prayer and spiritual life. In terms of faith, I've turned less
and less a perfectionist. In fact, I'm increasingly convinced that faith and
perfection contradict one another.

Every day, as I walk to my office in the Mia Hamm Building, passing
the spot where I collapsed on June 30, 2007, I say a brief prayer of thanks.
I still voice the prayer that came to me as a child, as I watched the dead boy
rise from Salters Pond, but not as fervently or as regularly as when I was a
child or a young man searching for himself. I still pray when I run, repeating the Lord's Prayer or reciting a mystery of the rosary, but not with the
same hunger and intensity as during my time of crisis.

I think that this ebb is natural and reflects neither a loss of faith nor a diminution of the truths I have struggled to glimpse. I still abide by the faith that's animated generations of the Salazar family. I realize that it's no wiser to try to maintain an intensity of the spirit as it was to maintain the Faustian intensity of training during my competitive career. Perhaps a mystic or saint could pray with an unceasing flame, but I am neither. I am simply a flawed man taught by death. I know full well that my teacher will visit again.

EPILOGUE

I MEET MO and Galen for a workout on the Nike campus the morning after my revelation about the hitch in Galen's stride. They warm up at a deliberate, almost desultory pace, savoring the late-morning sunshine. There's a bracing tang of autumn in the air, and a dry breeze washes through the trees lining the perimeter road. The guys are talking about Halloween, Galen explaining the rituals of the upcoming American holiday. Mo takes it in with a smile.

Meanwhile, I hustle across the parking lot to the running track, where I dump a load of sand on the red poly surface of the back-stretch. After more than a decade of coaching, I still savor these small moments: spreading sand, placing plastic cones around a field, screwing spikes into the soles of racing flats. They make me feel like a kid again, like in the days when Ricardo used to time me as I ran around our house back in Connecticut, on the shore of Salters Pond.

I finish raking and jog back across the parking lot toward the field, where Galen and Mo are still discussing Halloween. "Halloween," Mo says with his default sunny smile. "That's where the kids dress up in costumes?"

"And then they walk door to door in your neighborhood," Galen says. "People give them candy."

"How do they know where to go—the children?"

"You go out with them," Galen says. "It's a lot of fun."

It's time to start the workout, but I'm reluctant to rush the guys. They deserve a little bit of a break. I'll be asking a great deal of them in the long, crucial year ahead. On the other hand, we need to get our session in before lunchtime fitness classes take over the field. I'm eager to get to my stride-length experiment, and this afternoon, the pair are scheduled for a media photo shoot. Beyond these short-term insistencies, finally, lies my determination not to fail these men. I can't permit Mo to let down his countrymen or Galen to fail to realize his gift.

"Okay, guys," I say. "Let's do this."

They flow around the perimeter of the field, cycling between 300-meter surges and jogging recoveries, taking turns setting the pace, the slender bladelike Mo moving with a sinuous, flowing stride, arms swinging slightly akimbo, and Galen running with that gait whose flaw only I can see. Just for a moment, I relax my attention, reflecting on the odds stacked against us being here this morning: the native Somalian, the native Oregonian, and the native Cuban living a second, charmed life.

The workout winds up, and I lead Mo and Galen across the packed parking lot to the running track, where I explain my experiment. The guys listen closely as they help me smooth the sand. Galen volunteers to go first. He jogs to the starting line on the far side of the track, moving freely and easily on this golden fall morning. He takes his mark. I give a wave, and Galen starts to run.

Galen Rupp, Alberto Salazar, and Mo Farah after the 10,000 meters at the 2012 Olympics in London. Farah won the gold medal in 27:30.42; Rupp took the silver in 27:30.90. *(Photo by Victah Sailer @ Photo Run)*

ACKNOWLEDGMENTS

THANK YOU TO my mother, Marta Galbis, for her steady flame, and to my father, José Salazar, for his bright torch.

Thanks to my sister, Maria Cristina, and brothers Ricardo, José, and Fernando, my companions since Salters Pond.

My coaches and mentors molded me both as a runner and a man: Don Benedetti, Bill Squires, Bill Bowerman, and Bill Dellinger. My good friend Kirk Pfrangle's belief in me convinced me to believe in myself.

Almost every step I've ever run has been supported, in one way or another, by Phil Knight and his vision as embodied by Nike. Thanks to Geoff Hollister and other colleagues at the company for their encouragement and inspiration. Thank you also to Rudy Chapa for his lifelong friendship, to Darren Treasure for his insightful work with the Oregon Project, to my good friends Dr. Robert Cook and Shelley Cole, and to the runners I have coached over the years, who have given me more than I've taught them.

Were it not for the heroic efforts of Dr. Doug Douglass and Louis Barahona, I wouldn't be alive today. Dr. Todd Caulfield and the staff at Providence St. Vincent Medical Center provide me superb ongoing care. I wouldn't trust my heart to any other team.

John Brant, my collaborator, asked good questions that led to some memorable conversations.

The love of my wife, Molly, and children, Tony, Alex, and Maria, gives meaning to every moment.

Thanks to God the Father and the Blessed Mother for watching over me.

—Alberto Salazar

ALBERTO SALAZAR'S FAITH in me to help tell his story made this book possible. His honesty and insight made it come alive.

Dr. Doug Douglass and Dr. Todd Caulfield patiently explained the complex workings of the brain and heart and delineated the continually evolving border between life and death.

The superb editors David Willey and Charlie Butler have guided me through many memorable journalistic campaigns. John Atwood recognized the frame of this narrative and encouraged me to build it. Thanks to the talented, dedicated staff at *Runner's World*.

Shannon Welch and Jeff Csatari edited this book with a deft touch and generous spirit, and the people of Rodale Books have lent intelligent, unstinting support. Thank you, Sloan Harris, my agent.

During the writing of this book, my friend Ric Sayre collapsed and died of a heart attack at age 52, after returning from his daily run. I remember his gentle spirit, and the lives of other dedicated athletes who did not survive their versions of 14 Minutes.

As always, Patricia, Tom, and Mary inspire every good sentence I write.

—John Brant